T0357180

DEATH IN THE JUNGLE

ALSO BY CANDACE FLEMING

YOUNG ADULT

The Family Romanov: Murder, Rebellion, and the Fall of Imperial Russia

Fatal Throne: The Wives of Henry VIII Tell All

The Lincolns: A Scrapbook Look at Abraham and Mary

Murder Among Friends: How Leopold and Loeb Tried to Commit the Perfect Crime

The Rise and Fall of Charles Lindbergh

MIDDLE GRADE

Amelia Lost: The Life and Disappearance of Amelia Earhart

Ben Franklin's in My Bathroom!

Eleanor Roosevelt's in My Garage!

The Fabled Fifth Graders of Aesop Elementary School

The Fabled Fourth Graders of Aesop Elementary School

The Great and Only Barnum: The Tremendous, Stupendous Life of Showman P. T. Barnum

Strongheart: Wonder Dog of the Silver Screen

YOUNGER READERS

Clever Jack Takes the Cake

Imogene's Last Stand

Mine!

Narwhal: Unicorn of the Arctic

Oh, No!

DEATH IN THE JUNGLE

MURDER, BETRAYAL, AND THE LOST DREAM OF JONESTOWN

CANDACE FLEMING

a·s·b
anne schwartz books

 Published in the United States by Anne Schwartz Books, an imprint of Random House Children's Books, a division of Penguin Random House LLC, 1745 Broadway, New York, NY 10019.

Anne Schwartz Books and the colophon are trademarks of Penguin Random House LLC.
penguinrandomhouse.com
GetUnderlined.com

Library of Congress Cataloging-in-Publication Data
Names: Fleming, Candace, author.
Title: Death in the jungle / Candace Fleming.
Description: New York : Anne Schwartz Books, 2025. |
Includes bibliographical references and index. | Audience: Grades 10–12 |
Summary: "A chilling chronicle, written for young adults,
of Jim Jones and Peoples Temple"—Provided by publisher.
Identifiers: LCCN 2024018777 (print) | LCCN 2024018778 (ebook) |
ISBN 978-0-593-48006-9 (hardcover) | ISBN 978-0-593-48007-6 (lib. bdg.) |
ISBN 978-0-593-48008-3 (ebook)
Subjects: LCSH: Jonestown Mass Suicide, Jonestown, Guyana, 1978—Juvenile literature. |
People's Temple—Juvenile literature. | Jones, Jim, 1931–1978.
Classification: LCC BP605.P46 F546 2025 (print) | LCC BP605.P46 (ebook) |
DDC 988.1/1—dc23/eng/20241126

The text of this book is set in 11.3-point Warnock Pro.

Printed in the United States of America
10 9 8 7 6 5 4 3 2 1
First Edition

The authorized representative in the EU for product safety and compliance is
Penguin Random House Ireland, Morrison Chambers, 32 Nassau Street, Dublin D02 YH68, Ireland,
https://eu-contact.penguin.ie.

To Rebecca and Mac,
whose tireless work serves to remind us all
that “the bodies had names”

CONTENTS

KEY PEOPLE IN THIS BOOK

The following is not a comprehensive list of Peoples Temple members, nor of every name mentioned in this book. Rather, it is a list of those who play a primary role in this story. Note that italicized names indicate children under the age of eighteen at the time of the tragedy.

Peoples Temple Members

AMOS

Sharon: A single mother, she joined the Redwood Valley Temple in 1967 and quickly rose to become one of Jim Jones's trusted lieutenants, as well as a member of the "staff," his inner circle. In Guyana, she was permanently stationed at the Temple's headquarters in Georgetown, Lamaha Gardens, where she was Jones's eyes and ears regarding the goings-on in the Guyanese government. She had three children—Liane, *Christa,* and *Martin*—also members of Peoples Temple.

BEAM

Jack and Rheaviana: Fiercely devoted founding members from Indianapolis. Jack served on the planning commission (PC) and knew many of Jim Jones's secrets, while Rheaviana had an extraordinary talent for stretching a dollar. Their daughter, Joyce, married Dale (see Parks).

BOGUE

Jim: A disenchanted member of the Redwood Valley Temple, he was among the first "pioneers" sent to Guyana to begin the construction of Jonestown.

Edith: A dedicated church member, she divorced Jim and moved in with Harold (see Cordell) while he was in Jonestown. She and Jim raised four children in the Temple.

> **Teena:** Their oldest daughter.
> **Juanita:** Their middle daughter.
> **Marilee:** Their youngest daughter, she was an ultraloyalist.
> ***Tommy:*** The couple's only living son had a well-earned reputation for being a troublemaker. His best friend in the Temple was Brian (see Davis).

CARTMELL

Patty: She joined Peoples Temple in Indiana, migrated to California, and then went to Guyana. An ultraloyalist and member of the "staff," she did anything Jones asked of her, including spying on other members. She had two children.

Mike: An eleven-year-old when he first attended Peoples Temple, he later married Jones's daughter Suzanne (see Jones).

Trisha: Five years old when she first attended the Temple, she became a dedicated member.

COBB

Christine: A founding member from Indiana, she was devoted to Jones after he "healed" her son Jim's ear problems. She followed Jones to both California and Guyana. She had seven children with her nonmember husband, Jim Sr.

Jim Jr.: "Healed" by Jones in Indiana, he followed his family to Redwood Valley, gave up baseball, and became a trusted member. Sent to dental school by the Temple, he was also made a guard on Jones's security team. Eventually, he became a member of the Gang of Eight and, later, the Concerned Relatives.

Johnny: A close friend of the Joneses'.

Ava: The Cobbs' oldest daughter, she joined the Temple as a child in Indiana.

Teresa: The oldest of the Cobb children, she joined the Temple as a child in Indiana. She married fellow member Wayne (see Pietila) and became a member of the Gang of Eight.

Sandra: Born just a year before the Cobbs joined the temple, she married Tim Tupper (see Jones) right out of high school. They had a daughter, *Monyelle* (see Jones).

Brenda* and *Joel: Born into the Temple, they accompanied their mother to Guyana.

CORDELL

Harold: A follower from Indianapolis, he married fellow Temple member Loretta Mae Coomer, with whom he had five children: Candace, James, Mable, Chris, and Cindy. After divorcing Loretta, Harold became involved with Edith (see Bogue). Despite being a trusted member, Harold broke settlement rules by smuggling a transistor radio into Jonestown.

DAVIS

Brian: Though his father, Robert, was a steadfast member of the Temple, Brian's mother defected with his two younger brothers. A troublemaker, he hated Peoples Temple. His buddy in mischief was Tommy (see Bogue).

EDWARDS

Zipporah "Zip": From the moment she saw Jim Jones on "TV church," she never wavered in her belief that he possessed divine powers. In part because of her insistence on following Jones from Indiana to California (and eventually Jonestown), her sister, Hyacinth (see Thrash), also became enmeshed in Peoples Temple.

GEORGE

David: An Amerindian child taken in by Joyce and Charlie (see Touchette), he taught jungle survival skills to Tommy (see Bogue).

JAMES

Shanda: Not long after she arrived in Guyana, she attracted the unwanted sexual attention of Jim Jones. After a brief affair, she tried to break it off. An infuriated Jones ordered her held in the Extended Care Unit, where she was drugged against her will.

JONES

Jim: The charismatic founder and leader of Peoples Temple.

Marceline: The wife of Jim Jones, she played a vital role in the formation and growth of Peoples Temple.

Agnes Pauline: Adopted by the Joneses in 1954 after Jim saw her standing on his church steps, the eleven-year-old grew into a sulky and disobedient teenager. As an adult, she quit and re-joined the Temple several times. She eventually went to Guyana.

Stephanie: A Korean child adopted by the Joneses in 1958.

Lew: Adopted at the same time as Stephanie, Lew, also Korean, grew up in the church. A steadfast member, he married member Terry Carter and had one child:

> ***Chaeoke:*** The first Peoples Temple baby born in Jonestown, on April 4, 1977.

Suzanne: The biological sister of Stephanie, she was adopted in 1959 at age six. A devoted member of the Temple for many years, she married Mike (see Cartmell).

Stephan: The only biological son of Jim and Marceline Jones. As he grew, he recognized his father's deception and was often openly hostile toward him. He was a member of the Jonestown basketball team.

Jimmy: The first Black baby adopted by a white couple in Indiana, he was made Jim Jones's namesake. For most of his life, he willingly and unquestioningly did his father's bidding. He married his high school sweetheart, Yvette Muldrow, in Guyana. He was a member of the Jonestown basketball team.

Tim Tupper: Although he was the biological child of Rita (see Tupper), the Joneses formally adopted him. Like Jimmy and Lew, he was devoted to Jim Jones for many years. He married Sandra (see Cobb), with whom he had one child. He was a member of the Jonestown basketball team.

Monyelle: She was born in Jonestown on Valentine's Day 1978.

James Jon "Kimo" Prokes: The biological son of Jim Jones and Carolyn (see Layton). Jones covered up the truth by enlisting trusted member Mike (see Prokes) to marry Carolyn.

KATSARIS

Maria: An ultraloyalist and part of the innermost circle. Once shy and awkward, she became more confident after becoming one of Jones's mistresses in 1976. Along with Carolyn (see Layton) and a few others, she took control of managerial details in both California and Jonestown.

LAYTON

Larry: A conscientious objector and anti-war activist, Larry joined the Redwood Valley Temple with his wife, Carolyn. Despite her affair with Jones and the couple's resulting divorce, Larry remained an ultraloyalist.

Carolyn: An ultraloyalist, she was both Jones's longtime mistress and his administrative right hand. In California, she managed organizational details and implemented his ideas. She expanded this role in Jonestown and, along with a handful of others, took on the day-to-day management of the settlement. She and Jim Jones had one child together, James Jon "Kimo" Prokes (see Jones). Her sister was Annie (see Moore).

McELVANE

Jim: An ultraloyalist and head of security in California, he didn't arrive in Jonestown until mid-November 1978.

MERTLE

Elmer and Deanna: Trusted and loyal members, they both served on the PC until their defection in 1975, when they became two of the Temple's most vocal critics. Active members of the Concerned Relatives, they were among the first former members to talk with reporters Phil Tracy and Marshall Kilduff for the *New West* article.

MILLER

Christine: Independent and outspoken, she was the only known member to publicly argue against "revolutionary suicide."

MOORE

Annie: Joining the Redwood Valley Temple after high school graduation, she became, like her sister Carolyn (see Layton), an ultraloyalist and member of Jones's innermost circle. In Guyana, she served as Jones's private nurse.

OLIVER

Howard and Beverly: Lapsed members, the couple gave their two teenage sons, Billy and Bruce, permission to go to Jonestown for a brief vacation. They became vocal members of the Concerned Relatives, eventually traveling with Congressman Ryan to Guyana.

PARKS

Jerry: Packing up his wife, kids, and mother, he moved from Indiana to California. Later, the entire family went to Guyana.

Patricia: Married to Jerry, she was the mother of their three children.

> **Dale:** He married fellow member Joyce (see Beam). They adopted a son, *J. Warren Parks.*
>
> **Brenda:** She dated fellow member Chris O'Neil in Jonestown.
>
> ***Tracy:*** The youngest of the Parks children, she was only eleven when her family migrated to Guyana.

PIETILA

Wayne: A friend of Jim Cobb Jr., and a member of the Gang of Eight, he was married to Jim's sister Teresa (see Cobb).

PROKES

Mike: The Temple's public relations man, Mike was part of Jones's innermost circle and married to Carolyn (see Layton).

SCHACHT

Larry: A drug-addled college dropout who found salvation when he joined the Temple in Redwood Valley, he was sent by Jones to study medicine in Mexico. Before he could finish his medical training, he was relocated to Guyana, where he served as the only doctor in Jonestown. He was also responsible for the settlement's vast drug supply.

SIMON

Al: Along with Jim Bogue, he spent months cutting a trail through the Guyana jungle in hopes of escaping Jonestown. He was married to Bonnie.

Bonnie: A devoted follower and member of the Jonestown security force, she and her husband, Al, had three children: *Alvin Jr., Crystal,* and *Summer.*

STOEN

Tim: An attorney who joined the Redwood Valley Temple, he was one of Jones's closest legal advisers until his defection in 1977, when he became a vocal member of the Concerned Relatives. He joined in his ex-wife Grace's custody battle with Jones.

Grace: The former wife of Tim, she defected from the Temple in 1976, leaving her son, John Victor, behind. A year later, she began legal proceedings to regain custody of the boy, who had been moved to live in Jones's house in Jonestown.

John Victor: Was he Jim Jones's biological son, as the leader claimed? We still don't know. But Jones's refusal to return the boy to his mother, Grace, rocked the Jonestown community to its core.

THRASH

Hyacinth: An early church member, she believed Jones cured her of breast cancer. Because of her belief in his divine powers, and at the insistence of her sister, Zipporah (see Edwards), she migrated to California and, later, Guyana.

TOUCHETTE

Joyce and Charlie: The couple came to the Temple in 1970 through Joyce's parents, who had migrated with Jones from Indianapolis. Later, the couple was chosen by Jones as "pioneers," two of just a handful of members who began the construction of Jonestown.

> **Mickey:** Daughter of Joyce and Charlie, she joined the Gang of Eight.
>
> **Michael:** A friend of the Jones boys, he accompanied his parents to Guyana as a pioneer. He was the trainer for the Jonestown basketball team.
>
> **Al:** The Touchettes' oldest son, he went to Guyana as a pioneer.

TROPP

Harriet: She joined Peoples Temple in 1972 after visiting her brother, Richard, who was already a member. Once she earned her law degree, she quickly rose to the upper levels of Temple leadership. Unlike other members, she was not afraid to tell Jones things he didn't want to hear. In Jonestown she acted as his spokesperson, radioing responses to government officials, journalists, and the Concerned Relatives when necessary.

Richard "Dick": A college professor when he joined the Temple, he was trusted by Jones.

TUPPER

Rita: She arrived in Redwood Valley with her five small children—Ruth, Tim (see Jones), *Janet, Larry,* and *Mary*—after an unspecified personal trauma and quickly became a devoted member. She eventually moved to Jonestown with all her children.

WILSON

Joe: An ultraloyalist, he was on Jones's security force in California. In Guyana he was elevated to head of security.

Non-members

COBB

Jim Sr.: Husband of Christine, he never joined Peoples Temple, although he did move from Indiana to Redwood Valley with his wife and children so they could re-join their church community.

GARRY

Charles: A fiery lawyer who represented Jones and Peoples Temple in its last years, he accompanied Congressman Ryan on his fact-finding mission to Jonestown.

JONES

Lynetta: Jim Jones's unconventional mother.

Jim Sr.: Jim Jones's father, he was called Big Jim at first, then Old Jim when the injuries he sustained in World War I became more debilitating.

KATSARIS

Anthony: Maria's brother, he traveled to Jonestown with Congressman Ryan in hopes of reestablishing a relationship with her.

Steve: Maria's father, he was convinced that Maria had been "brainwashed" by Jones. A vocal member of the Concerned Relatives, he traveled with Congressman Ryan to Guyana but did not go with him to Jonestown.

KILDUFF

Marshall: A reporter who, along with Phil Tracy, wrote a critical article about Peoples Temple for *New West* magazine.

LANE

Mark: A lawyer working for Peoples Temple, he urged Jones to let Congressman Ryan visit Jonestown and eventually accompanied him to the settlement.

MOORE

Rebecca: Unlike her sisters, Annie (see Moore) and Carolyn (see Layton), Rebecca never fell prey to Jim Jones. Today she is a foremost scholar on destructive groups, and Peoples Temple in particular.

John and Barbara: Parents of Carolyn Layton and Annie and Rebecca Moore, they were also the grandparents of Kimo (see Jones). The couple grudgingly accepted their oldest daughter's relationship with Jones, as well as Kimo's secret paternity, to maintain family ties.

RYAN

Leo: Congressman from California's 11th Congressional District, he traveled to Jonestown at the request of the Concerned Relatives, who believed their loved ones were being mistreated and imprisoned there.

SPEIER

Jackie: One of two congressional staffers who accompanied Congressman Ryan to Guyana; she traveled to Jonestown and interviewed residents.

TRACY

Phil: With Marshall Kilduff he wrote the *New West* article that exposed Peoples Temple secrets and led to members migrating to Guyana.

A Note About Terminology

Out of respect for former members of Peoples Temple, I have adopted the terms they use when describing themselves. Thus, **survivor** is *anyone* who lived through their association with the organization, while **victim** is applied to the 918 people who died in Guyana.

Prologue

"The Horrors of Jonestown"

ON FRIDAY EVENING, NOVEMBER 24, 1978, CBS BROADCAST a special hour-long report: "The Horrors of Jonestown." The title, in blood red, was superimposed over a photograph showing piles of colorfully dressed corpses lying face down in the red soil of Guyana, South America. The bodies seemed awful yet orderly, not flung about like the dead after a battle, but neat, hand in hand sometimes, arms about each other's waists.

For the previous six days, news coming out of Guyana had been sketchy. First, Americans learned that a "strange religious cult" called Peoples Temple had assassinated California congressman Leo Ryan after he'd visited their jungle commune, Jonestown. Then the Guyanese government reported something even grislier: Everyone in Jonestown was dead. Followers of the Reverend Jim Jones had killed themselves by "sipping from a bucket of cyanide [mixed with] soft drinks." Guyanese officials estimated the body count at 383.

But that number was wrong.

On Tuesday, November 21, when U.S. troops arrived, they made a shocking discovery. A military spokesperson, his voice trembling with emotion, told reporters that far more people were dead, perhaps as many as 900. Almost all were Americans. When the press questioned the disparity between this count and Guyana's, the spokesperson blinked back tears. Under the groups of adults, he choked out, the troops had found the "bodies of children . . . more and more and more."

Back in the United States, citizens were both horrified and riveted by the news. What caused seemingly "normal" people to get caught up in something so fanatical? The elements of the event were dark yet fascinating—the mysticism, the intimacy of communal living, the bizarre deaths. Americans wanted to know every graphic detail.

And so that night, just after the dinner hour, CBS obliged them.

The report began with a film of U.S. troops lugging body bags and aluminum caskets. Many of them wore masks to block the stench of decomposing flesh. But the masks did little good. After days beneath the hot sun and intermittent tropical rain, many of the bodies had bloated and burst. The faces of the dead were no longer recognizable, and in some cases soldiers had to use snow shovels to scoop up the rotting remains.

"These metal caskets will be opened and filled and closed again and again," anchorman Bruce Morton said dramatically, "but the complete story of what happened to the members of the Peoples Temple settlement will remain open a long time."

Here the broadcast cut to commercial—an abrupt and ghoulish switch. Viewers went from death to dandruff shampoo and denture cleaner.

The broadcast returned. It recapped the Reverend Jones's life and career. Clips from Peoples Temple, the religious organization he'd founded, showed a sanctuary filled with rejoicing, happy people. "His people believed in him," narrated Morton, "in his goodness

[and] his love. His soft voice conveyed charisma. It was said he had the power to heal, the power to lead large numbers of people. [His followers] claimed they felt the power of Christ in him."

Former member Joyce Shaw recalled for reporters how he professed "to be God, to be immortal, to have been Jesus Christ [and] Buddha . . . every religious prophet from the past."

For an expert perspective, a newswoman sat down with psychiatrists Frank Ochberg and Frederick Hacker. "Why in the world would so many people agree to kill themselves?" she asked them. "What kind of leader could order mass suicide and be obeyed? How could Jones convince grown-ups to kill themselves and their children for him?"

Ochberg confessed to being "baffled." He didn't believe there was a single answer to any one of these questions. "I think you will find that for some it was a rational, conscious choice. For others it was . . . following people whose judgment you trust. Some were too young to make an informed decision. Some may have felt held hostage, or forced."

Hacker added his opinion: "Often these organizations start with good intentions, and then they gradually deteriorate as the leader assumes full power over the people. He becomes paranoid and totally uncontrolled."

The broadcast switched to an interview with longtime member Claire Janaro, who'd arrived in Guyana on the very day the deaths took place. Her husband, Richard, as well as their children, fourteen-year-old Daren and sixteen-year-old Mauri, already lived in Jonestown. But Claire had not gone with them. On Jim Jones's orders, she'd stayed behind to manage Happy Acres Ranch, the Temple's ranch for people with disabilities in Redwood Valley, California. The family's separation lasted eighteen months, but at last, Jones had given

Claire permission to move to Jonestown. Joyfully, she'd arrived at the airport in Guyana's capital city of Georgetown. But no one from the Temple was there to meet her. After waiting for hours, she'd checked herself into a hotel. She was still there, two days later, when she learned the terrible news. Now, as the press shoved cameras and microphones into her tearstained face, she said, "I was anticipating nothing but happiness, a dream come true." She told them about her family's long separation, then sobbed for several seconds before recovering her voice. "I made this sacrifice of being away from them to build a better world. That's all I can tell you."

Other shocked and grieving survivors expressed similar sentiments.

"No one joins a cult, they join a cause," replied one former member when asked why he'd involved himself in Peoples Temple.

And what was that cause? asked reporters.

"We were going to convert the world to brotherhood," explained another member. "And that was it. That was the dream."

The broadcast concluded on a reflective note. "Most of us, as the story unfolded this week, have thought, 'Not me. I'd never do that.' Yet one expert psychologist argues that under the proper pressures, *any* of us would; that thought control *can* reach us all. That point can be debated . . . and *will* be. Obeying orders to kill one's children? Unthinkable. And yet, it demands our thought."

Cult: What Is It?

The word cult *has been in use since the early 1600s. Originally it meant "a practice of religious veneration and the system based around such veneration." Around the turn of the nineteenth century, its definition expanded to mean a group displaying "veneration, devotion, misplaced or excessive admiration to particular person." Nowadays, when we hear the word* cult, *we think of a group or movement with an extreme ideology, headed by a charismatic leader. Some cults are religion-based, like Aum Shinrikyo, a Japanese group founded in 1984 with the goal of eliminating world sin. (It should be noted, however, that not all religious groups are cults.) Others are political (the Nazi Party), psychotherapy-based (Synanon), or focused on self-improvement (NXIVM). There are thousands of such groups—big and small—around the world that meet this definition. But that does not automatically make them bad or dangerous. The majority give members a sense of belonging and purpose* without *being destructive to the individual.*

Many scholars and scientists who study these groups no longer use the word cult *because it has become so sensationalized that it is inherently pejorative and is often associated with words like* deranged, depraved, *and* deviant. *Using* cult *or* cult follower *signals exactly how we should think about certain groups. It keeps us from engaging seriously with them. And using the word has real ramifications. After the press labeled the victims of Jim Jones "brainwashed cultists," Americans found it easier to distance themselves from the tragedy. They no longer needed to wrestle with the human component because these people weren't "normal," but rather weak, gullible, and crazy, not worthy of attention. (Let's not overlook the fact that 70 percent of those who died in Jonestown were Black, another reason that contributed to the ease with which a large segment of the American public considered the victims "subhuman.") The pejorative label allows us to feel morally smug and superior.* We'd *never join a cult.*

So what term should we use? Many experts prefer neutral-sounding labels like new religious movements, emergent religions, alternative groups, *or* fringe communities. *Others define groups as* healthy *or* unhealthy, constructive *or* destructive. *Which term best defines Peoples Temple? There is disagreement among experts about that, as well. Still, language is needed, so let's settle on* destructive group *as the best phrase to describe Peoples Temple.*

How can we determine if a group is constructive or destructive? Below are some characteristics of a destructive group.

1. It demands submission to leadership. Leaders claim to be prophets of God, specially anointed apostles, God himself, or simply strongmen who demand submission to their will. In truth, they are highly charismatic, persuasive people with authoritarian and narcissistic streaks. Money, sex, power, or all three typically motivate them.

2. It holds a polarized worldview. The group and its members believe they are the only good thing; everyone and everything outside is bad. Salvation, fulfillment, and happiness (or whatever is being promised) can be found only within the group.

3. It values feelings over facts. Emotions, intuitions, divinations, prophecies, and self-perceptions are considered more important than substantiated evidence or rational conclusion based on fact and logic.

4. It uses tactics to manipulate feelings. Leaders create false narratives and events to stimulate emotions in their followers—fear, mistrust, anger, devotion. They often employ group sessions involving gaslighting, love bombing, overloading of information meant to disorient or confuse, guilt, and physical punishment to control and coerce followers' responses.

5. It denigrates critical thinking. The leader, and ultimately the group, characterize independent thought as selfish, or anti-group. Individual opinions are forbidden. Questioning is not tolerated, and criticism is punishable. Followers must stick to "groupthink," those values and beliefs commonly held by the organization.

6. It believes that the end justifies the means. Both the leader and followers believe *any* action or behavior is justifiable if it furthers the organization's goals. This includes illegal acts. Since the leader is believed to be absolute and thus above all human-made laws, they may command followers to commit illegal acts for "the good of the group."

7. It values the group over the individual. The group's needs supersede any one person's goals, needs, aspirations, and concerns. Conformity is key.

8. It warns of severe or supernatural consequences for defectors. Leaders use fear, intimidation, and lies to keep followers in the group, warning that bad things will happen if they leave. Those who try to escape are made an example of; those who do get away are often harassed and intimidated.

9. It demands that followers sever from their family, friends, goals, and interests. The group becomes the followers' family—becomes their everything. Followers are discouraged from having anything to do with their former life to keep them from being pulled back into it.

Part One

Beginnings

To understand [Peoples] Temple, you have to know the *whole* story. You have to know my father.

—Stephan Jones, son of Jim Jones and Peoples Temple survivor

Chapter One

One Weird Kid

THE FIRST TIME JIM JONES ASKED FOLLOWERS TO PLAY DEAD was on an autumn night in 1941.

The ten-year-old urged the other boys to come with him.

They hesitated. Jimmy Jones wasn't a friend. Not really. Sure, they hung around with him, but they didn't like him. He was bossy and controlling. And he always got his way.

But there was something magnetic about him, too. Somehow, he coaxed them into doing things they knew they shouldn't.

Take the previous week, for example. They'd been playing in the loft over the Joneses' garage when Jimmy persuaded them to walk out on the rafters. They'd be like tightrope walkers in the circus, he'd said.

His playmates went first, slowly and in single file because the rafters were so narrow. Jimmy sidled out behind them. One of the boys looked down. It was a long way to the floor, at least ten feet. He tried to back off the rafter, but Jimmy wouldn't budge.

"Move back!" the boy yelled.

"I can't move," declared Jimmy. "The Angel of Death is holding me."

For several long moments the boys teetered precariously on the rafters. They begged him to move. All the while Jimmy watched them with “a weird look on his face,” recalled one of the boys. Then, finally, he claimed the angel had released him. They all inched their way back to safety.

Afterward, the boys agreed: Jimmy Jones was crazy. They swore never to play with him again.

And yet, just days later, they were sneaking out with him. His gifts of persuasion had once again been impossible to ignore. Beneath a harvest moon they followed their leader across the small town of Lynn, Indiana. No one noticed the little group. In those days most of Lynn's citizens went to bed early.

It didn't take long for the group to reach the warehouse on the edge of town. The boys stopped. What were they doing here? Jimmy sprinted to the warehouse door. It was unlocked. He beckoned the others to follow. They could trust him.

Trust? None of the others trusted Jimmy. Still, one by one, they slipped into the warehouse. Slowly, their eyes adjusted to the darkness, and they saw what was inside: coffins, dozens of them.

Jimmy opened the lid of one and climbed in. He insisted the others do the same. He instructed them to just lie there. That way, they might find out what it was like to be dead. He wiggled into position, arranged his hands across his chest, and closed his eyes.

It was too much for his companions. Yelping with fear, they bolted from the warehouse, leaving Jimmy behind.

He lay there alone, absorbed in morbid revelry. What happened to you after you died? What did it feel like? And how would it feel if your soul was raised from the dead?

The boy didn't find any answers that night. But he kept going back to the coffins.

Despite Jimmy's magnetism, the other boys never returned with him.

James Warren Jones had few memories of his parents' farm near tiny Crete, Indiana. Born on May 13, 1931, he was just three years old when the Great Depression bankrupted his parents. The financial loss sent his father, a physically disabled and unemployed World War I veteran nicknamed Big Jim, over the edge.

On the day the bank foreclosed, Big Jim beat his fists on the floor. "I've gone as far as I can go!" he cried.

"You go ahead and cry," Jimmy's mother, Lynetta, replied, "but I'll whip this if it's the last thing I ever do."

Moving her family to the slightly larger town of Lynn, just five miles away, she rented a cheap house and found work at the glass factory. She wasn't the only working mother in that sleepy little town. The Depression had forced plenty of women into the role of breadwinner. But she was by far the most unconventional. In those days people in Lynn did little more than earn a living, raise their children, and go to church on both Wednesday nights and Sunday mornings. Since there weren't any African Americans, Catholics, or Jews living within the town limits, there wasn't any reason for the Knights of the Ku Klux Klan to appear with their hoods and fiery crosses. (Around that time 30 percent of all native-born white men in Indiana were KKK members.) Alcoholic drinks were not sold within the town limits, and dancing, which many considered immoral, was prohibited at the high school. Crime was rare.

Into this conservative Christian community barreled Lynetta Jones. She cursed in public, wore trousers, and puffed on hand-rolled cigarettes. It was eyebrow-raising behavior, especially for a woman.

Her worst transgression, at least in the eyes of Lynn's citizens, was not attending church, and the town boasted six of them. There were the Nazarenes and the Methodists, the Disciples of Christ, the Baptists, the Quakers, and the Pentecostals. As in the rest of the state, evangelical Protestantism reigned. It was commonly believed that those who were not in a pew every Sunday were on the road to eternal damnation.

Lynetta Jones thought it all poppycock. It seemed ridiculous to her that some spirit in the sky decided who got into heaven. Those folks who went to church were, in her opinion, mindless dupes.

While Lynetta worked and Big Jim sat wheezing and in pain by the front window, their little boy wandered all over town, alone and unsupervised. Sometimes he was half-naked. Sometimes he scampered along the sidewalks gnawing on the sandwich Lynetta had left for his lunch. He loved animals, perhaps because they gave him unconditional affection, and he could often be found playing with the neighbors' cats and dogs.

The town's homemakers clucked about the neglected child. Was he going hungry? When was the last time he'd had a bath? Had anyone taught him the Lord's Prayer? They invited him into their homes, cleaned him up, and fed him. Jimmy—not yet five years old—quickly learned how to say or do whatever was necessary to get what he wanted. He had an instinctual ability to quickly surmise what was important to someone, and he could convince that person that he felt the same (even if he didn't). He swore to each woman that *hers* was the best pie, or biscuit, or cookie. He acted polite and grateful. He played on their sympathies, spinning false tales about his father's cruel and terrifying behavior. Having sussed out a homemaker's interest—needlepoint, gardening, baking—he claimed to share her enthusiasm. Each woman felt she had a special bond with Jimmy Jones.

Little Jimmy was simply trying to survive. "Manipulation was not a conscious thing for him," his son Stephan would later claim. But because of these early experiences, the act of manipulation became second nature, an ingrained part of his personality.

Across the street from the Jones family lived Myrtle Kennedy. Myrtle was dedicated to God. She led prayer meetings, organized church potlucks, and taught Sunday school at the Nazarene church, where her husband, Orville was pastor. With a glad heart, she followed the Nazarenes' strict rules: no dancing, no card playing, no short sleeves or short skirts. Like many of the other ladies in town, she felt sorry for little Jimmy Jones.

One morning while Myrtle stood in the grocer's line, she heard a neighbor talking about the child. Jimmy, now seven, had been playing on the tracks when a train came along. He'd almost been run over, exclaimed the woman. The wheels had actually grazed his cheek. The neighbor saw it as another example of Lynetta Jones's carelessness as a mother.

Myrtle, however, took it as a sign from God. The Lord, she believed, had saved the boy so she could take him under her wing.

Now whenever she saw Jimmy out wandering, she called him in for cookies or pie. She learned his favorite meals—macaroni and cheese, and grilled cheese sandwiches with tomato soup—and made them for him. Soon he went to Myrtle's home every day. Sometimes he even slept there overnight. Lynetta didn't care. It kept the boy out of her hair.

She might have been more concerned if she knew her son called Myrtle "Mom." The title pleased Myrtle, who had no children of her own. She saw herself as Jimmy's spiritual mother. And she set out to save his soul by reading to him from the Bible. The boy—bright and always eager to please—soon quoted scripture back to her. She was charmed.

Eventually, Myrtle got up the nerve to ask Lynetta if she could take the boy to church.

What could it hurt? decided Lynetta. She figured Jimmy was too smart to fall for all that church baloney. Besides, without the kid around on Sunday, she could put up her feet and drink a forbidden beer or two.

That first Sunday morning in the Nazarene church felt like a homecoming to Jimmy. People welcomed him warmly. Ladies patted his round cheeks with the soft tips of their white-gloved fingers. Men thumped his scrawny back congenially. Everyone said it was good to see him.

He slid into a pew beside Myrtle. An organ began to soulfully play, a signal that the service was about to begin. The air smelled of perfume and hair pomade.

But it was the preacher who transfixed Jimmy—his shiny satin robe, his booming voice and fiery words. He commanded everyone's attention. The entire congregation sat riveted. And they did *everything* the preacher told them to do—stand, sit, open their hymnals, pray. Jimmy suddenly wanted to be just like that preacher. Respected. Admired. The center of attention.

After that, Jimmy could hardly wait for Sunday. He memorized everything he heard at church. Within weeks he could repeat hymns, prayers, and lengthy Bible verses verbatim. His ability dazzled Myrtle.

What a whip-smart, marvelously gifted boy she'd been called to save. He was going to make a fine member of the Nazarene church.

When Jimmy was nine, he began wandering again—this time on Sundays. He rambled over to Lynn's other churches and plopped himself into their pews. The worshippers must have smiled at the child indulgently. He tried out the solemn Methodists, the pacifist Quakers, and the wealthy, well-attended Christ Church. But it was Gospel Tabernacle—the Pentecostal church located on the edge of town—that gripped him.

Pentecostalism especially appealed to the poor and working classes in both white and Black communities (although in the 1930s they did not worship together). Jim Jones would later call Pentecostals "the rejects of the community," meant as a compliment. Other Christians often looked down on Pentecostals because of the physical devotion of their services, in which people leaped spontaneously to their feet, burst into song, danced ecstatically, or fell shaking to the floor. They considered such displays both unsophisticated and unbiblical. But in the warmth of this church community, Jimmy claimed he found "immediate acceptance," something that had long eluded him.

The boy loved the exuberant services at Gospel Tabernacle. They were loud and boisterous, what folks called "holy rolling." One never knew what might happen next. God's spirit was on display every Sunday.

Jimmy felt attracted to Gospel Tabernacle for another reason, too. Pentecostals believe God bestows on them one or more spiritual gifts. Members might be given the ability to prophesize, or deliver messages from God. They might be able to heal the sick, or to speak in tongues, a language that bursts forth spontaneously when one is filled with the Lord's spirit. Jimmy, longing for attention and a feeling of specialness, desperately wanted those gifts.

He was eleven when he claimed the Lord had given him special powers. After gathering the neighborhood kids, he tied a cape around his neck (really just a towel) and commanded everyone to watch him fly. He leaped off his garage roof . . . and broke his arm. His Pentecostal faith, however, remained intact. He felt sure God would endow him with powers someday.

Around that same time, a new obsession seized Jimmy: Adolf Hitler. After the United States entered World War II in December 1941, the kids in Lynn often played soldier in the streets. All of them wanted to be American GIs battling the evil Axis. All, that is, except Jimmy Jones. He was impressed by the dictator's oratory skills. Imagine compelling an entire nation to goose-step to your will simply by speaking. In fact, Hitler's speeches reminded Jimmy of a preacher's sermons. Like a preacher, Hitler shouted and shook his voice, paused, fell silent, or spoke in whispered tones that slowly built to an emotional finale. And just like a preacher, he held his audience rapt sometimes for hours at a time.

Jimmy began studying Hitler's oratory craft. He'd watch the newsreels featuring the Führer that played daily (except for Sundays) at Lynn's movie theater. In the dark Jimmy closely noted the dictator's delivery, hand gestures, and body language. "I know that men are won over less by the written word than by the spoken word," Hitler wrote in the preface to his book, *Mein Kampf.* "Every great movement on this earth owes its growth to great orators and not great writers." Jimmy had yet to read those words, but—through Hitler's example—he was already learning that words well delivered could sway masses.

He began practicing his own oratory skills in the woods near his home. His sermons were part Pentecostal preacher and part Nazi dictator. He honed them for hours. Should he place his hand over his heart at this point? Should he shake his fist here? Every movement was carefully considered.

In April 1945, Hitler committed suicide to avoid capture by the advancing enemy army. Hitler was roundly declared a coward, but Jimmy didn't agree. The way he saw it, the dictator had chosen his own way of dying rather than leaving the choice in the hands of his enemies. Even more fascinating to him was the death of Hitler's bride, Eva Braun. How had Hitler convinced her to willingly take cyanide? *That,* the almost-fourteen-year-old marveled, was power.

It was around this time that Jimmy first became aware of racism. While the population of Lynn was all white, Black people did live in the area. Most African American men worked as farmhands, and on weekends they brought their families into town to shop. Jimmy, like the other white kids in Lynn, saw them every Saturday morning at the post office or standing in line at the grocery store. But he never engaged with them. In Lynn, as elsewhere in Indiana, this wasn't done.

All that changed the summer Jimmy turned fourteen. For the first time, he later claimed, he really *saw* his Black neighbors and recognized the bigotry of his white ones. He never explained the reason for this newfound awareness, but now on Saturday mornings, he began chatting with these families, offering his hand and asking about their homes and lives.

His behavior shocked both Blacks and whites. Jimmy was upsetting the town's unwritten social boundaries. But the teenager kept on. He earnestly wanted to learn about Black experiences, and the unfairness of their treatment bothered him deeply.

In high school Jim, as he now preferred to be called, became a loner. Yes, his teachers liked him. His public-speaking skills were extraordinary, he read voraciously, and he got good grades. Above all, he had ambition. Faculty expected him to head to college and break out of their small community. But he had few friends. Kids didn't so much reject him as ignore him. Once, while a group of schoolmates shot hoops, he walked over and suggested they sit down and read the Bible. When the teens refused, he grabbed the ball. They demanded he leave, but Jim wouldn't. It took a fist to the face to get rid of him.

His schoolmates *did* find Jim's Bible thumping useful in one instance, though.

As the Lynn Bulldogs prepared to take on a rival team, students asked him to conduct a funeral service for their opponents. Jim enthusiastically agreed. He both surprised and unnerved his classmates with how enthusiastically he "buried" the opposing team. Wearing a dark suit and with a Bible pressed to his chest, Jim stood in the center of the school gymnasium and intoned the solemn words of a graveside service, complete with obituary, eulogy, and benediction. Recalled one student: "He had a flair for the dramatic."

Over the years, Big Jim's physical condition had continued to deteriorate, so much so that locals now called him Old Jim. He coughed constantly and often didn't have enough breath to hold a conversation. Doctors could do little except prescribe pain medication. The pills left Old Jim numb. Sometimes he lay in bed, unmoving, for hours. Other times he staggered when he walked and slurred his words. People who saw him believed he was drunk, and Lynetta didn't contradict them. She had no sympathy for her husband's ailments and blamed him for her scraping-by life. She called him "a worm" for not pulling himself together.

By 1948 she'd had enough. Abandoning her sick husband, she moved to Richmond, Indiana, twenty-three miles away. Seventeen-year-old Jim went with her. His hometown held nothing for him. He had no friends, and he disdained his father even more than Lynetta did. He blamed the older man for his childhood poverty and neglect. "My worthless father was the reason I sought approval so damn much," Jim would later say.

With the move, Jim swept his father completely from his life. He never saw or spoke with him again, and when Old Jim died three years later, neither he nor Lynetta attended the funeral.

The first time Jim Jones preached in public was a Saturday morning not long after his move to Richmond. The teenager slicked back his hair, put on a clean white shirt and freshly pressed trousers, and picked up his Bible. He took the bus to an African American neighborhood on the north side of town. After selecting a spot on a busy sidewalk, he began pleading with passersby to allow the Holy Spirit into their hearts. Most ignored him or snapped "Get out of the way!" But four or five curious people stopped. Jim started preaching like he'd practiced, shaking a fist and waving the Good Book. But now he added a new message. "All men are equal under God," he exclaimed. "God wants us to be brothers, all of us, all races. . . . It says so right here." He held the Bible high.

More folks stopped to listen. Soon a small crowd of twenty-five or so stood around him. It wasn't just the teenager's Pentecostal preaching style that attracted them; it was his message. Incredibly, here was a white male publicly preaching for equal rights in a place where the Ku Klux Klan still held some sway.

Richmond, a bustling town with a population of forty-five thousand, was deeply segregated. While African Americans made up one-fifth of the population, they'd been pushed to the city's fringes on the extreme north and south sides. There they lived in cramped, overpriced, and poorly constructed buildings. Children attended inferior schools, and most Black parents could find only low-paying, unskilled jobs.

Racism was everywhere. And Jim Jones had noticed it. African American citizens couldn't share hospital wards with white people. They couldn't eat in the same restaurants. They were insulted, bullied, beaten . . . and worse. Jim hadn't encountered *this* level of racism in all-white Lynn, and he couldn't understand it. This was *not* Christian behavior. He found himself burning with the injustice of it.

When he finished preaching that day, the crowd surprised him by offering him a few coins. "The experience," noted one journalist, "was a turning point for Jim Jones: He'd discovered his platform."

Chapter Two

Husband and Healer

ON A SNOWY NIGHT IN DECEMBER 1948 AT RICHMOND'S Reid Memorial Hospital, a senior nursing student named Marceline Baldwin was left with the grim task of preparing a woman's body for the undertaker. She asked for an orderly's help. Minutes later a handsome, black-haired teenager arrived. Together they washed and dressed the corpse. Marceline noticed the orderly's solemn and respectful behavior. He even said a prayer under his breath. A devout Methodist, Marceline felt heart-warmed by this.

More impressive, the orderly went out into the hallway to speak to the grieving husband. Kneeling before him, he took the man's hand in his and spoke in a comforting tone. Marceline could not hear what the orderly said, but as she watched, the dead woman's husband hugged him. The orderly, Marceline later recalled, was "visibly touched by [the family's] suffering."

She soon learned the orderly's name: Jim Jones. A senior in high school, he'd been working the full-time night shift for the past several months. It could be an unpleasant job. Orderlies cleaned up vomit, emptied bedpans, and delivered the recently deceased to the morgue. Everyone who'd worked with Jones, however, marveled at the good-natured and kind way he tackled these tasks. He looked directly into patients' eyes, giving the impression that he saw beyond their illnesses. He held their hands, and prayed with them if they asked. He smiled and told them silly jokes. His wonderful memory allowed him to remember every sick person's name, as well as the names of their parents, spouses, children, and pets. He oozed empathy, convincing patients that he understood them. And the more it appeared they needed him, the more giving and compassionate he became.

After that first night working together, Marceline and Jim were inseparable. During her breaks, as she ate the sandwich she'd brought from home, he talked. Jim liked to talk, and Marceline was a good listener. With ease and confidence, he told her a pack of lies. To gain her sympathy, he claimed his mother was an alcoholic and his father physically abusive. To prove that he was anti-racist, he told her he'd been the star of the Lynn High School basketball team but had quit after the coach used racial slurs to describe their Black opponents. Another time, he said, he'd walked out of a barbershop with only one side of his hair cut because the barber made bigoted comments.

Marceline didn't question the truth of these stories. And when Jim explained that these painful experiences had inspired him to dedicate his life to uplifting others, she felt even more attracted to him.

Jones was learning how to sell himself. He'd discovered he had a knack for figuring out what people wanted to hear, and for saying it in the most convincing way. And if he had to lie, so be it. He saw lying as a useful tool, and he was good at it. His imaginative fibs rolled easily off his tongue.

Now he sized up Marceline Baldwin and rightly determined that she longed to dedicate her life to serving God by helping people. He also surmised that she didn't know how to go about it. And so, Jim talked about his unstinting faith in the Lord, about his desire to do Christ's work, about answering God's call to help the poor and downtrodden.

It was all a lie, or so Jones later claimed. He'd begun to cast off his religious faith not long after leaving his hometown of Lynn. Both his hospital experiences and those in Richmond's poor Black neighborhoods had revealed the truth to him. "I looked around at all the misery and suffering in the world and wondered how a loving God could permit it," he later said. The answer seemed obvious: God didn't exist. His mother had been right all along. Religion was a fraud.

He didn't, however, let on to Marceline. The more lies he spun, the more attractive Marceline found him. Within months of their meeting, he began talking about marriage. Together, he said, they had the power to serve humankind in meaningful and important ways. They would go wherever people were oppressed. It would be a godly life.

On the afternoon of June 12, 1949, to the bewilderment of her family and friends, twenty-one-year-old Marceline Baldwin walked down the aisle of Trinity Methodist Church and said "I do" to eighteen-year-old Jim Jones. Recalled one guest: "[Marceline] was angelic, just glowing, shining, a will-of-the-wisp and obviously special. I wondered, 'Whatever does she see in him?' "

That fall, Jones enrolled at Indiana University and moved to Bloomington, while Marceline remained with her parents. On campus, he fed his growing interest in politics and social welfare. He took Russian, World Politics, Psychology of Personality, History of American Social Welfare, and a sociology class called Society and the Individual.

Jones still didn't fit in with his fellow students, most of whom were older and far wealthier than he was. Often, "the guys" would head out together to go drinking or girl-watching. They never invited the married Jones to go along.

Withdrawing after his second semester, Jim moved to Indianapolis with Marceline. (He would, another ten years later, graduate from Butler University with a degree in education.) There he accepted a position as a student pastor at Somerset Methodist Church. He brimmed with ideas to revolutionize the staid and well-established church . . . so many ideas. He encouraged Somerset Methodist to spearhead a campaign to build a recreation center for the city's poor youth. He urged its members to invite African American families to worship with them on Sundays. He even tried to change the services themselves. In his opinion, Sunday morning in the Methodist church was dull and predictable, with every song, scripture, and prayer planned in advance. Who could feel inspired when every service felt like a funeral?

Jones thought back to his days in the Pentecostal church, where folks jumped up and sang and called out "Amen!" and "Hallelujah!" The services went on for hours if the spirit moved churchgoers. They hugged each other, whooped, and stomped. This, he decided, was the type of service he would conduct, one that brought people together through an infectious way of expressing faith; one that made people feel uplifted. Once people had bonded during worship, they could be moved to do the *real* work: helping the needy, lifting up the marginalized, working toward equality.

In his first sermon, he urged the all-white congregation to apply

Jesus Christ's values to everyday life. Christianity, he concluded, was incompatible with discrimination and segregation. His message fell on mostly disapproving ears.

When he tried to integrate the church by inviting Black visitors, several white families walked out. Jones felt disgusted. Obviously, it was one thing to nod passively when the pastor said all humans were created equal in God's eyes, and quite another to share a hymnal with a Black person. Jones had long suspected that mainstream denominations like Somerset Methodist were inherently racist, and this experience solidified his belief. He realized that if he wanted an integrated congregation, he would need to abandon the Methodists.

Jones had a more immediate problem, though: He and Marceline were strapped for cash. Because Jim's student pastorship was unpaid, he was working a series of low-paying part-time jobs. He even went door to door, peddling South American spider monkeys. He must have looked strange bicycling around Indianapolis with a cage of monkeys balanced on his handlebars. But his glib tongue and cute merchandise often got him in the door.

Still, the monkey business didn't come close to covering the couple's expenses. Marceline supported them, working full-time as a nurse, but in those days, wages for women were low. How to earn more money? It was Marceline who suggested the "revival circuit."

Traveling circus-like across the country, preachers on the circuit—men and women alike—stopped in small towns and big cities. After pitching a tent, they pounded their pulpits and preached up a storm. Most had no official church. In fact, few had any formal training. Instead, they claimed to have been called by God to spread the Gospel. Both Jim and Marceline knew that the most successful traveling preachers drew huge crowds. Their collection plates overflowed with cash. Some preachers even became famous.

Jones needed to see for himself.

On a muggy Saturday night in July 1952, he and Marceline drove out to a huge tent that had been set up ten miles south of Indianapolis. The tent's canvas flaps had been raised to catch the scraps of breeze. When they entered, about five hundred people already sat on hard wooden folding chairs inside. Despite the constant fluttering of the handheld fans provided by a local funeral home, the crowd dripped sweat. Unable to find seats, Jim and Marceline stood on tiptoe to see the stage. Dozens of others had been forced to do the same. Jim was impressed: standing room only.

It was common to have three or four preachers at a single meeting, each with their unique style. Some raged. Some soothed or cajoled. Some implored people to come forward, kneel at the tent's makeshift altar, and accept Jesus into their hearts. That night, the service began with an emotional mix of well-known hymns and Bible verses. Then the first of the preachers launched into a fire-and-brimstone sermon.

Jim studied the man's approach—and those of the subsequent preachers. What made the crowd gasp or weep? What made them leap to their feet? What filled folks with so much spirit that they stood, swaying like trees in the wind, their right hand raised and their eyes squeezed shut?

It was, he quickly realized, the faith healings.

Many Christians believe that God has the power to heal and that ministers have a direct line to him. As one preacher on the revival circuit told his tent congregations, "*I'm* not a healer. There's only one healer, and his name is Jesus. But . . . God sent me out and gave me power over sickness, over disease, over the works of the devil in his name."

As Jim Jones watched and learned, the preachers wowed the congregation.

"You're tormented by the demon alcohol," cried one preacher, taking a middle-aged man by the shoulders. "Do you believe God can cast out the demon?"

"I believe! I believe!" cried the man.

"So, here it comes," thundered the preacher. He tensed, and his right arm went around in circles, as if he were winding up for a pitch. Then . . . bam! He shoved the man in the chest.

The man stumbled backward. He would have fallen if not for two ushers who caught him and held him upright.

"Do you want a drink of that devil whiskey now?" shouted the preacher.

"No!" cried the man. He began to weep.

"And you never will again," the preacher declared.

The congregation exploded into applause and shouts of praise.

Next he asked an elderly woman to point out where she felt pain.

The woman rubbed the small of her back.

The preacher moved behind her and placed his hands on her shoulders. Then swiftly, roughly, he pulled her backward. "Lord, heal this old body," he prayed. "By the power of God right now."

The old woman groaned.

"Touch your toes right now," commanded the preacher. "Come on, touch them."

He didn't wait for her to try. Instead, he bent her forward, then jerked her upright. He did this again and again and again. With each jerk, he shouted, "Loosen up. Don't be afraid. Loosen up."

After the fifth time, he grabbed her arms and shoved them over her head. "How does your back feel?"

The elderly woman looked dazed. She fought to catch her breath. "Wonderful," she finally managed to say.

"Raise your hands to praise God," cried the preacher.

She did.

So did everyone else in the tent, except Jim Jones. He was looking around at the excited crowd, and the sweaty preacher getting ready to pass the offering plate. "If they can do it, I can, too," he later recalled thinking. It was, he realized, the best way "to get the crowd, get some money, and do some good with it."

Jones always claimed he couldn't remember much about his first act of healing, only that it "didn't work out too well." He did, however, have more to say about his second time.

In the summer of 1953, he and Marceline drove out to a revival tent in Columbus, Indiana. There, a white-haired preacher in a print dress noticed Jones in the audience. She pointed at him and uttered a prophecy: "I perceive that you are a prophet. . . . You shall be heard all around the world, and tonight you will begin your ministry." She called him up to the pulpit.

Jones hesitated before slowly taking the stage. He looked out across the audience. A sea of faces stared back at him.

He squeezed his eyes shut, and then "all this shit [flew] through my mind," he recalled, "and I'd just call people out, and they'd get healed of everything."

Unfortunately, there remains no record of the event beyond Jones's brief recollections.

Marceline didn't provide details, either, although she did claim amazement. "I felt as if I walked on air and I could not feel my feet on the ground and it was difficult for me to even speak."

Jones went on to say, "I don't know how to explain how people got healed of everything under the sun, that's for sure . . . or *apparently* got healed. How long [the healings lasted], I don't know."

Was it a miracle? Or the power of positive thinking?

In truth, it was a sham.

Jones had known he would be called to the stage that night. He'd arranged it in advance with the woman preacher. He even admitted to "taking little notes" before the meeting began. Mingling with the crowd, he had eavesdropped on conversations. Thanks to his stealthy reconnaissance and his excellent memory, he was able to call out names in the audience and talk about personal things that he should have had no way of knowing. He assured them that God would heal them. And folks, at least temporarily, believed he had.

Word spread about the twenty-two-year-old preacher with extraordinary powers. He still had his student pastor duties at Somerset Methodist, but on weeknights and Saturdays, he and Marceline drove out to prayer meetings and healing services in tents outside small towns in Indiana, Ohio, and Michigan. As more and more people—men and women, Black and white, old and young—turned out to see him, Jones's confidence grew. He was a natural showman, and in the weeks that followed, his healings became more dramatic. He wasn't making much money, but his reputation, as well as his following, was growing.

The young man who'd once felt marginalized reveled in the adulation of the crowds. They wept in his presence, reached out with trembling hands to touch him, praised his name. He experienced a heady feeling of importance and control. He asked them to drop to their knees, and they did. He proclaimed them healed, and they believed. He requested an offering, and they gave him the last few coins in their pockets. Later, recalled a witness to his healings, these believers packed their families back into their vehicles and left with one name "beat[ing] in [their] blood: Jim Jones, Jim Jones, Jim Jones."

Meanwhile, Jones's work at Somerset Methodist grew more and more stifling. There was no pounding on the pulpit or performing acts of healing in that staid, all-white church. There was no integrated congregation. In the fall of 1954, he decided it was time to leave and form his own church.

Starting a church wasn't complicated. All a self-anointed minister needed to do was rent a space and start preaching. These "storefront churches" had no affiliation with any established religion, and they conducted services in whatever manner they saw fit. Most, however, were short-lived. Indianapolis had hundreds of established churches, and it was hard for start-ups to compete. They simply couldn't grow a congregation. And without regularly attending members and their monetary offerings, the churches failed.

Remembering his teenage success in Richmond's African American neighborhoods, Jones rented a little space in the heart of a poor Indianapolis community. Jones named his church Community Unity (because *everyone* was welcome), then went door to door handing out flyers. He was at his most charming, smiling and shaking hands. That first Sunday a few people showed up. A few more came the second week. A dozen came the third.

By the fourth week thirty worshippers, mostly Black, arrived at the storefront. They settled in the rows of folding chairs and looked toward the simple wooden podium with a cross of Jesus mounted on a freshly painted wall. First-timers probably expected a typical church service—hymns, Bible readings, a sermon. Instead, the Reverend Jim Jones burst into the room. He slapped the men's backs and hugged the women, welcoming them all.

Jones didn't take his place behind the podium or open a Bible. He dragged a folding chair to the front of the room and sat. "What's bothering you?" he asked the attendees.

An elderly Black woman stood. She told Jones how her electricity constantly went out. She'd called the electric company several times, but no one came to fix it. They kept sending bills, though. Finally, she'd demanded maintenance before she paid. In response the electric company's white representative threatened to cut her power off. She guessed she'd just have to put up with spotty service. After all, she couldn't live in the dark.

"Let's write a letter," replied Jones.

Marceline, who sat off to one side, pulled out a notebook and pencil. Jones dictated a letter to the electric company spelling out the problem. Then he turned to the congregation. Was there anything else they should add? After some suggestions and revisions, he passed the letter around. Everyone signed it.

"Unity proves we're a real family in this church," he told them. "We work together to help each other."

He promised to take the letter to the electric company the next morning. He would sit down with the person in charge and talk with him. "A wonderful lady is being treated unfairly," he concluded. "Things have to be, *will* be, made right."

Then he turned to Marceline and asked her to lead the congregation in a hymn. He followed this with prayers, readings, and a sermon about love and tolerance. But Jim Jones, as well as the congregation, knew that it wasn't hymns and prayers that kept folks coming back. It was the direct help he offered them. In the 1950s a young white upstart preacher had far more clout with city officials than the most educated and established Black ministers . . . simply because he was white.

At that time Indianapolis, like many cities in America, was segregated, and many policies were racist. A practice called redlining separated the city's white and Black populations and allowed city governments to deny financial services based on race. When the federal government passed the National Housing Act (1934), it was hoped that home purchases would be made more affordable for all Americans. But it didn't turn out that way. In Indianapolis (and other cities across the country) property appraisers ranked residential areas on a grading scale from A to D, most desirable to least desirable. These color-coded maps, created by lenders, developers, and real estate appraisers, dictated how easy or difficult mortgage companies would make it for residents to secure loans. This appraisal process discriminated against areas where African Americans lived. An A-grade area, as one appraiser said, would not include "a single foreigner or Negro." The D-grade, or red, areas included "undesirable populations." Since appraisers purposely gave bad grades to areas where *any* African Americans lived, redlining made it impossible for Blacks to move into white neighborhoods. Areas were downgraded as soon as an African American moved into them. Even areas described as having "better class" African Americans were still classified as D-grade. In contrast, desirable A-grade locations, like the one near Butler University, boasted "native white; executive and other white-collar type residents with nominal foreign born and no black residents."

As a result, Black populations could not accumulate wealth through their homes' worth. Redlining also kept their children from receiving a better education, since the city school board divided different residential areas to feed into different schools. Racially segregated housing resulted in substandard, racially segregated schools. In some instances the drawn lines forced children to cross canals, railroad tracks, or busy streets to get to their schools, even though a closer, all-white school existed. Nor did the city provide crossing guards or any safety measures for Black neighborhoods. In 1952, around the time Jones began exploring the possibility of forming his own church, an African American child tragically died after being struck by a train on his way to school.

With little to no representation in their local government, the African American community had traditionally turned to their ministers for leadership. Time and again Black ministers requested a meeting with the mayor, the school board president, or the factory manager to discuss grievances. Often white officials listened respectfully. They sent follow-up letters. Sometimes they even formed a committee to look into the issue. But in truth these officials had no intention of solving problems, or improving Black citizens' lives. Instead, they placated the ministers while continuing on with business as usual.

Unable to get substantial results, Black ministers offered their flocks solace and comfort instead. Yes, they lived in poverty now, the ministers said, but better times were coming after death. God loved them, and He guaranteed them a place in the Promised Land; milk and honey would be theirs for all eternity. They just had to endure the here and now.

That felt wrong to Jim Jones. Why should African Americans have to wait until death? Why wasn't anyone working to raise them up *now*? He realized that as a white preacher he had influence that his Black counterparts did not. They couldn't go to the electric company and demand action. But because of his whiteness, he could initiate action on behalf of his Black members. This differed from what African American churches could offer, and it was a message that resonated. Every Sunday would bring new worshippers, not because Jones was a better preacher, but because he fully recognized his white privilege and chose to use it.

The next Sunday, Jones asked the elderly woman to stand up and tell everyone what had happened.

Her electricity worked, she exclaimed. Someone had come out and fixed it.

"See?" he said. "When you come to this church, you get something *now.*" He urged the congregation to bring their families, friends, and neighbors. Community Unity, he reminded them, still promised eternal life, but it didn't ignore life on earth.

Jim Jones had found a winning combination—a church that directly helped its members in crucial ways while still providing the Bible-based worship services they desired.

At the same time, the popularity of his faith healing on the revival circuit was also drawing members. He soon had to buy a building big enough to accommodate all who were coming to see him. He named this new place of worship Peoples Temple Full Gospel Church, intentionally omitting the possessive apostrophe in *Peoples* since his name referred to *all* the peoples of the world. The name, however, was soon simplified. It became known as Peoples Temple.

Another big change came to the Joneses in 1954. After service one Sunday, as Jim stood at the church door shaking hands with his congregants, he felt a tug on his robe. Looking down, he saw an eleven-year-old girl wearing ragged clothes and clutching a handful of wilting violets. She handed them up to the preacher. "I love you," she said with a terrible stutter.

Jones was instantly smitten. She must have reminded him of his own lonely childhood, because he made a snap decision: He would adopt her. The rest of the story is blurry. Obviously, Jim and Marceline tracked down the girl's mother. But how they managed to persuade her to give up her daughter is not known. What *is* known is that within weeks the child joined the Jones family. Her name was Agnes Pauline.

Chapter Three

Hyacinth and Zip

FIFTY-THREE-YEAR-OLD HYACINTH THRASH HADN'T BEEN TO church in a decade. She felt bad about it. Raised in the Pentecostal faith, she accepted as truth the mysteries and majesty of God's powers. She believed in prophecies, faith healing, and speaking in tongues. And she believed she knew God's work when she saw it. But she wasn't finding his hand in any of the all-Black Indianapolis churches she'd attended. The preachers, she claimed, were hypocrites. They demanded she put more and more money into their offering plates, while they carried on with women and drank liquor.

Now she stayed home on Sundays and watched "TV church" in her living room alongside her younger sister, Zipporah Edwards (Zip for short).

One such Sunday morning in 1955, a handsome young white preacher with shiny coal-black hair and burning eyes appeared on her tiny black-and-white screen. His name was Jim Jones, and he was broadcasting from his newly established Peoples Temple in Indianapolis.

Zip leaned closer to the television. "It was like Jim was just pulling her in," recalled Hyacinth.

Standing behind the pulpit, Jones seemed to focus himself entirely—every muscle, every nerve—on what he was saying. And his words astonished both sisters. Peoples Temple was a place whose "door is open so wide that all races, creeds, and colors find a hearty welcome to come in, relax, meditate, and worship God."

The TV camera panned to the Temple choir. Black and white members stood together, sharing hymnals and singing about God's love.

The sisters had never seen anything like it.

"I've found my church!" cried Zip.

The following week the sisters arrived at Peoples Temple wearing flowered hats, their best dresses, and white cotton gloves. The congregation greeted them cordially, and an usher led them up the aisle. He seated them next to a white couple.

The couple smiled a warm welcome.

Hyacinth looked around. Men, women, and children. Black and white. Young and old. They shared pews, handshakes, and hugs. She couldn't believe it.

Additionally, it felt like her childhood church. Hyacinth knew all the hymns by heart, all the Bible verses, too. And then there was the Reverend Jones, sounding like an old-time preacher on fire with the Holy Spirit.

"Amen!" one or another person would ecstatically shout. "Praise Jesus! Hallelujah!"

But it was Jones's spiritual powers that left Hyacinth awed. He began simply, with "discernment." In some Christian denominations such as Pentecostal or Southern Baptist, it is believed that preachers who have been touched by God can "discern" something about a person's past or present.

Falling into a trancelike state, Jones called out people's names, identifying what each carried in their purse or pocket. He disclosed past transgressions, financial problems, or present ailments.

Suddenly, he called out a man named Gilbert. He "discerned" that Gilbert had cancer. But the man shouldn't worry; Jones could heal him. He ordered Gilbert to the restroom. Minutes later Gilbert returned.

It was a miracle, the man cried. He'd passed a bloody, cancerous tumor from his bowels. He held it up so all could see. In a paper towel lay a putrid mass.

Hyacinth felt goose pimples break out all over her.

When the service ended, the sisters strode down the aisle to where Jones stood at the church entrance. He took their white-gloved hands in his. He looked deeply into their eyes and invited them back to next week's service.

In that moment, recalled Hyacinth, she felt respected, a feeling she'd never gotten from a white man. Despite all the morning's wonders, *that* was the biggest miracle of them all.

Not long after their visit to the church, Hyacinth and Zip found a flyer on their doorstep.

The Reverend Jones and a few church members would be in their neighborhood the next day and planned to stop by. He hoped they'd be home.

The sisters were thrilled. They tidied the house and made refreshments.

As promised, Jones and the others arrived. Sitting between the sisters, the preacher held their hands and prayed with them. "It was wonderful," recalled Hyacinth.

Peoples Temple gained two new members that day. The sisters joined a congregation that was already one hundred members strong. And they became part of what would be the church's largest demographic: Black women.

Hyacinth and Zip threw themselves into church life. Besides attending both Sunday morning and evening services, as well as Wednesday night meetings, they took part in the church's good works. They helped run the Temple's soup kitchen. They solicited donations of food and clothing. They fixed up baskets for the needy, which they handed out regardless of race. All the while Hyacinth experienced something new. Not only was she treated as an equal partner with the white members, but she started growing comfortable with them and forming friendships. This last part astonished Hyacinth. Having grown up in the Jim Crow South, both she and Zip were justifiably afraid of white people, particularly white men.

But now the sisters made friends with white people like Jack and Rheaviana Beam, a working-class couple who embraced Jones's emphasis on civil rights. A gruff man, Jack intimidated Hyacinth at first. But she soon saw beneath his rough exterior. Not only was he a good organizer, and handy at all sorts of equipment maintenance, but he was also fiercely loyal to Peoples Temple.

So was Patty Cartmell, an evangelical Christian with the heart of a civil rights activist. She'd dragged her kids, eleven-year-old Mike and five-year-old Trisha, to all kinds of religious experiences before hearing Jones preach. Afterward, she turned to her son and declared, "Mikey, he's got it all." She joined Peoples Temple and quickly became Jones's eyes and ears, mingling with the folks at the Temple and gathering information for him to use in his discernments and healings. She didn't feel guilty about these actions. He had convinced her that the end justified the means. Spying on behalf of the preacher was doing God's work.

Jones liked to begin his sermons with warnings that Satan was everywhere, working to destroy God's goodness. This made Satan the common enemy. The only way to fight him was to stand together, every member shoulder to shoulder. There could be no racism, or sexism, no disdaining of each other because of how much money or education one might have. Satan knew that a divided house could not stand. The only way to defy and defeat evil was to accept *everyone* as family.

The Reverend Jones also charmed and delighted. His congregation soon included dozens of children. He wanted them to think church was fun, not just something adults made them do. He often stopped preaching and told the kids to get up and run around the church a few times. Jones joined them, his blue satin robe flapping behind him.

One Easter Sunday he interrupted the story of Christ's resurrection and asked the children what song they wanted to sing on this holiest of Christian holidays.

"'Here Comes Peter Cottontail'!" shouted one kid.

Jones asked the congregation to sing it. And he started: "Here comes Peter Cottontail, hoppin' down the bunny trail. Hippity hoppin,' Easter's on its way. . . ."

Hundreds of voices joined him. Afterward, the Temple rocked with joyous laughter.

"Jim had a real good church program going," said Hyacinth. "It was so good."

It wasn't just the church program that held Zip. Like many

members, she gradually began putting more faith in Jones than in God. "She was sold on Jim," said Hyacinth. "She used to praise him up and down, and Jim praised her too. She did little things for him and got praises for that. She was so wrapped up in him."

⸻

In 1957, Lynetta Jones arrived in Indianapolis and took up residence in a second-floor bedroom of Jim and Marceline's house. Her son's reputation, as well as his congregation, was growing, and she wanted to bask in his accomplishments. She would live with the couple for the rest of her life.

Jones was happy to have his mother living under his roof. But Marceline found her mother-in-law's presence challenging. Lynetta hadn't changed much over the years. She still smoked and drank and cussed. And she still believed religion was a bunch of baloney. No way would she attend a church service . . . not even her son's.

⸻

That same year a young Black mother named Christine Cobb dragged her crying seven-year-old son, Jim, down the aisle. Christine had heard about the preacher's miracles. Abandoning her neighborhood Baptist church, she'd taken the bus across town to Peoples Temple. She hoped Jones could help her little boy, who suffered from dizzy spells caused by an ear problem. Doctors recommended surgery, but the idea terrified Christine. There had to be another solution.

Jones spied the Cobbs from the pulpit. He stepped down and made his way through the crush of people filling the aisle until he stood before them. He stared down at the child.

"You have an ear problem, my son," he said. He placed his hand on Jim's head.

Around him the congregation moaned and shouted. Some raised their hands, swaying with the Holy Spirit. The air seemed to pulse with anticipation.

Jones pulled his hand back. "Your ear will be fine, my son," he said.

Christine called out her gratitude as the preacher headed back to his pulpit. He turned around, then looked at little Jim. "You're going to be a leader someday," he prophesized.

As it turned out, Jones would get it half-right. He hadn't cured Jim. The boy would require ear surgery five years later. But Jim Cobb *would* lead a movement, one that would rock the Temple.

Chapter Four

All a Facade

JONES PREACHED THE GOLDEN RULE: "DO UNTO OTHERS AS you would have them do unto you." He emphasized traditional church outreach: distributing food and clothes to the needy, bringing casseroles to shut-ins, organizing programs for urban youth. Jones, of course, was the center of it all. He visited the sick and elderly, served meals in the Temple's soup kitchen, played basketball with the neighborhood kids, gave marital advice, ministered to the down-and-out, hugged strangers, bounced colicky babies on his knee, prayed for sinners, took in stray animals, praised the Lord at every turn, and was, declared Hyacinth Thrash, "so good": "He'd give a man the shoes off his own feet. . . . He was called of God."

It was all a facade. In the years since his marriage to Marceline, the last of his religious feelings had drained away. He no longer put his faith in God. He'd placed it in something else: socialism.

Broadly defined, socialism is an economic system in which all citizens share equally in property and material resources. It emphasizes cooperation; members of a socialist community work together for the greater good rather than for themselves.

Jones would later assert that he'd been a committed socialist since childhood, but there's no evidence to back up this claim. Early in his marriage he'd made sympathetic comments about socialism and said it was ridiculous that Americans treated it like a disease. He even attended a few communist rallies in Indianapolis. Around this same time, he'd also begun reading books like *The ABC of Anarchism* by Alexander Berkman and *The Communist Manifesto* by Karl Marx and Friedrich Engels. They'd led Jones to conclude that socialism was the only way to combat America's vast economic disparities and racial inequalities. "It seemed gross to me that one human being would have so much more than another," he later explained. "I couldn't come to terms with capitalism in any way." To his mind, it was both cruel and inescapable. The world was divided in half: socialist versus capitalist, or "good versus evil," as he said.

In those days the concept of socialism was virtually taboo, and anyone who espoused it was considered un-American. Jones knew that preaching socialism would never draw a crowd. In fact, it would almost certainly destroy his church. Jones concluded that he'd have to use religion as bait. He'd have to "infiltrate the church," using the cover of religion to promote socialism. He would make socialism his church's basic tenet and one day eliminate the Bible altogether.

He envisioned the socialist congregation he would create. Its members would donate all to the church—their time, labor, money, and possessions. In return they would live communally while the church provided for all their needs. Jones, of course, would be their leader, advising and mentoring them.

He even had a name for this new religious belief system: *apostolic socialism.* But in 1957 he wasn't yet ready to reveal his true goal to anyone, not even Marceline. Faith in God and the Bible was deeply ingrained in those he wanted to attract to Peoples Temple. Attacking what they devoutly believed would get him nowhere. No, he would have to chip away at their religious beliefs, as well as their notions about capitalism.

Jones first broached the topic at a Sunday-night service in 1959. He began by reminding members of Christianity's early days. The apostles—those first twelve men who'd chosen to follow Jesus—had forsaken all their belongings. They'd shared and lived communally, as had Christ. He looked at the congregation. "Now what are you gonna do with that?" he boomed. "Any opinion?"

No one answered.

"I didn't think so," said Jones, his voice filled with disappointment.

He went on. "God for some time has been putting it upon our hearts to sell what we have and give it to the corporate community of our church. Our Temple now is starting our restaurant, a mission that will feed people without cost. Running a grocery and no charge for food. We're asking people to give as God blesses them. No charge for anything because God is free and everything He has is free. It's been provided . . . on the basis of *from each according to his ability to each according to his need.*"

Did any member notice that famous line written by the founder of communism, Karl Marx? If so, no one spoke up.

Jones opened the Bible and read from it: "There was not a needy person among them, for as many as were possessors of lands or houses sold them and brought the proceeds of what was sold and laid at the apostles' feet; and distribution was made to each as any had need."

He was making a point: The apostles were socialists. Jesus was, too. So why weren't they?

He wrapped up. "Some of you don't like to hear this tonight. But you better get ready to hear a lot more of it. . . . *Amen.*"

With that sermon came new demands from the preacher. He insisted that families give 10 percent of their earnings to the Temple. He made work in the church's community projects mandatory, as well as attendance at all three weekly services. Additionally, he insisted all members follow his special rules: no putting on superior airs, no obsession with or discussion of material objects. He encouraged members to watch one another and report transgressions.

These demands were much greater than those made by other Indianapolis churches.

Jones also held weekly "corrective fellowship sessions," where people who were perceived to have acted inappropriately were called out before their peers. They were gentle procedures, usually ending with the wrongdoer promising to behave better. Jones then forgave them. After all, he reminded his congregation, no one could be expected to act perfectly, except for Marceline and himself. Surprisingly, most members appreciated the chance to receive constructive criticism. They worked even harder to meet the preacher's expectations.

Jones watched as, by increments, members changed their lifestyles to meet the Temple's needs. The distinctions between an individual life and a church life faded.

One night during a routine church meeting, Jones held up his hands for silence. He'd been wondering, Would everyone lie down on the floor if he asked them?

Members looked at one another quizzically. A few answered that they supposed they would.

Jones asked them to do it.

Some immediately slid out of their chairs and stretched out on the floor. Others hesitated before following suit. Soon, however, the entire group was on their backs.

Jones sat there, silently considering their still bodies. Then he remarked that he was "no better than they were" and slipped off his chair to join them.

It was the second time Jim Jones had asked his followers to play dead.

For some the strict rules and correction sessions were too much. They'd been looking for a church, not a lifestyle. They stopped attending the Temple. But Jones, feeling hurt and abandoned by their quitting, refused to let them go without a struggle. Didn't they see the personal bond he'd formed with them? Didn't they know they could call on him at any time for help or counsel? He inundated them with begging phone calls and letters. He appeared on their doorsteps to plead for their return. He beseeched them in the name of God, he said. To abandon Jones was to abandon the Almighty. In some cases he even claimed to have had a premonition. Something bad would happen to the quitter if they didn't return to the Temple. "You will be making a terrible mistake to leave me," he warned.

Still, most didn't return.

Life with his adopted daughter, Agnes, had not been as satisfying as Jones had hoped. By 1957, thanks to a year of speech therapy, the fourteen-year-old girl no longer stuttered. But she was sulky, stubborn, and rebellious. She talked back to her parents and refused to do chores and homework. This was *not* the happy-go-lucky child Jones had wanted. Darkly brooding Agnes did not fit with the wholesome Christian image he hoped to project. It was time, he decided, to add to the family.

Unfortunately, doctors had told Marceline, who suffered from back problems, that she would likely have difficulties with pregnancy.

This news didn't faze Jones. "[He] was always saying people should adopt rather than have children of their own," recalled Hyacinth. So, she wasn't surprised when the preacher and his wife decided to adopt. She *was* surprised, however, to learn that they didn't want a white baby. Instead, the couple planned to create what Jones called "a rainbow family." They would adopt multiple children of different races. His family would be, he said, "a living example of racial harmony."

At that time no white couple in Indiana had ever adopted a Black baby. Authorities weren't even sure if such an adoption was legal. Months passed as attorneys investigated the matter.

Frustrated, the Joneses set their sights on an Asian child instead. Since none were available in Indiana, they traveled to California. In October 1958 they returned to Indianapolis with two Korean orphans in tow: a four-year-old girl and a two-year-old boy. They christened the children with American names: Stephanie and Lew.

Jim and Marceline doted on the little ones. So did Jones's congregation.

On a rainy Saturday afternoon, seven months later, Stephanie climbed into the backseat of a family friend's car. She'd begged her father's permission to ride home with them after an outing to the Cincinnati Zoo. On the drive, a speeding vehicle struck the car head-on and killed everyone inside. Hearing the news, Jones hurried to the scene and watched as the sheet-draped stretcher bearing his daughter's body was slid into the back of an ambulance. Then he turned to speak to reporters. "It's hard to understand these things," he said, his voice faltering. "At least we have the consolation of knowing [Stephanie] received more love in these few months than in her entire life before."

He remained quiet for a few minutes. Then he pulled himself

together. As if remembering he was talking with the press, Jones regained his confident tone. Yes, he told them, the Temple still planned to hold regular Sunday services in the morning. And he fully intended to be there, praising God and delivering his word. He waited for the reporters to scribble down what he'd said in their notebooks. Then he revealed something extraordinary. He'd had a premonition about the crash, he told them. "For some strange reason I told my [congregation] that some of our people would not come back. I don't know what made me say it."

It seems no reporter verified this statement with his congregation, or questioned whether Jones was using his daughter's tragic death to promote himself and his so-called divine powers.

Meanwhile, Marceline rested at home, unaware of her daughter's death. Not long after Stephanie and Lew's adoption, she'd discovered she was pregnant. Now, eight months along, she'd chosen not to go to the zoo. According to her, she was just drifting off to sleep when she'd heard Stephanie's voice whisper, "Oh-boke needs a mommy and daddy. Oh-boke needs a home."

Soon afterward, Jones woke his wife to break the terrible news. At first, Marceline didn't believe it. Stephanie had just spoken to her. She repeated what she'd heard, then burst into tears. It must have all been a dream.

Jim told her that what she'd heard had been a vision. God had spoken to him through her.

Drowning in grief, Marceline clung to this explanation for comfort.

A child's funeral is always hard, but Stephanie's was made more difficult by the fact that no Indianapolis cemetery would allow the Korean girl's body to be buried in the white section. No white morticians would prepare her body for burial, either, insisting she be taken to a Black undertaker.

When Stephanie was finally interred, it was in the Black section of a nearby cemetery, swampy and sloping. On the day of the funeral, it poured, and the girl's grave was half-full of water when the pallbearers lowered her coffin into the ground. "Oh . . . it was cruel, cruel," Jones recalled.

The Joneses hadn't forgotten Marceline's vision. The day after the funeral, they contacted the adoption agency in California. Did they have a child named Oh-boke living at the orphan home?

Incredibly, they did—Stephanie's six-year-old sister, Oboki. The couple immediately adopted her. They renamed her Suzanne.

Was Marceline's vision a prophecy? After hearing her story, most church members believed it was. A few, however, claimed Jones had planted this "vision" in Marceline's mind—that he'd manipulated her into remembering something that never really happened, and that he'd done it to enhance his reputation as a man of divine powers. They suggested that Jones must have known all along about Oboki, from either the orphanage or Stephanie herself, although no proof of that exists. Marceline, however, clung to her vision unquestioningly and told it repeatedly and with conviction for the rest of her life.

Just three weeks after Stephanie's death, and days after Suzanne's arrival, Marceline went into labor. As doctors had foreseen, she had a difficult time. But at last, on June 1, 1959, she gave birth to a dark-haired boy. The Joneses gave him the first name Stephan in honor of his dead sister, and the middle name Gandhi after Mohandas Gandhi, the Indian political and social activist.

But the "rainbow family" wasn't complete. Months later, in 1960, authorities finally allowed the couple to adopt a Black infant. This son became the preacher's namesake. They christened him James Warren Jones Jr.

From the pulpit Jones now preached about his own experiences with racism. He reminded his congregation of how he'd been forced to bury his daughter in a segregated cemetery. He described how people spat on Marceline when she walked Jimmy down the sidewalk in his stroller. He even claimed to be a minority himself—part African American and part Native American—despite having no proof.

Not everyone bought it. Hyacinth found herself wondering if Jones's rainbow family was "for outside show." Did he adopt children from other races to make headlines, prove he was anti-racist, and gain followers? She struggled to ignore her skepticism. Time and again she reminded herself that Jones was "so good and had a real good wife." He wasn't trying to fool anyone.

Chapter Five

Hanging On to Jim

WITH THE ARRIVAL OF 1961 CAME A NEW CHURCH PRACTICE Jones called "witness to integration." After morning services at the Temple, Jones would drive a group of Black members to a white church. Led by Pastor Jones, the group would walk in, politely greet the ushers, and wait to be seated.

Jones had asked Hyacinth and Zip to be part of these missions, but Hyacinth felt reluctant to participate. She'd grown up in the Jim Crow South. Life had taught her that "most white folks [were] pretty tough towards blacks."

Jones told her not to worry, he would keep her safe. She simply had to trust in him and his powers. Besides, he added, God had called on them to do this work. It took individuals to overthrow racist systems. Look at Rosa Parks down in Montgomery, Alabama. She'd refused to surrender her seat to a white passenger even though the law required it, and her efforts resulted in the desegregation of Alabama's buses. Or take those four college students in Greensboro, North Carolina, who, just months earlier, had camped out at a whites-only lunch counter. They'd endured days of hatred and spittle, but they'd sparked a sit-in movement that spread across the country.

People were peacefully protesting segregation in restaurants, hotels, libraries, and other establishments. It was time, Jones said, to protest segregation in Indianapolis's churches, too.

Motivated by his words, Hyacinth gathered her courage and joined Jones's protests. But every mission left her shaking with both anger and fear. At one all-white church the pastor encouraged his congregation to sing "Old Black Joe," an offensive song about formerly enslaved African Americans. Recalled Hyacinth: "That really hurt me." She tried to hide her pain. With a dignified expression and a straight back, she sat until the end of the service.

At another white church on a cold, snowy Sunday, Jones's group sat down in the front pew. Moments later the ushers—at their pastor's bidding—opened the windows next to them. He hoped to freeze the Black visitors out. Once again, Hyacinth sat through it, shivering.

The fifty-nine-year-old began to dread these missions. With each witness to integration, her anxieties grew. She couldn't sleep. She couldn't eat.

Things came to a head when the Temple group visited a white church on the south side. Right after the congregation recited the Lord's Prayer, a man turned to them and said the church would be bombed if they didn't leave. The threat terrified Hyacinth. She scrambled to her feet and left, along with Jones and the others. But instead of driving back to the safety of the Temple, Jones led them to a field next door. He started preaching about inequality at the top of his voice.

"I was afraid," Hyacinth admitted. "I couldn't take it anymore." She urged Zip to leave with her, but Zip refused. For the first time since joining his church, Hyacinth turned her back on Jones. Alone and still trembling, she went home.

In her kitchen she sat down with a cup of tea. It seemed to her now that Jones was using her. He didn't care about her personally. She was just another body in the pew, another five dollars in the offering plate, a pawn in his quest to make a name for himself. Right then she decided to quit Peoples Temple. She would tell Jones the following Sunday.

That Wednesday she went for her annual medical checkup. After examining her and doing a few X-rays, the doctor said, "Hyacinth, you have cancer."

She could feel the tumor herself, a hard little lump under her left armpit. She returned home believing she was going to die.

On Sunday, Jones approached her before the service began. "You've had bad news," he said. "Don't worry. . . . We'll pray." He laid his hands on her chest.

Three days later she could no longer feel the lump.

Hyacinth returned to her doctor, who reexamined her and took another round of X-rays. The tumor was gone! "How do you explain that?" the doctor wondered out loud.

"Divine healing," she confidently replied.

Was it actually a miracle, or could it have been a misdiagnosis?

The truth didn't matter, not to Hyacinth. She believed Jones had healed her. "[I] hung on to him," she said. She would follow the preacher anywhere.

Jones was doing good work in segregated Indianapolis. He set up a soup kitchen that fed hundreds every day. He organized an employment assistance program in which church members helped the jobless find work and gave them appropriate clothes to wear to job interviews. Always ambitious, he preached not just from his pulpit but also on the local radio and television stations. He even advertised his preaching in the city's newspapers. He stuck to his core message: inequality and the racial problems in Indianapolis. And he walked the walk by pressuring storeowners and theater managers to stop discriminating against Black customers. In one instance he convinced a restaurant owner to integrate his dining room by arranging for dozens of Temple members to eat there, offsetting the loss of bigoted customers who refused to eat with African Americans.

Then, in the fall of 1961, Jones collapsed and fell down the church stairs. Crumpled on the ground, he trembled and gasped for breath. Those around him helped him sit up. The preacher blinked, obviously confused. He mumbled about the loud, clashing noises in his head. Marceline took his pulse. It was racing.

The episode soon passed. Getting to his feet, Jones reassured those around him: He was fine; there was nothing to worry about.

In truth, he'd recently begun experiencing sudden and overwhelming bouts of fear. He obsessed about heights, drowning, flying in airplanes, choking. Sometimes these fears crept in and nagged at him for days. Other times they came on quickly, causing heart palpitations, dizziness, and breathlessness. Jones recognized these fears as irrational, but he couldn't shake them.

A visit to his doctor confirmed what Marceline had suspected—he was having a nervous breakdown. In those days, before the availability of anxiety medications, Jones had two treatment options: hospitalization or time off work.

He chose the latter.

On the last Sunday in October, Jones stepped out from behind the pulpit, interrupting the choir midsong. He raised his hands for silence. He had something urgent to tell the congregation. "I have received a vision," he declared, "a terrible, prophetic vision."

A murmur ran through the congregation.

Jones continued. It had been revealed to him that America would soon be under nuclear attack and everyone living in Indianapolis would be obliterated. This apocalypse would come on the sixteenth of some month, although the vision hadn't specified which month, or even what year. The preacher *did* have a time—3:09—although he didn't know if that was a.m. or p.m. Again, the vision had been vague.

His words must have terrified his followers. Most of them believed in his prophecies, and this one especially struck home. At that time Americans lived in fear of nuclear holocaust, and had since November 1955, when they learned that the Soviet Union (modern-day Russia) had produced their own thermonuclear bomb. The prospect of World War III loomed large. Soviet premier Nikita Khrushchev repeatedly threatened to annihilate the West, while in schools across America, students practiced duck-and-cover drills in their classrooms, and President John F. Kennedy urged families to build fallout shelters in their backyards.

What could the congregation do? Jones had the answer: relocate to a safer place, away from nuclear targets. And while his vision had not revealed the name of this place, he claimed God would lead him to it. He vowed to leave immediately on a divine quest.

The congregation went wild—weeping, hugging, shouting praises. The Temple choir burst into a favorite church song, "The Glory of Love," and people bopped along to the upbeat tune.

"Mmm-hmm!"

"Amen!"

Pastor Jones would save them.

Chapter Six

Strange Odyssey

DAYS LATER A GROUP OF FOLLOWERS GATHERED AT THE AIRport in Indianapolis to see Jones off. He carried a single suitcase, along with his passport and a few thousand dollars drawn from the church's bank account. Where was he going? None of them knew, not even Marceline, who remained behind. She stepped forward to hug him goodbye. Bending down, Jones kissed each of his children. Then he turned and shook hands with member Russell Winberg, who would be doing the preaching until Jones returned. When would that be? No one knew that, either. But Jack Beam, who'd agreed to take on the day-to-day management of the church, hoped it would be soon. With a final wave, Jones boarded his plane.

The next afternoon he landed in Guyana, located on the northeast coast of South America. Why did he visit here? Again, no one knows. For two days he explored the capital city of Georgetown. He found the English-speaking country with its large Black population interesting. Guyana, he concluded, might make an excellent relocation site . . . someday.

Next he took off for Hawaii. Ostensibly, he was still searching for a nuclear-free haven, but in truth, he was vacationing. Marceline and the children met him there, and for the next several months, they swam and sunbathed. The lush islands acted as a balm for Jones's troubled mind. His dark fears subsided.

It was during this Hawaiian respite that Jones read an article in *Esquire* magazine titled "Nine Places to Hide," which listed the cities and/or regions where people had the best odds of survival following nuclear war. On the list was Belo Horizonte, an impoverished city in Brazil. After doing some research, Jones decided to move his family there. His idea was to establish himself as a prominent preacher before sending for his followers.

Jim and Marceline, along with nine-year-old Suzanne, five-year-old Lew, two-year-old Jimmy, and two-year-old Stephan, arrived in Brazil in April 1962. (Nineteen-year-old Agnes remained in the United States.) Jones had high hopes. He felt sure his charm and energy would immediately open doors.

But Jones didn't speak Portuguese, and he struggled to find work. He'd expected the Temple to fund this mission. And it did send an occasional small stipend. But in Jones's absence, membership, as well as donations, dwindled. Services that once attracted more than two thousand people now drew less than two hundred. Even stalwart members like Hyacinth and her sister, Zip, started church shopping. Without Jones's showy performances, the Temple faced extinction.

Back in Belo Horizonte, Jones finally found a low-paying job teaching English in an American school. In his spare time he volunteered in orphanages and ministered to those living in the city's favelas. He planned to establish a church in one of these impoverished neighborhoods, then relocate his Indiana congregation there. But without sufficient funds, this scheme was impossible.

By early 1963 he was ready to throw in the towel. There was no future for Peoples Temple in Brazil . . . and there wouldn't be one in

Indianapolis, either, if he didn't get back soon. Thanks to his earlier prophecy of nuclear attack, however, he couldn't go home for fear of losing all credibility with his remaining followers. He needed a plausible reason to return without having fulfilled his quest.

World events provided that excuse. On November 22, 1963, President Kennedy was assassinated in Dallas. The event seared the nation. Many blamed his death on a national climate of violence, hate, and extremism. They believed America was coming apart.

Amid this turmoil Jones cabled his congregation: He was returning home. In these troubled times, he declared, his flock needed his leadership.

Weeks later he was back in his pulpit. Looking out over the mostly empty pews, he realized he'd have to start recruiting new members all over again. He'd have to rebuild his congregation and reestablish himself as a powerful pastor, healer, and community leader.

But Indianapolis had changed while he'd been away. For the first time the Indianapolis city council included two Black members, who'd helped push through laws guaranteeing that all restaurants and stores served customers of all races. They'd also helped craft an ordinance outlawing discrimination in housing and were working on laws that would make decent housing available at affordable prices. Jones tried to recapture his place as a leader in the integration movement, but Black citizens no longer needed him. Now they could go directly to the city council, which wielded far more clout than Pastor Jim Jones.

Additionally, the church faced a mountain of bills, and the phone and utility companies were threatening to cut off service unless Jones paid up. Unable to make ends meet, he was forced to sell the big church he'd bought years earlier and move into a smaller building. This galled him. More galling were the charitable donations sent to him by other local churches after the *Indianapolis Star* ran a story about the Temple's financial plight. How could he hold up his head in the community?

Jones's fears returned, but this time he submitted to them. "They became a part of him," wrote one biographer, "like a chronic injury."

One such fear was for his children's safety. Worried that they might be kidnapped, he refused to let them ride bikes in front of the house. And he prohibited them from playing near the chain-link fence that separated the Joneses' backyard from the alley. He marked off an invisible line and made the youngsters promise never to cross it. But time and again toy planes and baseballs landed near the fence, and the children scampered after them.

One overcast day in the fall of 1964, eight-year-old Lew and his friends stood in a circle tossing a ball as five-year-old Stephan and six-year-old Jimmy watched. Stephan wished the older boys would let him play.

Suddenly, the ball whizzed between Lew's legs and skittered toward the fence.

Lew raced after it.

That's when Stephan saw it. On the other side of the fence, a monster wearing a black robe was shuffling toward him. In its black-gloved hands it lugged a heavy stone.

"Look out!" hollered one of Lew's playmates.

Lew whirled and froze at the sight.

The monster lifted his arms and heaved the stone over the fence. It thumped to the ground just inches from the terrified boy.

Lew wheeled and dashed for the house. "Bogeyman! Bogeyman!" he screamed. The others followed, except for Stephan.

He stood, eyes fixed on the figure as it shuffled away. There was *something* familiar about it.

"Stephan!" cried Marceline. As the little boy squirmed, still trying to see, she dragged him inside. Then she wrangled all the kids into the living room. She looked them over for injuries.

At that moment Jones barreled through the back door. "Is everything okay?" he shouted. He'd had a premonition that something bad had happened, so he came running right away, he told them.

Something felt off to Stephan. He couldn't put his finger on it, but . . . He pushed the feeling aside. His father was there to protect them. Nothing mattered but that.

It would be another decade before Stephan learned the truth: His father had been the bogeyman.

Part Two

Relocating

I was totally converted the moment I walked into Peoples Temple. The kids—integrated children—the singing, the dancing, the talk of socialism, and a life away up in the hills . . . where we were safe from nuclear attack. I was overwhelmed. . . . I was turned on to gospel music. And when we'd go to the big meetings . . . I'd be jumping and clapping, and Jim would remark, "There's Claire, she hasn't got any rhythm, but she sure has enthusiasm." I loved it. . . . I loved everything about it.

—Claire Janaro, Peoples Temple survivor

Chapter Seven

California Dreaming

IN EARLY 1965, JONES TOLD HIS FOLLOWERS THAT HE'D HAD another vision about nuclear holocaust. This time he'd been shown a mushroom cloud over Indianapolis. He'd also been given specifics. The terrible event would occur on July 16, 1967, at 3:09 p.m. But fear not, he quickly added, because the vision had also revealed where they should go to escape nuclear fallout: Northern California.

To be fair, Jones's fear of nuclear holocaust *was* real. But other considerations factored into his decision, too. After struggling to reassert himself and his church, Jones realized his time in Indianapolis was up. If he wanted to recover his image as an activist, while still holding on to the last of his followers, he needed to relocate his church. But where? He returned to the *Esquire* article and its list of nuclear-safe locations. His experience in Brazil had discouraged him, at least for the present, from the idea of moving Peoples Temple to another country. That left the only place on the list that was in the United States—Eureka, California, a small town 270 miles north of San Francisco. But a handful of trusted church members sent to scout settlement sites convinced Jones that the rural community of Redwood Valley, 150 miles south of Eureka, better suited Temple needs. It was also, they explained, still within the "Eureka safe zone."

Jones liked the idea of California. He saw it as a progressive state, a place more likely to support a socialism-based church.

Now he told his congregation that he intended to take his family to California. Who would go with him?

It was a test of faith. Which members were loyal enough to uproot their lives and move across the country? Who among them truly, deeply believed that he was a prophet able to speak with God?

—

In the summer of 1965, Peoples Temple had two hundred members. Most, however, refused to move with Jones to Redwood Valley. They had enjoyed their time in the church, but they weren't leaving their jobs and homes.

Eighty-six members, however, *did* join in what Jones called "the migration." They auctioned off or gave away everything they owned, sold their homes, and quit their jobs. Then, banding together in a caravan of loaded-down vehicles, they set off on a two-day cross-country trek. Among them were some of Jones's first followers, including the Cartmells and the Beams. These "migrants" would become Jones's core membership in California. Most would never leave his side.

Zip was wild to go, too, but Hyacinth held her off. She hated the idea of selling their home. She'd saved and struggled for it. Surely, the Lord wouldn't ask her to sacrifice that.

—

Jones regularly called congregants who had stayed behind, using all kinds of tricks and ploys to get them to California. He told some that he'd "seen" they had cancer, or crippling arthritis, or some other serious ailments. Of course, he could cure them. All they needed was to come to Redwood Valley.

Still others were regaled with descriptions of idyllic California. Everyone had jobs, he told them, far better ones than they'd held in Indianapolis. The air was fresh and healthful; fruits and vegetables shot up with almost no effort; the people in town were friendly and welcoming. Indeed, the Lord had sent them to the land of milk and honey.

He convinced dozens of families.

Too bad that Redwood Valley wasn't as Jones described it. The preacher didn't bother to tell these families about the hostility area residents exhibited toward members of Peoples Temple. This was mostly due to the sudden influx of African Americans into their almost entirely white and conservative community. Small-town racism was rampant, and some residents turned Black members of the Temple away from restaurants. They refused to rent them apartments or sell them homes. Those who did serve Black members often did so with cold, hard glares and stony courtesy. During a church trip to Lake Mendocino, local bigots shouted racial slurs at the group. They jeered at the sight of Blacks and whites together, catcalled, and threw trash.

All this harassment made Temple members feel persecuted. Jones turned this to his advantage, telling them that this persecution made them special. In the face of adversity, they were fighting for their dream of racial equality. Naturally, Jones said, they would be forced to endure the slings and arrows of the white status quo. Look at Gandhi. Look at Jesus.

At Jones's coaxing, the congregation began to divide the world into "insiders" and "outsiders." They isolated themselves. While they projected a public image of do-gooders eager to engage with their new neighbors, members were growing suspicious, even paranoid, about outsiders.

Jones encouraged these feelings. He constantly stressed that it was the Temple against a mostly unfriendly world. Only within the group would they be protected. He reminded them that they were setting an example that would eventually inspire the rest of the country. They might be a small group now, but soon the masses would come. And he would lead them.

To do this, however, they needed more people. They would have to convert outsiders into church members. Recruitment followed a plan. As a first step, the Temple made donations to local charities. Next Jones set up meetings with public officials in which he stressed the church's commitment to contributing to their new community. Then he began a letter-writing campaign. Anytime a school board member cut a blue ribbon, or a county politician made a speech, or an elderly citizen had a milestone birthday, that person received a flurry of well wishes from Peoples Temple. Jones assigned a group of members to this last task. They scoured the local newspaper for announcements. Births, deaths, graduations, and anniversaries—nothing went unnoticed.

Before a member of the writing committee could send a card or letter, however, Jones had to approve it. Sometimes, if Jones considered a recipient potentially useful, the committee sent a homemade cake with a card that read: "From the Ladies' Aid Society of Peoples Temple Christian Church." Those who received these cakes usually sent Jones a thank-you note—just as the preacher had hoped.

Connection made, he telephoned them and invited them to a service. Some accepted his invitation. Some even joined.

Not long after the Lake Mendocino incident, Temple members built a pool in the Joneses' front yard so they could swim in peace. They did all the work, and the experience empowered the group. Since their arrival, they'd been renting a space to hold services, but now they decided to erect their own church. They constructed it directly over the pool. Inside the simple redwood building, the space was equally divided between the pool and a large open area for meetings. Together they painted walls and sewed curtains, installed tile and hung wallpaper. They even built Jones's pulpit. From then on whenever members attended church meetings, they felt a deep pride. They'd built this church with their own hands, as a family.

And as a family, they shared meals, fellowship, advice, and encouragement. They didn't mix with nonmembers or pursue outside friendships. Even their children played only with Temple kids. At Jones's insistence members cut themselves off from their non-Temple relatives and friends. They stopped accepting their phone calls and discouraged visits. The church was becoming their everything.

Jones did have one teensy problem—his mother. Lynetta, who'd moved with them to California, was a bit of an embarrassment. He had to explain away her drinking by telling members she imbibed only on doctor's orders. He hid her cigarette smoking by allowing her to light up only on the back porch, where no one could see or smell her habit. And when members remarked about never seeing her in church, Jones lied and told them she donated heavily. Sometimes Lynetta turned up for church potlucks. She liked the fawning she received as Jones's mother. But she wasn't a follower. She knew her son too well to fall for his "sky god stories."

Within a year of the Temple's arrival in California, Jones began to publicly question the Bible. From the pulpit he pointed out every error, contradiction, and inconsistency it contained. He highlighted the atrocities condoned by God: enslavement, rape, murder, and hundreds of other violent acts. He eventually collected his findings in a twenty-four-page booklet called "The Letter Killeth."

In his booklet Jones didn't entirely dismiss the Bible—instead, he used scripture to support his belief in socialist theories. But above all the tract was a tool to legitimize his divine powers. "Who raises the dead, makes the blind to see and the deaf to hear? Who corrects bones? Truth can still be found in the Bible, but a prophet is needed to make it clear," he wrote. Happily, for them, "there is a prophet in our day who unquestioningly proves that he is sent from God. He has all the gifts of the spirit as given in the Bible: word of wisdom, word of knowledge, faith, gifts of healing, working of miracles, prophecy, discerning of spirits, tongues, and interpretation of tongues. We must have a prophet who is living the Christ life to direct us in this hour." Obviously, that prophet was Jim Jones.

A handful of members found this claim heretical and left the Temple. But most stayed—some because they agreed with Jones's logic, others because his shift in dogma wasn't enough to cause them to abandon the church community.

In Redwood Valley, church was an all-day commitment that included two services and a potluck in between. Congregants spent their entire Sundays together. But they weren't bored. Pastor Jones preached up a storm. He was exciting, exhilarating, surprising, and electrifying. Integration. Social change. A hint of revolution. The place would be "booming, stomping, rocking, vibrating," recalled his son Stephan. Bounding off the stage, Jones "would just hug and kiss elderly women and pick children up in his arms, tapping into something that was real."

It was *this* Jim Jones who drew people. A handsome man with a charming smile, a genuine playfulness, and a seemingly huge heart. "He had people hooked," said Stephan. "People were either hooked on him or hooked by him."

Chapter Eight

Joining Jim

ALMOST TWO YEARS AFTER PEOPLES TEMPLE MOVED TO California, Hyacinth Thrash's leg went numb. Doctors discovered a tumor on her spine. She needed surgery.

Zip, who'd been speaking by telephone to Jones weekly since he'd left, contacted the preacher. She asked him to heal her sister.

Jones promised to pray.

The next morning Hyacinth went under the scalpel. But while removing the tumor, the surgeon nicked a nerve, leaving her with permanent damage. Ever after, her leg ached painfully, and she walked with a cane. She wondered why Jones had let this happen. Why hadn't he cured this tumor like the one in her breast?

"He was losing his gift," she told Zip.

Zip disagreed. Jones was all the way across the country. How could he heal someone he couldn't lay hands on? She begged Hyacinth to go to California. Not only would they be safe from nuclear bombs, but Jones would also cure her.

Hyacinth gave in. After selling the house and packing up their possessions, they climbed into Zip's car. Despite her initial reluctance,

Hyacinth felt excited. The year—1967—had been a good one for civil rights. President Lyndon Johnson had recently appointed Thurgood Marshall to be the first Black justice on the United States Supreme Court. And that same court had just overturned laws banning interracial marriage.

Still, on their first-ever cross-country trip, the sisters packed a cooler with enough sandwiches to last the entire two days to avoid whites-only restaurants. Driving west on Route 66, they marveled at the mountains and the desert. Both imagined a brighter, better life in California. "Oh, it was a fine time," declared Hyacinth.

Once they arrived in Redwood Valley, the sisters flung themselves into Temple life. With Jones's help, they moved into a two-bedroom apartment. The only African Americans in the building, the sisters soon formed close friendships with their neighbors—Temple members all. A middle-aged couple, Alfred and Mary Tschetter, often stopped over to the sisters' to watch television. An Italian woman named Mrs. Landini shared herbs from her garden. And the Parks family, who lived next door, sat beside the seniors' beds, administering fluids and medicine when both sisters came down with the flu. Hyacinth thanked the Lord each morning for leading her to California.

Zip, on the other hand, thanked Jim Jones.

Hyacinth soon bought a four-bedroom ranch house. At Jones's suggestion, the sisters converted it into a care home for patients who'd been discharged from the local mental hospital, and the sisters took in four women with minor mental health problems. The state paid them $270 a month per patient. Hyacinth found joy in her new job and took pride in "doing things right," she said. She treated the women with love and respect, served nutritious meals, and kept everything spotless. And since she'd scrimped most of her life to get by, she knew how to stretch a dollar. Each month—after paying all her expenses—she had a little money left over. This she put into the Temple's offering plate.

Hyacinth was one of the rare members who purchased her own property. Using money brought from Indiana, the Temple had acquired multiple properties in and around Redwood Valley. These were converted into church-owned care homes. Some, like Hyacinth's, provided shelter for mental patients. Others became nursing homes for the elderly. Still others took in foster children or juvenile delinquents. There was even a rehabilitation center for drug addicts. Temple members served as administrators and staff, and all profits went to the church. Not only did this scheme provide jobs for members, but it also served as an outreach program. Those living in clean, caring homes often joined the Temple, as did those who successfully kicked their addictions. The children placed in Temple homes by the state attended services, too. Many remained devoted members as they grew into adults. At the same time, the money made from these businesses was used to fund even more outreach efforts—pamphlets, radio programs, TV spots, newspaper ads—which attracted even more people to the Temple.

In their spare time Hyacinth and Zip folded and stamped pamphlets soliciting funds for Jones's ministry and made pastries for the church's weekly bake sale. Zip's cranberry-sauce cake was especially popular.

The sisters grew vegetables, too, and put up jars of zucchini, corn, peaches, string beans, and tomatoes. Other members did the same. By November the shelves in the church pantry groaned. These preserves were distributed to the church's care homes and the community's poor. "We all helped each other," said Hyacinth. "It was so much fun. . . . It was like heaven."

Meanwhile, Jones made the rounds from one member's home to the next, chatting and listening, showing concern for their well-being, praying with them, giving advice. He insisted that no problem or concern was too small to bring to his attention. And he wasn't above menial work himself. It wasn't surprising to find Pastor Jones with his sleeves rolled up, scrubbing toilets or taking out garbage. His actions made clear that they were an ad hoc family, and he was, in essence, their father, a model of love.

Hyacinth had just one complaint about life in California. Jones hadn't healed her leg. She longed to feel his hands on her head and hear the words that would draw out her lameness. But Sunday after Sunday passed without him calling her forward. Why? she wondered.

After years of nagging, Christine Cobb—mother of Jim Cobb Jr., the boy whose ear Jones claimed to have healed—gave her husband an ultimatum. "I'm going [to California]," she told him. "If you want to come, you can."

Jim Cobb Sr. gave in. In the winter of 1967, he left his well-paying job as a steelworker and traveled across the country with his wife and six of their seven children. Christine was overjoyed at being reunited with her church. But Jim, a nonmember, regretted the decision immediately. Racist Redwood Valley and its surrounding towns reminded him of the South, and he couldn't find a job worthy of his skills or experience. He ended up changing truck tires for minimum wage. Worse, he desperately missed his oldest son, Jim Jr.

Jim Jr. had stayed behind with his aunt in Indianapolis so he could finish the season with his high school baseball team. Now seventeen, he was eyeing college athletic scholarships and the possibility of playing professional ball.

In June 1968, after his team got edged out in the state playoffs, Jim boarded a Greyhound bus to join his family in California. When he reached San Francisco, his spirits soared. There was Candlestick Park, home of the Giants. Wouldn't it be something to take his place alongside the likes of African American greats like Willie McCovey and Bobby Bonds? But as the bus rumbled northward into open farmland, his heart sank. Redwood Valley was out in the sticks, far from major-league baseball.

Jim also felt shy around the Temple people, especially the teenagers. It had been three years since he'd last hung out with any of them. In that time they'd been steeped in Jones's socialist philosophies and isolated from anyone who wasn't part of the church. On Friday and Saturday nights, they hung out together, spinning records and dancing, making peanut butter fudge, or playing board games. Jim began counting the days until his return trip to Indianapolis and the start of his senior year.

But Jones had no intention of letting the boy go. He insisted the other teens throw a party for Jim. The entire congregation showed up. They showered him with attention, most especially the pastor. Oozing charm, he insisted Jim teach them some "big-city dances." Blushing, the boy did. Soon everyone—even Pastor Jones—was doing the "tighten up" to Archie Bell and the Drells. Members giggled and got silly. Some of the elderly members demonstrated the foxtrot. Pastor Jones and Marceline did a goofy version of the twist.

And over the next few weeks, Jones reminded the teen that it was his heart, not his skin color, that mattered; that only in *this* place could he nurture the spirit of compassion and giving that Jones knew existed inside him.

Jones also railed from the pulpit about the evils of competition. "If you got hurt, then you would be dumped," he told the congregation, although Jim felt the message was meant especially for him. The preacher went so far as to use competitive sports as a metaphor for capitalism: In America everyone competed for the dollar. Those who grabbed the most won, while the poor were reviled and ignored.

That summer Jones pried Jim away from his dreams of scholarships and professional baseball. The teen didn't return to Indianapolis in August. Instead, he stayed with the church.

At the local high school, Jim played football in the fall and basketball in the winter. He'd had to ask Jones's permission to do so. The preacher now required his followers to seek his approval before making decisions. Everything from getting engaged to choosing one's high school class schedule had to be sanctioned. Surprisingly, few members objected to this new level of control. They believed Jones was a prophet; he knew what was best for them.

When spring came, it was time for Jim's favorite sport: baseball. Worried Jones would withhold permission to play, he signed up without asking.

Two weeks into the season, the preacher called out Jim's name during Sunday service. He ordered him to the front of the church.

The other members turned to stare at Jim. They tsked with disapproval.

The teen, feeling hot with both shame and embarrassment, stood. He moved toward the pulpit.

Jones's dark eyes bored into him. "You played football, and that's a savage game," he thundered. "Then you played basketball. Okay, there's nothing wrong with that. But *baseball*?" The preacher knew

Jim's passion for the game, and he couldn't allow it to compete with the Temple. "What are you going to do with your life?" he demanded.

Jim scanned the faces of his church family. Would anyone take his side? He turned toward his mother. Would she speak up on his behalf? But everyone, including his siblings, looked stern.

He continued to stand there, feeling intense pressure. He didn't think he could bear the group's disappointment. Worse, though, would be Jones's response. He'd begun meting out punishments to members who needed correction. Jim had seen people paddled, or forced to clean the church's bathroom tile with a toothbrush. And these had been for minor infractions.

Jim felt he had no choice. Though it hurt him deeply, he would quit the baseball team and give up his dreams of playing college and major-league ball.

Jones praised him for making the right decision, and the congregation cheered and applauded. Jim was part of the group. So why did he feel so terrible?

Chapter Nine

Reeling In Members

THE YOUNG COUPLE HELD HANDS AS THEY WALKED ALONG a country road on that Sunday afternoon in 1968. They took in the colorful fall leaves and the ripening apples in the orchards. The woman—twenty-three, lean, and taciturn, her long, dark hair caught back in a tight ponytail—was fretful. What were they going to do about a church? Since their move to the Redwood Valley area, they'd visited several different services. But none had been a good fit.

Her husband didn't have an answer. He was the same age as his wife, but his beard and heavy brow made him look older, and the sandals he always wore gave him a hippie vibe. A vocal anti-war protester, he had, until their move, participated in sit-ins and rallies on his college campus at the University of California, Davis. He'd met his wife there at a draft-card burning.

A car pulled up alongside them. The driver, a handsome, black-haired man, asked if they wanted a lift.

Carolyn shaded her eyes and looked into the backseat. Two boys—one white and one Black—grinned at her. The man introduced them as his sons Jimmy and Stephan. He introduced himself as Jim Jones, pastor of Peoples Temple in Redwood Valley.

The couple got in. They told him their names: Carolyn and Larry Layton. Under Jones's warm and friendly prodding, they explained that they'd moved there after Carolyn accepted a job teaching French at Potter Valley High School, about thirty miles away. Larry had found work, too, in the nearby state mental hospital. The government had classified him as a conscientious objector, which meant he wouldn't be drafted or sent to Vietnam, but in return he was required to do work that contributed in some way to the nation's health or safety. His hospital job met that requirement.

Larry must have wondered if Pastor Jones would kick them out of the car. Refusal to serve in the military was seen by many as cowardice and a lack of patriotism. Words like *draft dodger* and *commie sympathizer* were often hurled at conscientious objectors.

But Jones smiled and nodded. Peoples Temple, he told them, was committed to peace and fervently opposed the Vietnam War. It believed in countering violence and racial injustice with nonviolent activism. Would they like to attend one of his services?

The following Sunday, after a warm welcome from the church's greeters, the couple took their seats. Carolyn looked around. Black and white congregants sat together, sharing handshakes and songbooks. The sight bowled her over. The daughter of a Methodist minister, she'd participated in civil rights and anti-war protests alongside her parents and younger sisters as a child. To her, activism was a part of daily life. It appeared to be that way at Peoples Temple, too.

That first service, Jones bounded onto the blue-carpeted platform. Applause erupted, but Jones quieted his people with hand motions. Then he invited them to greet their neighbors. Everyone hugged. The whole church felt filled with love.

When it came time for the sermon, instead of preaching, Jones unfolded a newspaper and discussed current events. He criticized the government. Unfair laws reflected the racist beliefs of arrogant legislators determined to retain wealth and power at the expense of the downtrodden, he said. There were two Americas. One was public and relatively powerless. The other was the deep state, the *real* government—white men devoted to maintaining the status quo who used the FBI and the CIA as their muscle.

Heads around the sanctuary nodded, including the Laytons'. The U.S. government was keeping folks down, but the Temple would raise them up.

Then the healings began. Jones called up a woman, told her she had cancer, and sent her to the bathroom. When the woman reemerged, he claimed she'd passed a malignancy from her bowels. One of his church aides held up a bloody mass as proof.

Carolyn knew this wasn't real, but she decided to look past it for now.

She and Larry returned the following week, and the week after that. Both quickly reconciled themselves to Jones's theatrics. Without these performances, folks who believed in faith healing might walk away from this place of love and return to the cruel outside world. Jones was saving them, not lying to them.

Carolyn soon became an enthusiastic member . . . and an enthusiastic devotee of Jim Jones. She called her parents, John and Barbara Moore, and raved about the preacher. "It was the only subject that seemed to matter to her," said her mother. Her parents found this worrisome. Such gushing was uncharacteristic for their serious, methodical daughter. What kind of church had she joined?

Temple membership spread through the families living in Redwood Valley and beyond. By the end of 1968—a little more than three years after the original group had moved west—close to two hundred people called themselves members.

As in Indianapolis, the majority of Temple members (75 percent) were poor and disenfranchised African Americans—a reflection of the alienation they felt within U.S. society. In the wake of Dr. Martin Luther King Jr.'s assassination, as well as those of Medgar Evers, Malcolm X, and Robert F. Kennedy, they found themselves wondering how to live Dr. King's dream. Would they ever be judged solely by their character instead of their skin color? Peoples Temple seemed to offer a solution.

Another group began joining the Temple around this time, too: people in their twenties and thirties, some white, some Black, some college-educated, some dropouts. Many sprang from California's counterculture. In the summer of 1967, tens of thousands of young adults had headed to San Francisco with a shared desire for peace and freedom. The American dream cherished by their parents was no longer a goal for them. They rejected consumerism, advocated peace, and demanded social reform. Some protested the Vietnam War. Others fought for civil rights and women's rights. Most were searching for meaning, purpose, and a sense of community. Once, they would have joined organized religion as their parents had, but conventional faith no longer satisfied. They were interested in the metaphysical, the spiritual. Some studied Eastern religions. "We had a saying," recalled one activist who joined Peoples Temple. "One person can only whisper. You need to be in a group to stand strong."

Many others who joined the church were going through life transitions—moving to a new town, returning from military service, losing a job, getting a divorce, battling addiction, and so on. They were searching for security, stability, and a helping hand. The Temple offered all this and more.

Jones understood these varied reasons, and like a chameleon, he "appealed to anyone on any level at any time," recalled one former member. To some, like Hyacinth Thrash, he spoke the language of a Pentecostal preacher. To others, like the Laytons, he referenced political theory and metaphysics. "His vocabulary could change quickly from . . . backwoods and homey to being quite intellectual," recalled another former member. He drew on these people's deep yearning for some kind of alternative life . . . and exploited it.

Chapter Ten

Carolyn

ONE NIGHT IN 1969, TEN-YEAR-OLD STEPHAN JONES SAT beside his father in the front seat of the car. Stephan didn't know, and didn't care, where they were going. He was out with his father, just the two of them, and it made him feel special.

They pulled up in front of a house, and the front door opened. A woman stood there. She was willowy, with long, dark hair and a nervous smile. Stephan didn't recognize her, but he could tell by his father's behavior that she meant something to him. Maybe more than he did. Jealousy stabbed at the boy.

Jones told him the woman's name: Carolyn Layton.

Stephan didn't understand. Why were they here?

Jones smiled at his son. "This is good for me, so it's good for you," he explained. "She lifts me up. She strengthens me and brightens my spirits. . . . You'll see. I'll be the dad you need, now that I've found what's missing. Look at how different I am already. This is good for us."

To Carolyn, he said, "Look at how much you mean to me. I've brought my son to meet you. . . . You will be his mother."

He turned to Stephan and added, "She will be your mother."

Stephan felt sick. He already had a mother.

When the three sat down to dinner, he couldn't eat a bite.

Afterward, Carolyn made up a bed for him on the sofa. Then she and Jones went into her bedroom and closed the door. The boy sat there. He felt "helpless and lost." Through the walls he heard sounds he didn't understand. He covered his head with a pillow.

Days later he sat on the edge of his mother's bed. She'd just spent hours with weights strapped to her ankles in hopes of pulling her vertebrae apart (part of the treatment for her chronic back pain), and she seemed pale and tired. She also seemed sad.

Stephan couldn't look her in the eye. He felt guilty about what his father and Carolyn had done, and ashamed for having been part of it. "His world," he later said, felt "warped."

"Your dad told me where you went the other night, honey," Marceline said. "He told me about Carolyn, about them."

Stephan's thoughts whirled. "Not only had I been polite and quiet, but there were moments when I had even felt special. Dad had . . . talked to Carolyn of his special love for me. I had been too afraid, hurt, and *proud* to act, and Mom was suffering as a result."

Marceline seemed to know what her son was thinking. "I'm sorry, honey. Are you okay?"

He nodded, but he really wasn't. His father, he realized, had made him part of the betrayal. Why would he do that? That afternoon Stephan felt the first licks of anger toward his father. Over time they would grow into a wildfire.

Marceline Jones contemplated divorce. It wasn't the first time. Back in Indiana, after discovering her husband wasn't the Christian he'd claimed to be, she'd considered ending it. But her Christian beliefs had held her: A woman married for life. If she was dutiful enough, loving and persistent enough, she could fix her husband's flaws.

But now, after twenty years of marriage, Jim had committed adultery. It was a devastating betrayal. She saw his actions as not only cruel and selfish but also, to her mind, a mortal sin. The Ten Commandments spelled it out: "Thou shalt not commit adultery." Of course, Jones didn't believe in the Bible or its tenets, but Marceline did.

Jones warned her not to make a fuss. No angry confrontations. No storming back to Indiana. Her life wouldn't change much, he promised. She'd still retain her role in the church. In public and within the Temple, she'd still be his wife. No one else would know about his relationship with Carolyn. He and Marceline would continue to act as a loving, monogamous couple. Jones claimed to still love her but said he "needed this."

Marceline didn't believe him.

Jones changed tack. This wasn't about him. It was about the church. His extramarital affair was vital to the Temple's purpose. He worked so hard—sometimes twenty hours a day. All that preaching and faith healing and glad-handing sucked him dry. Being with Carolyn made him healthier and more energetic. She reinvigorated him in a way that allowed him to go on with their important work.

His twisted but persuasive logic succeeded. Marceline accepted the situation. She justified her decision as a sacrifice for the Temple.

One Sunday, not long after confronting Marceline, Jones asked Larry Layton to stay behind after church.

"Larry, I'm in love with your wife," he blurted out when everyone else had gone. He made it clear that it wasn't the same kind of love he had for his other members. His relationship with Carolyn was special and sexual. Then he smiled, squeezed Larry's shoulders, and called him "son." Radiating fatherly concern, he talked Larry into divorcing his wife.

No one knows what Jones said, but it was obviously persuasive. Not only did Larry immediately head to Nevada to arrange a quickie divorce, but once it was granted, he also returned to Peoples Temple and resumed his place in its membership. Incredibly, this experience left him even *more* devoted to his leader. Now an ultraloyalist, Larry Layton would do *anything* for Jim Jones—steal, cheat, even murder.

Carolyn Layton's parents, John and Barbara Moore, hadn't heard from their oldest daughter for several weeks. Concerned, they made the 130-mile trip from their home in Davis, California, to Carolyn's tiny house in Potter Valley, a short drive from Redwood Valley. They took along their other daughters, fifteen-year-old Annie and eighteen-year-old Rebecca. All four wondered what Carolyn's reaction would be when they appeared on her doorstep.

To their relief, Carolyn invited them inside and brewed some tea. Once they were all settled, she made an announcement. She and Larry were divorcing. But that wasn't all. She wanted them to meet her pastor. Carolyn picked up the telephone receiver and called Jones.

He arrived within minutes. At first, he talked about social action and God's love. Then, to the Moores' horror, he revealed his relationship with their daughter. "Up to now," he told them, "I've never had a sexual relationship with anyone but my wife."

This fact did *not* comfort the parents.

Carolyn added that the Joneses could not divorce because Marceline was mentally ill. Jones had to remain by her side. After all, he'd taken a sacred vow: *in sickness and in health.*

John Moore, a Methodist pastor, must have wondered about the rest of the vow: *to love, honor, and cherish.* His daughter's logic was warped. Jones wasn't virtuous—he was cheating on his wife.

Carolyn beamed. "I can't express how completely every need for companionship and romance is fulfilled by him," she said.

Her parents interrupted. They turned to Annie and Rebecca. Would the teens mind stepping outside? As the two sat on the grass, they wondered what was being said in the house. Annie wrinkled her nose in disgust. She thought the thirty-eight-year-old Jones was gross and old.

When the teens went back in, their mother was crying—and she continued to cry most of the way home. Between bursts of tears the adults agreed not to criticize or question Carolyn. That would only drive her away. Maybe, just maybe, she'd come to her senses and return home.

In the backseat Annie seethed. She hated Jones for making her mother sad, and she heartily agreed with her father: Jim Jones was nothing more than "a charlatan."

Chapter Eleven

Brother Tim and God the Father

ON A SUNDAY IN 1971, DURING A BREAK BETWEEN THE hours-long services, Temple kids raced around the parking lot, yelling and laughing and blowing off steam. Eleven-year-old Stephan Jones, scrambling headfirst after a ball, ran smack into a tall, skinny, blond kid named Tim Tupper. Stephan knew they were the same age. He also knew Tim and his family were new members.

Rita Tupper, along with her five kids, had arrived in Redwood Valley like "refugees from a shipwreck," recalled one member. No one knew what crisis had led the family to the Temple, and tight-lipped Rita never said. No matter. They'd been welcomed with open arms. Jones and the members gave Rita a home, a job, and friendship. In return she gave them her unwavering devotion.

Now, as the boys bonked heads, Stephan felt like he'd found a missing part of himself. "I loved [Tim] almost the minute I met him," he said. The two became inseparable, and soon Tim was spending all his free time at the Joneses' home. He reveled in Marceline's motherliness and the warm attention he received from Jones. He loved the boisterous energy of the household, too. Agnes, at twenty-eight, no longer lived with her parents, but nineteen-year-old Suzanne remained. Smart and confident, she joked around with Stephan, as well as fifteen-year-old Lew and eleven-year-old Jimmy. They acted like typical goofy, high-spirited kids. Tim hated leaving.

Jones encouraged this feeling. Tim didn't have to stay with his mother and siblings, he told the boy. His family included everyone in the Temple. He could live with anyone he chose.

Tim chose the Joneses. It wasn't that he didn't love his mother or siblings. He still claimed them as his biological family and spent time with them. But within weeks of his arrival in Redwood Valley, he'd moved his stuff into Jimmy and Stephan's bedroom and called dibs on the top bunk. He took to calling Marceline and Jim "Mom and Dad" and began using the name Tim Tupper Jones (although the couple wouldn't legally adopt him for several more years).

Stephan was thrilled. His best friend had become his brother.

But one wonders what Rita Tupper thought. The record doesn't say, but she obviously didn't resist. A devoted member, she likely saw Tim's adoption as an honor. Besides, you didn't contradict Jim Jones.

It began as an ordinary Sunday morning. Shortly after eleven o'clock Jones bounded into the sanctuary. His presence was like a jolt of electricity—the crowd leaped to their feet, burst into explosive applause, shouted his name. Jones's satin robes swirled around him as he moved briskly down the center aisle to take his place behind the pulpit. He pushed back the shock of black hair that angled across his forehead and grinned boyishly at his congregation. He took a moment to organize his papers and sip some water. Then he gave a nod to the organist, who began pounding out a song.

The musicians followed along—drums, tambourine, electric guitars.

Jones began to sing in his deep baritone voice, and the others joined in. "We live and die for freedom! We live and die for freedom! Freedom! Freedom! Freedom!"

The song came from the Peoples Temple songbook. These days the congregation rarely sang traditional hymns. Instead, their music reflected the roots and aspirations of the Temple and included songs from the civil rights era, as well as pop standards and even Broadway tunes such as "You'll Never Walk Alone" from the Broadway musical *Carousel.*

As Jones sang, he raised his right fist in the air. So did his followers. It was a symbol of socialism. Solidarity. Strength. Resistance.

The crowd swayed and clapped to the music, whooping it up to gospel and soul. By the time the final strains of the song ended, they were ready for Jones's message.

This morning he had an unorthodox but important one. His purpose for being, he told them, was to prove they didn't have to depend on religion. "There [is] no need for God or any other kind of ideology. Religion, the opiate of the people, shall be removed from the consciousness of humankind. There shall no longer be any need for anything religious when freedom comes. . . . And the only thing that brings perfect freedom, justice and equality, perfect love in all its beauty and holiness, is social. *Socialism!*"

The congregation roared its agreement.

Jones looked out at their fervent, excited faces.

"I come as 'God socialist'!"

"All right. *All right.* Yeah!" The members' shouts drowned him out.

Jones yelled louder. "I shall show you, from time to time, proof of that, so that you will have no further need of religion. . . . I come to you doing all the things you have ever imagined God to do and you have never seen done. . . . It's beautiful to know God is a socialist worker. He is one of the people. He is all you have desired, all the freedom [and] justice."

He paused.

"And I must say," he added, "it is a great effort to be God."

He looked out over the congregation. Most people were clapping and praising and rocking in their seats. They were so whipped up that few likely considered his words.

Jones quickly switched from his message to faith healings—a congregation favorite.

With each "cure" Jones hollered above it all. "If you still need a God, I'm going to nose out that God. He's a false god. I'll put the right concept in your life. . . . The only happiness you've found is when you've come to trust *this* earth God."

The Temple reverberated with the sound of adoring worshippers.

"You prayed to your sky god, and he never heard your prayers. You asked and begged and pleaded in your suffering, but he never gave you any food. He never gave you a bed, and he never provided a home. But I, your socialist worker God, have given you *all* these things."

The congregation reached fever pitch. Amen!

Feeding on their energy, Jones came from behind the podium and flung the Bible to the floor.

The congregation roared its approval.

"No, it's not sacred. You won't die if you drop it." Jones stepped on the Bible. "You won't die if you stand on it." He bounced up and down. "You won't die if you jump on it."

Laughter filled the sanctuary.

His voice went from fiery to soothing. “When your world has failed you, I’ll be standing, because I am freedom. I am peace. I am justice. *I am God!*”

“A lot of people believed it,” recalled Hyacinth. “Zip sure believed he was God. I wanted to believe, too.”

Behind his pulpit Jones dabbed the sweat from his brow. It was done. From now on most of his followers would call him Father.

Chapter Twelve

Secrets Behind the Temple's Doors

AN ORGANIZATION BASED ON DECEIT REQUIRES CLOAK-AND-dagger work. Jones chose eight to ten white women—most of them young and college-educated—to do his dirty work. With absolute loyalty and unquestioning obedience, this group—known as "the staff"—carried out Father's "heavenly deceptions."

One of their most important jobs was collecting information on current and potential members. They went about this creatively. Donning clever disguises, they weaseled their way into people's homes by pretending to be a senile senior citizen, or a suddenly faint expectant mother, or a door-to-door makeup saleswoman. Once inside, they noted the furnishings and the photographs. A trip to the bathroom often led to the medicine cabinet, where personal information—prescriptions (indicating health problems), dates of illnesses, doctors' names, the person's level of hygiene—was found. Even a brand of toothpaste could be useful.

Other times they carried out nighttime garbage raids. Dressed in black, they scaled fences and crept down dark alleys to rummage through members' trash cans. In among the coffee grounds and dirty diapers, they might find whiskey bottles or cigarette butts, proof the member wasn't following Temple rules against drinking or smoking. A phone bill might indicate that a member still communicated with her outside family. A bank statement might reveal that a member was holding out on the church; a credit card statement could prove that they remained materialistic.

Returning to the Temple—with no one the wiser—the staff typed up all they'd learned on index cards. Locked in a special room, this information was available only to themselves and Jones, who used it to astound people with his revelations and healings.

Among those on the staff were Carolyn Layton, Sharon Amos (a loyal member who'd joined the Temple in 1967), Patty Cartmell, and Patty's daughter, Trisha. These women believed that the end justified the means. They accepted that "heavenly deceptions" were for the Temple's greater good. Wrote one journalist: "Only by surrendering their moral reservations could they lure people to the Temple, deceive them, and strip them of their possessions in the name of saving them."

Jones knew that his staff, with their knowledge of his most sensitive personal issues, could do tremendous damage if they ever turned on him. Because of this, he chose them carefully (although his criteria remain a mystery). He praised them and flattered them. And it wasn't long before he was having sex with most of them so they would, as he told them, "know how special you are to me."

But it wasn't Father's personal attention that motivated these women. Their biggest reward was the responsibility and power he bestowed on them. Unlike rank-and-file members, they had the freedom to make decisions. They carried out Jones's orders, but in their own way. They planned *how* to get a thing done and put it smoothly into motion. This placed them at the very top of the church hierarchy, just below the leader himself. It was a heady place to be.

Peoples Temple also had an advisory board called the planning commission, or the PC for short. Formed soon after the church moved to California, it originally consisted of thirty-seven members but grew over time. No one other than Jones understood how members were selected. The Temple's acknowledged leaders all sat on the commission. This included the staff, as well as Marceline and representatives of some of the families who'd followed Jones from Indianapolis. But the preacher also used PC membership for other reasons—to reward his most devoted followers, impress women he intended to sleep with, or keep a close eye on followers he didn't trust.

Most of those appointed were, like Jones's staff, white, college-educated, young, and female. Jones rarely appointed Black members to leadership. Rather, rank-and-file African Americans were "patronized in the [historical] tradition of a caring slave master and his family," says James Lance Taylor, chair of the department of politics at the University of San Francisco and a foremost scholar on the Peoples Temple movement. Though Jones clearly cared about the welfare of his Black members—valuing and depending upon their commitment and hard work—he didn't consider them capable of church leadership. Adds Taylor: "Jones was in essence an 'anti-racist racist.'"

While Jones claimed the PC's purpose was to develop and direct the overall activities of the church, everyone on the board understood that it existed solely to do Jones's bidding.

To keep up pretenses, he allowed PC members to debate ideas and express their opinions during their weekly meetings. He remained quiet, watching for signs of disloyalty or hints that someone wasn't completely committed. One member recalled how Father reclined comfortably on a pillow-covered couch while everyone else—

packed into a small, stuffy space above a Temple-owned laundromat known as "the loft"—sat on the hard wooden floor. The meetings went on for hours, sometimes until dawn. No one ever got up for a drink or went to the toilet because Father frowned on it. Cans of soft drinks, as well as a platter of lunch meats and cheeses, sat next to him on a table. Occasionally, he passed around the platter, but no one took a bite. They knew better. Father never let them forget how hard he drove himself, that he needed that fuel more than anyone else. He didn't waste energy going to the toilet, either. If he had to use the bathroom, he discreetly relieved himself into a can while a chosen PC member held up a towel.

Soon after the PC's formation, Jones began insisting that members divulge private things about themselves through gossip sessions, written assignments, questionnaires, and reports. They spent hours talking about their own sex lives, more hours talking about other people's sex lives. Jones urged them to reveal their intimate experiences graphically and in lewd detail. He wanted to know their secret desires. He required them to make a list of everyone with whom they'd slept.

He shared stories, too, about the women (and some men) with whom he'd had intercourse. His accounts were crude and graphic and usually humiliating to his partners. Declaring himself the ultimate lover, he confessed to having a strong sex drive. But he never admitted to selfish pleasure seeking. Instead, his lovemaking was a selfless gift, he claimed. Wasn't it only natural that PC members should turn to him with their sexual needs, just as they turned to him for advice and guidance?

Often he asked those who'd had sex with him to stand up in PC meetings and testify to his greatness as a lover. Many exaggerated their encounters, to Jones's delight and approval. Said one member:

"At [my] first meeting, everyone was businesslike and cordial. Then at the next meeting, all they talked about was who [was having sex with] who."

One night, after being humiliated by the raunchiness of a meeting, Marceline insisted on knowing why her husband wanted to share such personal details.

Because he wanted those on the PC to know how deeply he trusted them, he replied.

Many PC members came to see his sexual advances and obscene boasts as gifts bestowed by Father on those to whom he felt closest. Most did not realize that Jones was using sex as a means of control, that the affairs were a form of blackmail, that compromising sexual encounters could be used to silence a person or keep them in the church. Instead, PC members accepted his adultery and kept it secret from the rank and file.

Back in Indiana, Peoples Temple had practiced corrective fellowship sessions, in which Jones and others gently criticized individuals for less-than-Christian behavior. But in the years since the move to California, the sessions, now called catharsis sessions, had grown more violent.

Closed to the public, these meetings were held on Wednesday evenings. To guarantee that no one else got in, Jones posted guards at the door. He didn't want anyone on the outside—especially potential members—to see what was happening.

The meeting always began with Jones calling someone to the front and announcing what they had done wrong. Perhaps an adult had been caught smoking a cigarette, or a child had talked back to his teacher. "What do you say to that?" he'd ask the congregation. It was their cue to gang up on the transgressor, shouting out other offenses the person may or may not have committed: He hadn't put any money in the offering plate; she'd skipped a meeting; he'd called another member a bad name. Jones framed these transgressions as acts against the Cause.

Jones encouraged members to verbally attack transgressors. He whipped them up, encouraging them to say what they really thought, and in the crudest ways possible. His high-pitched giggles often accompanied their cursing and shouting. The message was clear: Father approved.

Week after week the congregation's virulence increased, and sometime in 1971 it spilled over into physical violence. Corporal punishment quickly became the norm. Soon a wooden plank—three-quarters of an inch thick and two and a half feet long—replaced the belt that had been used previously, and it was wielded without mercy. How many whacks should the offender get? Jones alone acted as judge and jury, dictating the number.

He gave a kindergarten boy five whacks for eating a piece of candy without sharing it with his friends. The terrified child cried and said he was sorry. "Five whacks," insisted Jones. As the little boy screamed, ultraloyalist Jack Beam held a microphone to his mouth, amplifying the boy's pain and fear. At last, beating over, he was forced to say, "Thank you, Father."

A fifteen-year-old got far worse. Accused of calling someone a "crippled bitch," he was sentenced to 120 whacks. Two adults had to hold him in place. Afterward, he collapsed and had to be carried offstage.

Jones meted out other kinds of punishment, too. A middle-aged woman accused of flirting with an outsider had her hands tied before being tossed into the church's swimming pool. Jones let her thrash and struggle for a few moments before ordering aides to haul her out.

An elderly man who forgot to address Jones as Father was forced to stand for six hours.

A three-year-old was assigned to work all night, scrubbing floors with a toothbrush, after biting another child. Jones also instructed an adult to bite the little boy so he'd know what it felt like.

And then came the boxing matches. At first, they were used as punishment for the children. An accused youth would be told to put on boxing gloves. Then they were made to fight a tougher, stronger opponent. If the wrong child won, even tougher opponents were called on to fight the offender. As they pummeled each other, the congregation cheered and shouted.

The matches soon extended to adult members. The brutality turned severe as people donned gloves and pounded away, bruising and bloodying each other. On more than one occasion, noses were broken and opponents knocked out. If adults tried to escape injury by not fighting back, they were punched anyway.

Jones demanded the wrongdoer's family be the harshest critics during these sessions. Sometimes he even asked them to administer the punishments. If they balked or expressed anything other than agreement, Jones accused them of disloyalty. Did they want to be called up next? They certainly didn't, and so they behaved as Jones expected. Some truly believed in the rightness of the punishment, but many others put on a performance. "Remember," they whispered to their loved ones, "I have to do this for the Cause. But I still love you."

Afraid of looking foolish or, worse, unenlightened about the purpose of the punishments, followers learned to squelch their opinions.

No one wanted to seem lesser. "We did a lot of thoughtless things because of fears about how we looked," admitted Stephan Jones.

Many times, Stephan disagreed with what was happening. He'd wonder, "Am I the only one who thinks this is crazy?" Everyone else appeared to be fine with it. And so he would fake his own approval. "It was peer pressure, pure and simple," Stephan admitted. "Everyone wanted to be seen as a good [follower], not just to Dad but to each other." He added, "I now believe at least half of [the members] were doing and thinking the same thing I was."

Part Three

Radicalizing

You got this guy who sounds like he's on fire. . . . Jones had a way of *talking*, and he'd take his voice and go *up* and go *down* and bring it back *around* and *show* you. . . . I jumped into [the Temple] with both feet, even though I was doubtful of some of the things that I heard, and even some of the things I saw. . . . I was afraid to question. Then I got to the point that I was afraid to walk away from it, too.

—Hue Fortson, Peoples Temple survivor

Chapter Thirteen

Multiplying

SOMETIME IN 1971 IT BECAME CLEAR TO JIM JONES THAT membership from the Redwood Valley area had peaked. The Temple's membership, now numbering around four hundred, had more than quadrupled since the move to California in 1965. So, too, had Jones's ambitions. He wanted to lead thousands, have a national, maybe even international, ministry. To do so, he needed more followers and more cash.

Jones didn't intend to abandon the Redwood Valley Temple. But the cities of Los Angeles and San Francisco, with their pockets of deep poverty, seemed like perfect recruiting grounds. Black neighborhoods struggled with widespread unemployment, school and housing dislocation, police violence, and discrimination. Additionally, in San Francisco, white city officials had undertaken gentrification projects that ultimately dismantled Black communities and business districts and created unnatural borders between more affluent white neighborhoods and traditionally Black areas. The worst result of these efforts was the containment of 96,000 African Americans (13 percent of San Francisco's population) in the

Fillmore District, which quickly gained a reputation of being a "bad" neighborhood.

Fillmore resident Hannibal Williams noted: "[When] a community is broken up, when the relationships that bind people together fall apart, the time is always right for a religious scoundrel. . . . [City officials] literally destroyed our neighborhood and in the process made it ripe for anybody with some kind of solution. People were desperate for solutions, something to follow. Jim Jones [presented a] solution. He had a charismatic personality that won the hearts and souls of the people."

It wasn't charisma alone. He also won hearts and souls through cultural appropriation. Said the Reverend Dr. J. Alfred Smith of Allen Temple Baptist Church, a Black church in Oakland, California: "If you closed your eyes and just listened to him preach, you would swear you were listening to a Black man." Jones appropriated traditional Black music, too—spirituals, rhythm and blues, and freedom songs. Many of California's urban African Americans, particularly older ones, found Jones's intentional use of Black idioms and Pentecostal religious practices highly attractive.

Recruitment was also helped by the Temple's projection of itself as a successor to the civil rights ideals of Dr. Martin Luther King Jr. After Dr. King's assassination, traditional Black churches wrestled with the changing needs and expectations of their congregations. Admitted Smith: "The 1970s were dark days for the Black church in San Francisco." Jones saw a need for a Black-church-centered civil rights movement. Appropriating the ideals of Dr. King (and in many cases Dr. King's very words), Jones echoed them during his services. Repeatedly, he represented himself as having "a black soul, a black heart, and a black consciousness," says historian James Lance Taylor. He posed as a "black messiah advancing black liberation."

To attract more politically progressive young African Americans, Jones combined what Taylor calls his "white power and privilege with the stagecraft of Black Power." He preached racial pride and economic empowerment and demanded recognition and inclusion of African American culture in political and educational institutions. But his words rang hollow. For the most part Peoples Temple remained insular. While members did occasionally join picket lines and participate in political rallies, Jones's purpose in sending his people was a selfish one: to enhance his public image.

In Los Angeles the Temple purchased a huge old church on South Alvarado Street that could seat fourteen hundred people. On Sundays those seats filled quickly. Many became new members; others came out of curiosity. Around and around went the offering plates, often as many as six times a service. Much of this money went toward neighborhood outreach programs: after-school youth programs, vaccination clinics, food pantries, soup kitchens, and more. While these good works were a boon to the communities, they were also a boon to the Temple.

San Francisco copied the Los Angeles model. The church bought yet another huge building, this one on Geary Boulevard in the city's Fillmore District. The two-story yellow stone monstrosity had an auditorium big enough to seat eighteen hundred people. It also had a warren of rooms that the Temple renovated into apartments. As in Los Angeles, members instituted a slew of social programs, attracting recruits from the neighborhood.

When the press came to see what had been achieved in the Fillmore District, Jones put on his most pious face. He explained that the Temple's good works were modeled on Christ's example. Members aspired to nothing beyond loving service. While he touted the Temple's commitment to racial and economic equality, he didn't say a word about its devotion to socialism and corporal punishment.

A new and grueling schedule accompanied the addition of the new churches. On Fridays, after school and work, the entire Redwood Valley membership would pile onto a fleet of used Greyhound buses that the Temple had purchased earlier. Built to hold a maximum of forty-three passengers, the buses usually had seventy to eighty riders squeezed aboard. People sat in the aisle and overhead in the metal luggage racks. Some even climbed into the cargo bins beneath the bus, using a wire to prop open the bin doors so they wouldn't die of carbon monoxide poisoning.

Meanwhile, Jones rode in his private bedroom on bus number seven. "The last two [rows] were taken out and a door put across it," remembered one member. "Inside there was a sink, a bed, and a plate of steel so no one could ever shoot [him]."

Everyone would arrive in San Francisco hours later for a service that might last until midnight. Then they'd drive through the night toward Los Angeles, Jones's packed-in followers trying to get some sleep while their leader snoozed comfortably in his private sanctum. After arriving in Los Angeles around eleven, they ate breakfast (usually peanut butter sandwiches) and changed into their church clothes for the two p.m. Saturday service. On Sunday the Los Angeles services would go from eleven to around four in the afternoon. Then the entire Redwood Valley membership piled back on the buses, arriving home early Monday morning. Disheveled and exhausted, they had just enough time to return to their jobs as students, city employees, teachers, social workers, caregivers, janitors, and attorneys.

The expansion reeled in hundreds of new members. It brought

in thousands of dollars in revenue—sometimes as much as $25,000 a weekend (approximately $187,000 nowadays). It did something else just as important, too. It kept followers so busy that they had little time left for their families or themselves. They felt harried and exhausted and consumed by the church . . . just the way Father liked it.

Chapter Fourteen

Pill Popping and Paranoia

JIM JONES WORKED AS HARD AS HIS FOLLOWERS. AMBITION gnawed at him, often pushing him to put in twenty-hour days. He insisted on micromanaging every aspect of the Temple. He decided how every dollar was spent. He read and approved every word in the church's newsletter. He signed off on every marriage or divorce. He chose where members lived, and each of their church jobs. No detail escaped his focus. He alone decided on the number of hand towels to be purchased for the Redwood Valley Temple bathrooms, and he vacuumed the church sanctuary when there was no one else to do it.

This constant pressure and effort took its toll. How could he keep up? He turned to amphetamines, also known as speed.

As a child, Jim Jones had seen how his father, Old Jim, found respite from his war injuries in painkillers. Now, four decades later, Jones emulated the father he'd despised. Members recalled that as far back as 1965, Jones would occasionally pause midsermon to complain about his need for pain medication. He claimed to suffer from a litany of ailments—liver problems, anemia, heart palpitations. Was Jones already abusing pain pills back then? The record doesn't show, although his son Stephan believes he was. Others close to Jim Jones insist his drug problems didn't truly blossom until 1971. That's when, exhausted by his frenetic schedule, he began taking speed to fuel his long days.

This chemical boost worked . . . but it quickly led to abuse. Soon Jones was using drugs regularly—speed to propel him through his days, and quaaludes, a sedative, to put him to sleep. The more he took, the more he needed.

It wasn't long before he couldn't function without them.

Jones's inner circle—the staff and PC—helped him procure the drugs. Sometimes they bought them on the street. Other times, if they worked in hospitals or care facilities, they stole them. They even fooled physicians into writing prescriptions for themselves, then passed the medication on to Jones. He praised them for their efforts. They were helping the Cause, he told them, in a "very special, very *private* way."

Of course, they weren't allowed to breathe a word of this to the congregation at large. Not only was recreational drug use against Temple rules, but the church also bragged publicly and frequently about its successful drug rehabilitation program.

Still, there were signs of Jones's abuse, including his mood swings. One minute he'd be pleasant and loving; the next he'd turn nasty and critical. His temper grew sharper, too. He had always been impatient, but now he snapped for the slightest reason. He also began wearing dark sunglasses everywhere. He told followers this was because his inner powers were so great that anyone looking into his eyes would be scorched. In truth, his eyes were often red from drug use. By far the worst side effect, however, was paranoia. Jones, a man already plagued by fears, became rabidly suspicious.

A trained nurse, Marceline recognized what was causing these behavioral changes. She begged her husband to quit.

He denied he had a drug problem.

One morning toward the end of 1971, when Jones's words sounded especially slurred and his step was stumbling, a frustrated Marceline flung open his medicine cabinet and grabbed his stash.

Jones demanded she give them back. He gripped Marceline's arm with one hand while frantically snatching at the pill bottle with the other.

She wiggled free, darted to the toilet, emptied the pills into the bowl, and flushed.

Jones howled with fury.

Despite Marceline's bold action, nothing changed. Jones easily replaced the pills.

Jones had long warned his followers about outsiders, certain individuals and organizations who were out to get them. With drugs fueling his dark imagination, his stories grew more bizarre. He claimed the CIA and FBI had been tapping Temple telephones because Peoples Temple had proved that "generous socialism" was a better economic system than "cruel capitalism," and *that* made them dangerous to the U.S. government. He warned about infiltrators and spies. Was the person sitting beside them really committed to the Cause, or were they an impostor working for the CIA? Be constantly alert, he cautioned. Be suspicious of everyone, even family and friends. Report anything and everything.

Jones even claimed he was on the government's hit list. Operatives had already assassinated anyone else who'd tried to lead Americans to a better life, he told members from the pulpit—President John F. Kennedy, Dr. Martin Luther King Jr., Malcolm X, Medgar Evers, and Robert F. Kennedy—and he was next. The government feared and hated him. It feared and hated them, too.

Like a malignancy, Jones's paranoia spread through his rank-and-file followers. Unaware of his drug use, they came to believe that shadowy enemies were everywhere, and the only way to protect themselves was by cleaving even closer to Father.

Spring was in full bloom that Sunday afternoon in 1972. Their spirits buoyed by both worship and the fine weather, Temple members gathered in the Redwood Valley Temple parking lot. In these happy between-service hours, men set up tables and chairs. Women laid out casseroles and desserts. Teens huddled in groups, bantering and joking, while kids played. Moving among his people, Jones chatted and laughed. He ate cake from a paper plate, then hugged the beaming lady who'd baked it.

Suddenly, three large booms drowned out the happy chatter.

"Rifle shot!" shouted Jack Beam.

Everyone screamed and scattered—everyone but Jim Jones. He lay on the asphalt, a dark red stain spreading across his shirt. He appeared to be dead.

Marceline dropped to her knees beside him and began sobbing. Meanwhile, Jack Beam and a group of ultraloyalists carried Jones into the church. Marceline, still crying, followed. The door slammed behind them.

In the parking lot followers wailed and prayed. Old ladies trembled. Children clung to their parents in fear.

Half an hour later Carolyn Layton returned to the parking lot. Solemnly, she asked the crowd to come inside. They shuffled to their seats, sniffling and shaking.

Then—hallelujah!

A shirtless Jim Jones came striding out onto the stage. Marceline, Carolyn, and Jack Beam followed.

"Tell them," Jones said to Beam. "Tell them about the hole I had in me."

Beam held up the bloody shirt while a Temple nurse testified, "I could stick my fingers in [Father's] wound." The preacher, she told them, had died.

Jones invited his followers to examine his naked chest. See? No wound. Not a scratch. He had resurrected himself and healed his fatal wound.

The congregation stomped, shouted, whirled in circles, and raised their hands to the heavens. It was the greatest miracle of them all.

In truth, Jones and his close aides had staged the whole thing.

When the congregation finally settled down, Jones stepped behind the podium. To stay safe, he told them, they needed constant vigilance. There was sure to be another assassination attempt on him. Security at all three churches would need to be stepped up, and guards would be armed. Additionally, church services would be open only to those specifically invited. Current followers would be required to show membership cards to gain admittance. Men wanting to enter would be patted down. Women's purses would be searched.

Peoples Temple was becoming a fortress. No one got in. No one got out.

Chapter Fifteen

Truth by Trickles

SINCE SACRIFICING BASEBALL FOR THE CAUSE, JIM COBB—twenty-two years old in 1972—had grown into a committed, hardworking member of the Temple. He did whatever Jones requested, no questions asked. So, when the Temple had suggested he attend college in Santa Rosa three years earlier, he'd gone eagerly.

Jones hoped to create a group of professionals who believed in a socialist life. He envisioned the Temple's future—lawyers providing free counsel, doctors and nurses caring for the sick at no cost, teachers educating young students in the ways of socialism. To achieve this, members purchased three apartments close to Santa Rosa Junior College. These college communes, as they were called, each housed twenty of the Temple's brightest and most dedicated youths. Keeping them together limited their contact with outsiders on campus. It also created peer pressure that kept them in line. No one wanted to break a rule only to be confronted by the other students or, worse, Father and the congregation.

Jim Cobb brimmed with idealism. Longing to devote his life to others, he chose a socially useful occupation: dentist. He envisioned being a part of a Temple-built medical complex where he would care for everyone regardless of race or economic status.

One Friday evening, as usual, Jim returned to his Redwood Valley home for weekend services. He looked forward to hanging with his siblings—Ava, Teresa, Sandra, Johnny, Brenda, and Joel—and sharing the events of the week with his dad.

Jim Cobb Sr. had never joined the Temple. He didn't mind that his family belonged, though, and he even lent a hand around the church from time to time. A hard worker, Jim Sr. provided for his family despite his low-paying job, and he had a close and loving relationship with his children.

Jones saw Jim Sr. as a threat. He wanted the Temple to be his followers' only means of support, the congregation their only family. But Cobb's presence put a crack in the fortress of isolation the leader was building.

At first, Jones waged psychological warfare on the churchgoing part of the Cobb family. He publicly criticized Jim Sr. for smoking and drinking, and attacked him for eating chicken during the Temple's short-lived foray into vegetarianism. This, in turn, encouraged the membership to shame his wife, Christine, for having a husband who wasn't dedicated to the Cause. They called her bourgeois for living with the comforts his hard work provided. They questioned her commitment to socialism and economic equality.

"He's out to destroy you," Jones told her.

Jim Jr. felt conflicted. He believed Father was right, but he loved his dad.

That Friday night when he walked into his parents' house, he found a gang of Temple men in the kitchen.

Jim asked what was going on. Where were his parents?

One of the men spoke up. Jim Sr. had turned drunk and violent, he said. He'd threatened to kill Christine and kidnap the children. They'd ordered him to leave Redwood Valley . . . or else.

Jim didn't believe it. His mild-mannered dad never drank more than a beer or two, and he'd certainly never laid a hand on them.

He rushed to Jones's house. Shaken, he listened as the leader explained the danger. "Your father has changed," he said. "You have to accept it."

Jim begged that his father be allowed to return home.

Jones pretended to think on it, then finally agreed, but on one condition: If the young man's father grew violent again, Jim had to promise to kill him.

"I won't kill [him], but I'll make sure he doesn't hurt anybody," Jim said.

Jones shook his head. It wasn't enough.

And so Jim gave in to the separation from his father, as painful as it was. His mother and siblings did, too. They didn't dare ask where he'd gone or try to contact him. Jim Sr. simply disappeared from the family's life that day.

Jones had long meddled in the family life of his followers, but by 1972 he was routinely breaking up marriages, recommending divorces, and suggesting alternative partners for adults. This mixing and matching weakened family ties. And without those strong bonds, Father could exert more control.

But though Jones physically removed Jim Sr., he couldn't erase the man's memory. Jim Jr. never stopped missing his dad, and eventually, he came to believe that the Temple gang had threatened him. Jim would never discover with what. Years later, after he tracked his father down, Jim Sr. refused to tell him. Jim Jr. was convinced that on Jones's orders, they'd threatened the Cobb children's lives.

By the late spring of 1972, about forty Temple guards patrolled the church perimeter, kept vigilant watch at all the exits, and went everywhere Jones did. Even during services they surrounded him as he made his way to the pulpit, then spread out across the sanctuary, eyeing the congregation. Jones chose these men and women carefully. While all were well trusted, some were picked because they were physically intimidating, others because they knew how to handle firearms. All orders came directly from Jones. They were his personal police force.

That summer, while on break from school, Jim Cobb was placed on security detail. He took his job seriously, participating in the Temple's weapons-training lessons and scrutinizing church crowds for suspicious individuals. And at each meeting he checked the podium for bombs and listening devices. Father, he'd learned, was especially paranoid about tapes of his socialist sermons falling into enemy hands. Jim even had a uniform: a leisure suit complete with a beret like the ones worn by Black Panthers—another appropriation.

One Sunday morning in July, members of the Redwood Valley Temple were singing "Deep in my heart, I do believe, I know, I know you're God" when—

BAM!

Gunshots rang out.

Jim rushed toward Father as the congregation began screaming. He reached the stage just as Father stumbled out from behind the podium and fell to his knees.

The screaming and crying grew louder.

Father squeezed his skull between his hands.

"Calm down!" he commanded. "I've been shot in the head."

The congregation's screams turned to soft, shuddering sobs.

Tense moments passed.

At last, Jones stood. "I'm all right," he assured his followers. "I dematerialized the bullet."

The sobbing turned to roof-raising shouts of joy and praise.

But Jim Cobb almost laughed. Then he chastised himself. If Father said it happened, it happened . . . right?

Of course, it was another manipulation meant to terrify followers. Yet again, an inner-circle member, hiding outside, had shot a gun into the air. Jones had faked the rest.

When the service ended, Jim Cobb looked around for bullet holes in the walls or furniture. He found none. Questions bombarded him. Why were the people who were trying to kill Father so ghostlike? They seemed to have a magical ability to just up and disappear. Even their bullets never left any trace. And if Father could cure himself, why did he need security guards?

Jim tried to silence his doubts, push down the questions. But he'd let something into his head, and he couldn't get rid of it.

A few days later during weapons training, a couple of guards mentioned to Jim what they'd found in Father's closet. "An overnight case," said one. "We were worried it was a bomb, so we opened it."

As they raised the lid, a sickening odor had escaped.

"Made me want to puke," added another.

Jim asked what it was.

"A glob of fermenting chicken guts," replied the first guard.

It was the alleged cancers. Father hadn't cured *anyone.*

Chapter Sixteen

Going Communal

TWO BLOCKS FROM THE SAN FRANCISCO TEMPLE STOOD A peeling two-story house owned by the church. On the first floor, in front, a former addict named Odell Rhodes lived with six boys between the ages of seven and twelve. The Temple had given Rhodes, who had no experience raising children, complete responsibility for his young charges. He cared for them without any input from their biological parents.

On the same floor, in back, lived a single woman with three young girls. Two of them were her biological children, but the other was her Temple daughter. She was expected to treat them all as her own.

Upstairs lived four more adults, as well as three teenagers. None of them were biologically related, but rather a Temple-made family.

The entire household took their meals together at the Temple dining hall, and the church paid all their expenses. Two of the adults had outside jobs; the others all worked for the church.

This was typical of communal living.

Jones had long urged members to move into Temple-owned housing. By 1972, however, he was insisting on it. The Temple had leased houses and apartments across Redwood Valley, Los Angeles, and San

Francisco, and already half the congregation had gone communal. After selling their homes and possessions, they'd given *every cent* to the church. They'd turned over bank accounts and life savings, too, and signed over their salaries, pensions, Social Security checks—*everything.* Said Deanna Mertle: "Our life savings were gone. Our property was gone. All we had left was Father and the Cause."

It was exactly what Jones wanted. Communalism made it easy for him to keep track of his members' behavior and whereabouts, and it left them entirely dependent on him and the church.

The Temple bought members clothing now—in bulk. Most communals wore jeans and T-shirts, with nicer clothing reserved for those who worked in schools, banks, or offices. Jones didn't want anyone connected with the Temple looking ratty in the professional sphere. The church, after all, had a public image to maintain.

The church bought everyone's food, too. Communal diets were simple and cheap—oatmeal for breakfast, peanut butter sandwiches for lunch, scrambled eggs and canned vegetables for supper. These meals were eaten in shifts in the Temple dining hall. Boasted Jones, "[I'm] feeding six hundred, seven hundred, eight hundred people a night."

Members following Jones's dictate to go communal found themselves crammed into tight quarters together. Bunk beds allowed for as many as six people to occupy one small bedroom. Cots and sofa beds were squeezed into living rooms. Privacy was a rarity. One couldn't shower without somebody else coming in to use the toilet. If a member complained, Jones replied, "Modesty is a bourgeois affectation. True socialists would never be ashamed of their bodies, or their natural bodily functions."

Few complained about these conditions. For those who came from poverty, like Odell Rhodes, communalism improved their lives by providing food, shelter, and medical care. For senior citizens, it promised a lifetime of loving care. And for members of economic means, going communal was proof of their fierce commitment to the Cause.

Under Jones's tutelage, the congregation was shifting from a purely religious group to one focused on the tenets of socialism: working together in a coordinated way, pooling resources, creating equality and economic security, and eliminating class distinctions. To achieve these goals, most members were willing to share *everything,* including family.

Usually families weren't housed together when they went communal. More often, unrelated members were placed together, usually by age. Seniors lived with seniors. Married couples lived with other married couples. A group of teenagers might be placed with a guardian couple, while younger children were typically removed from their parents and placed with other adults. Jones claimed this last separation was a requirement of a good socialist. Equality meant that *everyone* should share in the joys and sorrows of parenthood, he said.

The flowers and trees around Hyacinth's Redwood Valley home bloomed in an explosion of bright color. Birds of every kind flitted cheerfully around the feeders she'd put up. At night she often sat in her backyard, listening to crickets and counting the flashes of lightning bugs. Sometimes folks from church joined her. They made small talk and looked up at the stars. "It was like heaven," said Hyacinth.

Then Father paid a visit. It was time for Hyacinth and her sister,

Zip, to move into communal senior housing, he told her. He had a place for them in a cozy apartment in San Francisco, a place where they'd be entirely taken care of.

Hyacinth objected. She didn't need to be taken care of. She still had plenty of good years left.

Jones pressed harder. He asked whom she and Zip would rely on if they needed care. Neither woman had children. If they didn't go communal, he warned, they would most likely end up in some squalid nursing home, forgotten and alone. They didn't want that, did they?

Both women agreed they didn't.

He went on to say that Peoples Temple would soon be leaving the valley. He'd recently made the San Francisco Temple the new church headquarters, and the Redwood Valley organization would become a satellite church. Services would still be held, but Marceline would lead them. Most members were making the move to the city to remain close to Father. All their friends would soon be gone.

Still, Hyacinth demurred. "I just didn't know what to do," she later said. "I just wanted a place of my own."

Zip, however, made up her mind instantly. She didn't want to be anywhere Jim Jones wasn't. She was going to San Francisco, with or without her sister.

Looking back on this event years later, Hyacinth recognized Jones's manipulation. "He knew he could twist Zip around his finger," she said. He also knew that where Zip went, Hyacinth followed. All he had to do was "work on Zip."

Finally, reluctantly, Hyacinth agreed to go as well. She deeded over her beloved home with its flowering garden, and immediately church workers swarmed over the property, boxing up a lifetime of possessions to sell at the Temple's thrift store. At the last moment Hyacinth snatched back a well-worn book. It was a biography of Abraham Lincoln, one of the few items her family had brought with them when they'd moved from the Jim Crow South.

In San Francisco the sisters, along with an elderly couple, Henry and Mildred Mercer, moved into a small, seedy apartment near the Geary Boulevard Temple that overlooked an adult bookstore and a massage parlor. The place smelled like urine, and cockroaches scampered out from under the baseboards.

Because of the sisters' ages, workers delivered their food. In Redwood Valley, Hyacinth had eaten fresh fruit and vegetables, but now her meals consisted of hot dogs, macaroni and cheese, and pudding. She was disgusted. Additionally, Jones had promised to give her a hundred dollars out of her Social Security check each month. "But [he] never did," she said.

Hyacinth was afraid to say anything. Jones had recently told the congregation about a member who had complained about communal living and been struck down, thrust into a coma from which she still hadn't recovered. She didn't want *that* to happen to her.

In San Francisco every member had a church job, and Hyacinth's was to sit next to invited visitors during the public services and talk up the Temple. Meanwhile, Zip stood on street corners, handing out pamphlets and begging for contributions. She did so willingly. "She thought of it as an honor," explained Hyacinth.

Each pamphlet pictured a hungry mother and child. Below it a Bible verse read:

> *For I was hungry and you gave me something to eat,*
> *I was thirsty and you gave me something to drink,*
> *I was a stranger and you invited me in.*

Zip understood, as did most members, that Christianity was being used as a front for the group's socialist beliefs: that the persistence of a church image legitimized them. By appearing Christ-centered, the Temple retained the support of city officials and continued to reel in those who might otherwise have steered clear of the group. As historian Catherine Abbott noted: "Posing as a purely Christian church was an ideal hiding place for a radical group such as Peoples Temple."

But Hyacinth still clung to both her Pentecostal roots and Jim Jones.

While his disrespect toward the Bible disgusted her, she continued to believe in his healing power. At every service she limped down to a front seat so he could see her with her cane propped beside her. She waited for him to call her name, but he never did. Why did he refuse to heal her?

Chapter Seventeen

Annie

ANNIE MOORE ARRIVED IN REDWOOD VALLEY ON A SATURday morning in August 1972. The recent high school graduate had come to spend the weekend with her sister Carolyn Layton before heading off to live with her middle sister, Rebecca, in Washington, D.C. The eighteen-year-old looked forward to seeing Carolyn but hoped she wouldn't have to spend any time with Jim Jones. She still recalled how, years earlier, he'd disclosed his affair with Carolyn and made her mother cry. The memory made Annie angry.

Two days later Annie joined the church. How it happened remains a mystery. It had long been Temple policy for members to proselytize to the rest of their relations, and the Temple's membership included as many as three generations of some families. But though Carolyn would have liked her parents and sisters to join, John and Barbara were committed Methodists, and Rebecca was immune to what she considered Jones's nonsense. That left young, impressionable Annie. Obviously, Carolyn and Jones had given the teen the "hard sell," said John Moore.

"Oh God, isn't one child enough?" cried Barbara when she learned of Annie's decision.

The teen tried to explain her choice in a letter to Rebecca: "The reason is because (and you'll probably groan) . . . I am convinced that [the church] is a good place to be. Jim Jones has and knows more secrets about the world than any other group or person. Also, their church is socialist in the real sense (the kind of socialism Jesus was talking about)."

Annie was an activist. In high school she'd organized peace vigils and hikes against hunger. She'd distributed anti-war leaflets and headed an anti-war demonstration. In her spare time she wrote songs and played her guitar, made ceramic sculptures, painted, and drew. She wore long, flowing tie-dyed skirts, and had long, thick hair. Young, passionate, and intense, Annie planned to commit her life to social service. She'd thought to do this by becoming a nurse—until her visit to Peoples Temple. Now she believed she'd found a better way.

Annie took to heart the Bible passage Jones quoted to her: "Go, sell your possessions and give to the poor." Before she left home for good, she cut her long hair into a short crop and sold what little she had—her record collection and spare clothing—giving the proceeds to Peoples Temple. She planned on selling her guitar, too, but Jones stopped her. Music, like money, was a gift she could share with the congregation, he told her. Her father would later say that Annie entered Peoples Temple "in the same way a nun might enter a convent . . . with a vow of poverty."

Rebecca tried to convince her sister to change her mind. She criticized both the church and Jones and reminded Annie of her earlier feelings about the preacher.

Annie responded angrily. "You obviously think Peoples Temple is just another cult or religious fanatic place or something. Well, I'm kind of offended that you would think I would join some weirdo group. I'm a pretty sensible person, and I can tell what's real and what's not. . . . This is the largest group of people I've ever seen who are . . . fighting for truth and justice for the world."

At the beginning of September, Annie moved in with Carolyn, who had been allowed by Jones to remain in her own home in Potter Valley. Temple members quickly discovered how different the sisters were from each other. Annie possessed a sweet spirit and offbeat sense of humor. People warmed to her. But most found Carolyn cold and emotionally distant. Although her sexual relationship with Jones remained a secret, it was obvious to all that she was the leader's right hand. As a member of his staff, Carolyn was the one who made sense of Jones's instructions. She conveyed his wishes to others through memos and announcements.

Until Annie moved in, Carolyn had lived alone so that Jones could alternate between her and his "old family" without anyone knowing. Now he persuaded Annie that he needed his time with Carolyn to harness the energy and power necessary to lead the Temple. Annie could never let on about his relationship with her sister.

Jones's appeal made Annie feel special. Father trusted her with his most private secrets. In just a few short weeks, she, too, had become an insider.

The Temple found Annie a job as a nurse's aide in a Redwood Valley nursing home. Annie immediately noticed the inequities in care. The patients with money stayed in the bigger rooms and were fawned over by the medical staff, while those whose care was paid for by the state found themselves crowded into small rooms. As a result, they had fewer visitors and received far less attention.

Annie made a point of spending time with the impoverished patients. She smiled and asked about their families. She played guitar for them and held their hands. She told them about Peoples Temple and its commitment to caring for everyone, regardless of race or economic status. Some of these patients transferred to nursing homes run by Temple members. Some even became members. This buoyed Annie. Already, her proselytizing was helping to grow the Cause.

Chapter Eighteen

"I Know a Place"

IN THE FALL OF 1972, JIM COBB JR. MOVED TO SAN FRANcisco to start dental school. For months doubts about Jim Jones had been plaguing him. The more he thought about Peoples Temple, the more misgivings he had. And there was one thing that particularly troubled him: He now saw that the Temple wasn't a true integrationist movement. Sure, the congregation was diverse. But diversity wasn't the same as racial justice, which required a purposeful struggle against white supremacy. For all Father's talk about equality, the church leadership was almost completely white. While most Temple members were Black, like Jim, only two currently served on the church's governing board, the PC, which now numbered around a hundred members.

Doubt and anger finally overwhelmed him. He decided to take a break from services.

His absence was quickly noticed. But Jim ignored the phone calls from family and Temple friends. He tossed letters from Jones into the trash unopened. It pained him, he said, to "realize how someone could put together a movement with so many good people . . . yet could be so rotten."

In December, while studying for final exams at the university library, Jim looked up to see his mother, Christine, heading straight for him. She'd come to tell him that she and the kids had just moved to San Francisco. They'd taken up communal life in the city. Wasn't that wonderful? His family lived just blocks away from him.

Jim shook his head. "Mama, I don't want to pop no bubbles," he said. "I love my family and I love my friends, and there are good people in the church. But I've looked at it, and you know what? Jones is the [bad] one."

Christine argued. Jones wasn't to blame; it was his staff, especially that Carolyn Layton. She bossed him around and gave him bad advice.

"No," he replied, "I've seen things you haven't. . . . He's behind it all; it's him."

"If you can't come back for anything else, come back for the family," Christine begged. "The kids need you. They're asking where you are and what you're doing."

Jim couldn't do it.

He did, however, visit his mother in her church-owned apartment. His two youngest siblings were living communally with other families. Some Sundays he even walked her to services, but he never went in.

One spring morning in 1973, while taking his mother to church, a wave of longing washed over Jim. He missed the community so much—the sense of belonging, the feeling of acceptance. This emotional wave swept him through the Temple's double doors. Tearfully, he stood before the congregation and apologized. "I've been out in the world, and there's nothing out there," he said. "There are a lot of bad things and bad people out there, and there are a lot of loving people and good things going on here."

Jones crowed with delight. The prodigal son had returned.

But no matter how hard Jim tried, he couldn't ignore the truth. Father was a fake who kept his followers in "crisis mode," as one member termed it. In almost every sermon he peddled fear, uncertainty, and distrust in the U.S. government. Fueled by his amphetamine-induced paranoia, he spun dark and sinister tales. Jones declared that the president at the time, Republican Richard Nixon, was a modern-day Hitler. He and his modern-day Nazi Party hated the poor. They hated people of color. They hated socialists. And they had a secret plan to round up everyone they hated and place them in concentration camps. Oh yes, they were coming for Jones and his followers first. Peoples Temple represented everything the U.S. government hated.

That April—just weeks after Jim's return to the church—Jones claimed that concentration camps had been built in California, Pennsylvania, Alabama, and Oklahoma. "I've prophesized the date, the hour, the minute, and the year it's going to happen," he shouted. "They've got them all ready. They did it to the Japanese, and they'll do it to us."

His words caused fear to flow through the sanctuary, recalled member Deanna Mertle, "like electricity."

Jones went on. "I tell you, we're in danger tonight, from corporate dictatorships [and] the great fascist state of America. If we don't build a utopian society, we're going to be in trouble."

Did politicians and white men ever go to jail? he asked, then answered himself. "Never, never. But if a Black takes a piece of bread, he'll go to jail."

"Mmm-hmm!"

"Amen, Father!"

But Jones wouldn't let them down. When the fascist government came for them, he intended to give the enemy "one hell of a fight."

The congregation hollered, warlike cries that must have made the back of Jim Cobb's neck prickle. None of what Father was saying was true. Didn't anyone else realize how crazy he sounded?

Jones shushed them. His voice turned calm, and he spoke slowly. Instead of fighting, perhaps there was another way. "Now what we have in mind when [the Nazis come] is we're going to [go] abroad. . . . We'll leave quietly . . . till we get to the border . . . and then we're going to get some land where we can raise food, that's our hope, and some animals."

He didn't name a destination that day. But a few weeks later, he returned to the subject. "I know a place where I can take you, where there'll be no more racism, where there'll be no more division, where there'll be no more class exploitation. I know the place. Oh yes, I do."

What was Father alluding to? He was playing games with his followers, scaring them, teasing them with promises. Jim Cobb couldn't take it anymore. He *had* to leave the church . . . and for good.

Chapter Nineteen

Escape!

FATHER'S WARNINGS ABOUT QUITTING THE CHURCH HAD grown more and more threatening. During one sermon he described how a defector had fallen ill and died after leaving. He told of how another had been killed in a work accident. "Leave and you will die," he said. "You cannot escape this movement!"

Jim Cobb wasn't worried about Jones's divine powers. He no longer believed in them. He was, however, scared of what Jones might ask his followers to do. Would he have someone tail him? Kidnap him? Kill him?

Even years after quitting the church, former members received threatening letters from the Temple. Jones's staff cut words from magazines and arranged them into terrifying messages before smearing the pages with poison oak. "We know where you live," read one. "We're watching all the time." Sometimes former members picked up the phone to hear heavy breathing on the other end. Other times a gruff voice would tell them to "keep your mouth clamped up." Other tactics included publishing a newspaper obituary in the defector's name or renting a hearse and letting it idle in front of their house.

To escape, Jim would need a secret plan. Not even his family could know. And he'd have to go far away without leaving any tracks. He'd have to simply disappear.

Days after his decision, friend and former dorm mate Wayne Pietila dropped by Jim's commune and asked him to go for a car ride. "But don't tell anyone else [you're going]," he cautioned.

Jim hesitated. Wayne was acting suspicious. Was he spying for Jones? Still, Jim went along.

They drove in silence, wending their way through the city streets. Wayne seemed to have no destination in mind, and he kept glancing nervously into his rearview mirror.

Minutes passed. Jim's anxiety built. At last, he blurted out, "I want to tell you I'm leaving the church. I wasn't gonna say that, but I don't give a shit. If you're here to spy on me, that's okay. Whatever, man. But I can't take it anymore."

Wayne jerked the car to the curb. "Man," he said, "that's what I wanted to tell you. We're going, too!"

Months earlier twenty-year-old Pietila had been elevated to the PC, but the meetings left him feeling both disgusted and disillusioned. Why did they waste so much time on scandal and sex talk? What about socialism and integration? His wife, Teresa Cobb (Jim's twenty-one-year-old sister), also had serious misgivings. The couple wanted to defect but worried they couldn't do it alone. Then they heard whisperings about some others who felt the same: twenty-two-year-old John Biddulph and his nineteen-year-old wife, Vera, also a newly appointed PC member, and three Santa Rosa college students—nineteen-year-old Tom Podgorski, eighteen-year-old Lena Flowers, whose family had followed Jones from Indianapolis, and, most surprisingly, nineteen-year-old Mickey Touchette. Mickey came from a bedrock Temple family—her parents, Joyce and Charlie, served on the PC.

Now Jim Cobb joined them. They believed that by leaving together, they'd have a better chance of escape. A large group could better defend itself against the search parties that surely would be sent out. But what if Jones notified the highway patrol? Yes, they were over eighteen and not breaking any laws, but the young people knew Father would make up some story to put the police on alert. They'd have to take back roads.

Other plans remained vague. A few in the group felt they needed time to prepare, but delay made Jim nervous. What if someone saw them whispering or noticed they were spending more time than usual together? All it took was one report to Father for their plans to be discovered. No, they had to go—immediately!

On an October night in 1973, the group gathered in the dark outside Wayne's house in Redwood Valley. They packed everything they could—food, clothes, books—into three vehicles. Then, silently, they drove off.

In a letter they left behind for Jones, they explained their decision to quit the Temple, pointing out that whites advanced more quickly in Peoples Temple than Blacks. How could Jones advocate racial equity when he didn't practice it? Additionally, they claimed the Temple's actions and concerns didn't match its rhetoric. "For the past 6 years all staff have concern[ed] themselves with [disgracing] people, calling them [names], sex, sex, sex. What about socialism?"

The young people headed for Canada. As their little caravan made its way northward, the Gang of Eight, as they came to be called, kept a nervous lookout. They expected to see headlights behind them at any moment.

Wayne showed those in his car the gun he'd brought along. He discovered he wasn't the only one who'd packed a weapon—Jim and some others also had firearms. As former guards, they'd known where the Temple guns were hidden and had helped themselves.

When Jones learned they'd gone, he dispatched search parties and even rented an airplane to scan the highways, but the defectors weren't found. Jones became furious. He felt under personal attack, betrayed and insulted.

He called an emergency meeting in Redwood Valley, summoning members from both San Francisco and Los Angeles. The potential damage to the church had to be immediately stanched. Defection could threaten morale. It could start a domino effect with other members leaving right and left.

Still, Jones knew he had to proceed cautiously. These were not rank-and-file members. They were promising would-be professionals, essential contributors to a future self-sufficient socialist society. Additionally, he didn't want to rattle the defectors' faithful families with threatening sermons or calls to violence.

Instead, Jones tried another approach. "If I had a leader—oh, how I would love to have a leader," he began one sermon. "If I had a God—oh, how I wish I had a God like you do . . . because I'm the only one there is as far as I can see. And I have searched all over heaven and earth and I certainly looked through the belly of hell." He said that he'd warned the young people not to leave. He'd tried to protect them. But they were headstrong and thought they knew better than God. Already, they were paying the price. "The adventure has turned into a bitter, bitter agony already. They're a black and white suicide squad. . . . An accident looking for a place to happen." The ignorant children had turned their backs on Father, and in doing so, they'd turned their backs on Peoples Temple. He wasn't angry. But shouldn't *they* be furious? The Gang of Eight had abandoned *them,* and for nothing but selfish, capitalist reasons.

For weeks the same wheedling message turned up in meetings and sermons. Soon members were branding the eight as political terrorists and racists. Seeking vengeance, and coerced by Jones, friends and families of the defectors signed false affidavits attesting to the students' wicked past acts—theft, sexual misconduct, drug use. Not only did these documents shred the eight's reputations within the church community, but they also gave Jones something to threaten them with should any speak publicly against Peoples Temple.

While all this was happening, the young people drove. At the Canadian border they froze with fear. They felt sure Jones had notified border authorities to watch for them. Deciding not to chance it, they turned and headed for Montana instead.

For weeks they traveled from place to place, camping beside lakes, swimming, and fishing. Eventually, they arrived in Spokane, Washington, where they moved into a house together and found work. At night they talked about the Temple and Jim Jones. None of them intended to ever go back, especially Jim. Little did he know that he would come face to face with Jim Jones one last time.

The incident shook Jones. It would be so easy for Jim Cobb and the others to bring down the church. They knew about the fake healings. They knew about the armed guards and catharsis sessions.

He decided to exert even more control over his followers.

At the next PC meeting, just days after the defection, he had Carolyn hand out blank pieces of paper and ask each member to sign one. She explained Father's new policy. If anybody displeased or angered him, Father would write any "confession" he chose above their signature—drug trafficking, rape, pedophilia. He'd thus own a signed document attesting to their guilt. Maybe he'd show the document to the rest of the congregation. Or maybe he'd show it to the police.

This was blackmail. If they signed, Jones would always have something on them, and he could ruin their lives. Still, under Jones's watchful eye, everyone signed. "It was a test of our faith," explained Deanna Mertle. They didn't think Jones would really *use* them.

At yet another PC meeting a few days later, Jones, who'd been popping more pills than ever, asked, "How many of you here today would be willing to take your own lives now to keep the church from being discredited?" His words slurred.

Jack Beam asked what he meant.

Jones explained. He'd been thinking about what to do in the face of public attack, and he'd come up with a plan: revolutionary suicide.

Jones hadn't coined the term; he'd appropriated it. Black Panther leader Huey P. Newton had recently published a memoir titled *Revolutionary Suicide,* in which he wrote: "Revolutionary suicide does not mean that I and my comrades have a death wish; it means just the opposite. We have such a strong desire to live with hope and human dignity that existence without them is impossible. When reactionary forces crush us, we move against these forces, even at the risk of death." Newton pointed out that those who'd been killed while involved in a movement to overthrow the white racist establishment had committed "revolutionary suicide." They'd willingly laid their lives on the line for racial justice. In short, revolutionary suicide was martyrdom.

But Jones twisted Newton's idea into something entirely different. He suggested everyone on the PC commit suicide at the same time. They'd be revolutionaries in service of apostolic socialism. "We will go down in history," he said. He claimed he was ready to do it that very day. "Life is a bore," he added. "Surely, no one here is enamored with his existence." And such an extraordinary act would generate lots of news coverage for the Cause.

"I want to take a vote today to find out how dedicated you all are," Jones said.

Jack Beam jumped to his feet. "I don't want to die. I don't know about the rest of you people, but I don't want to kill myself." He stormed out of the meeting.

A handful of others also refused.

Most, however, agreed.

Deanna Mertle was one of them. She didn't believe Jones really meant it but thought her acquiescence would get her on Father's good side. She believed most of the others felt the same.

Jones made a list of those who wouldn't die. "[These] are people who can't be trusted," he said when he'd finished. "A person is not fully trustworthy until he is ready to lay down his life for the Cause."

Mike Cartmell stood and said, "We could all take our lives, and it certainly would be newsworthy. But there is a possibility that the public might think of us as the biggest fools of all time, instead of as courageous revolutionaries."

Jones considered this.

Deanna added her opinion. "More than one hundred bodies lying dead in this church might indeed make [us] look insane."

Without another word Jones dropped the subject and moved on to other topics.

But he didn't give up on the notion of revolutionary suicide.

Chapter Twenty

Father's Grand Plan

FOR MORE THAN A DECADE, JIM JONES HAD HARBORED A grand plan: to create a socialist utopia in the wilderness far from established society. He'd put aside his dream to focus on other issues—expanding the Temple, recruiting followers, and tightening control over them. But now, shaken by the Gang of Eight's abandonment, he knew it was time. He would take his followers someplace so far away that devotion to the Temple—and to Jones—would be their only option.

He already knew the place: Guyana. He'd been impressed by the South American country when he'd visited twelve years earlier. He'd liked that the country was socialist, and that its national language was English. He'd liked that 90 percent of the army and police were Black, as were most government ministers and high-level bureaucrats. Best of all, he'd liked its isolation. Most Guyanese lived along the Atlantic coast, except for the indigenous people, the Amerindians, who inhabited the jungle in the country's interior, a vast, tangled wilderness that was completely unconnected by roads to the cities or the coast. Jones envisioned his members living there, cut off from the modern world, creating a self-sustaining community.

In October 1973, not long after introducing PC members to the concept of revolutionary suicide, he called them in for an emergency meeting.

Once everyone had arrived, he presented his project. To start, the Temple would send five hundred members to Guyana, he explained. These would be volunteers, folks who wanted to go. They would clear land, cultivate crops, and build a town, a process Jones expected to take ten years.

What about the California Temples? Was Jones suggesting that eventually they'd all move to South America? a PC member asked.

No, he replied. Despite having told the congregation that he knew a place where they could all go to avoid the concentration camps, he had no intention of relocating everyone. All three California Temples would continue to operate as usual. If U.S. members wished, they could travel to the settlement on a short-term basis. Jones envisioned rotating people in and out for varying lengths of time. It would be like mission work, or summer camp.

And where would Father be?

Jones explained that he would remain headquartered in San Francisco, although he'd visit the settlement often to provide spiritual leadership.

It was time for the committee to vote on Jones's plan. The leader, of course, didn't need their approval. But Jones knew it was important that they feel a sense of ownership in the project, that they'd make a group decision.

The verdict was unanimous. A "Peoples Temple Agricultural Project" would be established in Guyana. Members, however, called the project Jonestown.

The following Sunday, Jones announced the agricultural project to the congregation, calling Guyana the Promised Land. He'd purposely chosen this motif because it resonated with many of his African American followers. In traditional Black churches the Bible story of Moses leading the Jewish people out of enslavement to the Promised Land held special meaning. Enslaved persons in the American South had seen the Jews' plight as parallel to their own. And in the following decades, the story continued to inspire hope.

Jones went on to describe Guyana as a tropical heaven with ripe fruit bursting from every tree. Food was so plentiful, he claimed, all you had to do was sit back and let it drop into your lap. They'd have so much that they'd be able to feed the hungry communities along the South American coast. Imagine it, he told them, "Temple boats loaded with food and Temple hands of all colors providing nourishment to the poor."

But the community couldn't be built without money. He urged everyone to look for previously unconsidered sources of income. Life insurance policies. Burial plots. It was time to give it all to the church. For those few who still had not gone communal, he demanded that each Sunday they give him a minimum of 35 percent of their weekly salary. Better yet, he said, why not just go communal and hand over the entire paycheck? Those who already lived communally should find unnecessary personal items—the extra pair of shoes, the matching silverware, the bedside lamp—and give them to the Temple thrift store. Every sacrifice brought them closer to a glorious life in the Promised Land.

Despite his announcement, Jones had yet to consult with the Guyanese government. It wasn't until December that he and a handful of aides flew to Georgetown to meet with officials. A deal was quickly struck. The Guyanese offered the Temple three thousand acres of rainforest near the Venezuelan border for the bargain price of twenty-five cents per acre. In return Jones promised to cultivate at least half of the leased land. If successful, the Temple could, after five years, expand its holdings. The deal satisfied everyone. Jones got his Promised Land, and the Guyanese got Americans on their border.

For decades, Guyana and neighboring Venezuela had been in a dispute over the exact location of the border between them. Venezuela, insisting its territory extended hundreds of miles into land claimed by Guyana, threatened to invade. If this happened, there was little that Guyana—economically depressed and with almost no military—could do to stop it. The country would be easily overrun. Venezuela's leaders, however, feared American military might. If an American settlement established itself on Guyana's border, Venezuela wouldn't dare invade. And so, Guyanese officials eagerly welcomed Peoples Temple.

Chapter Twenty-One

Pioneers

THERE WAS NOTHING BUT JUNGLE. NO ROADS. NO VILLAGES. No visible human mark of any kind. Michael Touchette peered into the bush—just unbroken, impenetrable green cut through by meandering, muddy rivers. The thick trees grew so close together that they created a wall. "And this is no joke . . . you could walk, say, fifty feet into the jungle, close your eyes and turn around, do a couple . . . three sixties, open your eyes and you would have no clue where you came . . . from."

Coils of underbrush embedded with needle-sharp thorns wound between the trunks, creating a natural barbed wire. The heavy, humid air was loud with the buzzing of stinging, biting insects, the cawing of brilliantly plumed birds, and the shrieking of howler monkeys. The first time Michael heard the monkeys' cry, his hair stood on end. It sounded like a person being murdered, but after a few months, he became used to it. He was also used to forever being on the lookout for venomous snakes and columns of stinging ants. He hadn't seen any jungle cats yet, but he knew they were out there.

Since their arrival in mid-March 1974, Michael and twenty

others, including his family, Charlie and Joyce Touchette and his older brother Al, had toiled to clear the land. They were the Temple's first settlers, chosen for their skills and muscle. Father called them "pioneers."

Jim Bogue also arrived with that first group. He, too, was strong and skilled, but he'd been sent to Guyana for a different reason.

The Bogue family had joined the Temple in 1968 after the accidental drowning of their two-year-old son, Jonathon. Mired in grief, Jim Bogue had found hope and compassion within the church. So had his wife, Edith. The couple, along with their children, Teena, Juanita, Marilee, and Tommy, quickly became active members. Like Hyacinth Thrash, they ran a care home in Redwood Valley. But as time passed, Bogue couldn't accept the changes he saw in the church—the disrespect toward the Bible, the insistence on communal living, the violence of the catharsis sessions. He decided to quit.

His wife reported him to Jones, who advised Edith to drain all the money from their joint bank account—the couple had yet to go communal—and to take Bogue's name off the facility's license. Edith did so. And she threatened Bogue, too. If he didn't stay, she said, she'd get a divorce and take the kids. He'd be left penniless and without a family.

With little choice, Bogue stayed. But he'd lost Jones's trust. The leader didn't want him around, giving other members ideas—yet he had no intention of letting Bogue leave. Instead, after services one Sunday, he pulled Jim aside and asked him to be a pioneer. It was a shrewd calculation. Jim's relationship with Edith had been in tatters ever since he'd tried to leave the church. Jones knew the man would do anything to repair it. "Don't worry," he told Bogue. "As soon as you get settled in, I'll send Edith and the kids down to you." He intimated that it would be a new start for them, away from the Temple.

Bogue accepted.

And Jones found a new strategy for dealing with problematic followers: He would send them to Guyana.

The pioneers flew to Guyana's capital city, Georgetown, then chartered a small plane to take them to Port Kaituma, a tiny, poor village deep in the remote jungle where a handful of people, mostly Amerindians, lived. Built on an inlet of the Kaituma River, the village boasted a few dozen simple homes on stilts, two bars, and a gravel airstrip. There were no regularly scheduled flights; all air transportation in and out had to be chartered, or you could take a boat. To get to the nearest pocket of civilization, a small Guyanese military base called Matthews Ridge thirty-five miles away, villagers had to travel by train or on a dirt path. There were no direct roads leading anywhere else.

The pioneers lived in Port Kaituma as they struggled to get to the site of their future settlement. A little over six miles of jungle stood between them and it. They needed to build a road through this wilderness, but cutting through the foliage quickly became a lesson in frustration. Axes didn't make a dent. Neither did chain saws. The blades of their tools simply broke against the hard wood.

The Amerindians came to their aid. They showed the pioneers how to take down trees using a pulley system with ropes. One at a time the trees were levered out of the ground. It was slow, backbreaking work, but finally a rough road—twenty-five feet across—was cleared.

At last, the pioneers reached their site. They found more trees.

"We cleared the jungle to get to the jungle," said Michael.

With a road cut, the pioneers brought in heavy equipment rented from the Guyanese government. They paid the Amerindians to continue clearing trees while they flattened the site's center.

This entailed burning the fallen trees, then using a bulldozer to clear away the debris. Michael taught himself to drive the machine. "I got really good at it," he said. Six months into their efforts, they finally began planning the town.

Since none of them were architects or draftspeople, they simply drew things on a piece of paper. "We planned by ourselves at night," recalled Michael. "'This is where we want the garden,' someone would say. 'This is where we want to build a well. This is where we'll build the outhouse.' We didn't know what we were doing. We just did it."

Jones expected the settlement to grow its own crops. He didn't know that soil in a rainforest is poor. The topsoil is acidic and only a few inches deep. Below it lies a hard clay. The pioneers tried all sorts of ways to improve the soil. They added fertilizer. They used crushed seashells. Nothing worked. Again, the Amerindians came to their aid. They showed the Americans how to use ash from the burned vegetation and trees to add nutrients.

The pioneers planted corn, carrots, celery, and asparagus, but nothing grew. After the Amerindians suggested planting local crops—sweet potatoes, cassavas, pigeon peas, bananas, pineapples, and oranges—they started over. Jim Bogue, especially, threw himself into the challenge of tropical agriculture.

Without Jones's presence everyone felt calmer, although no one said that out loud. They lived happily, almost autonomously, something twenty-one-year-old Michael hadn't experienced since his parents had joined the Temple four years earlier. On a typical day the pioneers woke at sunrise and got to work. Food, shipped from Georgetown, allowed them to eat three hearty meals a day. They quit around five-thirty. Evenings were free, something that never happened back in California. They read, played dominoes, caught up on their sleep, or just hung out, talking and laughing. Sometimes they watched movies sent from Georgetown, which they ran on a sixteen-millimeter projector. Back in the States followers were prohibited from going to the movies, but here in the jungle the pioneers took in the musical *Hello, Dolly!* and Bruce Lee's *Enter the Dragon.* Their favorite film, though, was *Dirty Harry,* and they watched it over and over. "It got so we could recite every line," claimed Michael.

On Sundays they gathered for a weekly meeting. If a problem arose, they dealt with it thoughtfully and reasonably. In the jungle they depended on one another for survival, and they decided that discipline would only hurt their efforts.

Michael Touchette loved his days in the jungle. "It was a lot of fun, I'll tell you that!" he said. He became a skilled bulldozer operator, as well as an expert problem solver. "[If] you have a machine breakdown, you can't run out to the hardware store . . . ," he explained. [W]e were . . . a day trip by boat to get to [Georgetown]." Even if they did get to the city, it was usually impossible to find what they needed. Guyana was still a developing nation, and Georgetown had few materials. Said Michael: "We sit there and we try to figure out the problem by ourselves and we did the best we could."

In Guyana, Michael discovered his best self. Despite the sunburn and the bugbites, the cuts and the sprained muscles, the jungle felt like home. "This new way of life, to me, was everything," he said.

Chapter Twenty-Two

Kimo

IN THE SPRING OF 1974, CAROLYN LAYTON DISAPPEARED from the Temple. "I sent her away on a crucial and secret mission," Jones explained.

That summer he added more details. Carolyn had gone to Mexico to buy parts for an atomic bomb, he told members. He'd hoped that having the bomb would keep government agents from harassing the Temple. But before Carolyn could purchase the final piece—the detonator—she'd been caught and thrown into a Mexican prison.

"It was an astonishing story," remarked one PC member, "but absolutely believable since it came from God."

Only a handful of people knew the truth: Carolyn was pregnant with Jones's baby.

Annie Moore knew. In the year and a half she'd been in the Temple, she'd risen to a place of prominence. Most assumed this was because she was Carolyn's sister, but there was more to it. In Annie, Jones saw a foot soldier—a deeply committed, trustworthy young woman who was smart, capable, and an unwavering believer in both socialism and Jim Jones.

"I'm the gladdest I've ever been to be in this church, working for social justice and brotherhood," she wrote to her sister Rebecca. She went on to say that Jones "averages two hours of sleep a week because he is up all night doing counseling and church work. . . . He would not kill the slightest bug or pull up a weed unless it was harming man[kind] as a whole. I've never seen such dedication in a person before."

Jones knew Annie could be trusted with the secret. Not once did Annie let on that Carolyn was living—at Jones's suggestion—in Berkeley with their nonmember parents.

Annie visited often. "Aren't you excited about being a grandmother?" she asked Barbara Moore one day.

"No," replied Barbara. She detested lying about Carolyn's situation, but there seemed nothing else to do. Her daughter needed her.

Jones, too, frequented the Moore home. At these times he didn't act like a charismatic leader. "Instead, he was a quiet, concerned individual with a pessimistic view of the world," recalled Rebecca.

John and Barbara treated Jones pleasantly. They hoped that by accepting him, they'd be allowed a closer relationship with their daughters and future grandchild.

There was, however, one member of the Moore family who refused to warm up to Jones—Annie's dog, Willie. He barked and growled whenever Jones was nearby. The one time the leader tried to pet him, Willie bared his teeth. Jones became the only person Willie ever snarled at.

On January 31, 1975, Carolyn went into labor. Annie stayed with her until the moment of birth, then Jones accompanied her into the delivery room. Soon after, little James Jon was born. The baby, said new grandmother Barbara Moore, "is very cute. Pug nose, brown hair . . . Healthy and happy and so far, good."

For obvious reasons the leader of Peoples Temple couldn't give his last name to the baby. Instead, he arranged for Carolyn to quickly and quietly marry Mike Prokes, the church's public relations man, who'd been sworn to secrecy. Like so many Temple unions, it would be a paper marriage. Mike and Carolyn would never live together or share a bed. They did, however, record the baby's name as James Jon Prokes. Carolyn called him Kimo, Hawaiian for "Jim."

When Carolyn returned to the church almost a full year after disappearing, she explained to members that she'd adopted her cousin's unwanted son. But rumors flew, most likely started by Jones, that she'd been raped while in the Mexican prison and gotten pregnant.

The congregation welcomed the baby. Father especially doted on him, carrying Kimo around, tickling him, bouncing him on his knee. He made an exception for the baby, too. After six months of age, all Temple children were raised communally—but not Kimo. He stayed with his mother.

Chapter Twenty-Three

Tommy and Brian

FOURTEEN-YEAR-OLD TOMMY BOGUE FELT ADRIFT, ORPHANED, and *angry.* After his dad, Jim Bogue, had been sent to Guyana, Tommy began acting out—skipping school, ditching church services, talking back.

His mother, Edith, couldn't control him. She turned to Jones, who placed him in the care of a member known to be a strict disciplinarian. The woman beat Tommy with a rubber hose for little things like arriving home from school fifteen minutes late. In the summer of 1975, after another member noticed the bruises covering the boy's body, Jones had him moved into the San Francisco Temple.

When he first walked into his new home, Tommy wasn't impressed. A closet-size upstairs room at the back of the church, it boasted a bare double mattress that lay on the cracked linoleum floor. On top of the mattress sat his roommate, a redheaded kid named Brian Davis. Brian, who was watching *Creature Features* on a tiny black-and-white television set, didn't even look at Tommy.

Tommy plopped down next to Brian. Together they watched TV in silence for a few minutes. Then they started talking. They discovered they had lots in common. Said Tommy, "We both enjoyed the TV series *Night Gallery* and *Twilight Zone* (our favorites), and we both played musical instruments. We were both to start the ninth grade in the fall at Presidio High."

They had something else in common, too: their hatred for Jim Jones.

Like Tommy, Brian had watched his family crumble at the hands of the church. The boy saw his father, a true believer, only at services. His mother had defected years earlier and now lived in a suburb of San Francisco with his two younger brothers. Brian desperately wanted to go home to them.

The teens quickly became "comrades in mischief," recalled Tommy. At night they creeped out through a side door and shimmied through a hole in the fence that surrounded the church property. Avoiding the security guards became a game to them.

Once outside they felt exhilarated in their freedom. They explored all over the city by sneaking onto buses. They skateboarded down to Ocean Beach and flirted with girls. It felt good to act like normal teenagers.

Eventually, though, they had to go back. After creeping into the Temple, the boys would find an out-of-the-way spot and wait. Sooner or later some sputtering adult would come upon them, demanding to know where they'd been.

"Right here," they'd reply innocently. "We didn't know anyone was looking for us."

Back in their room they'd laugh about fooling the grown-ups.

One night they decided to try smoking marijuana for the first time. "Wouldn't you know it, we were caught sneaking back in," said Tommy.

Jones handed down their punishment. For an entire night the

teens were forced to crawl around on their hands and knees, picking lint off the sanctuary's red carpet.

Another time they got caught smoking cigarettes. For this offense Jones gave them the night job of scraping the yellowing linoleum off the kitchen floor. By morning their knees were embedded with hundreds of sharp particles that had pushed their way through their pant legs and into their skin. "It made us miss the carpet," Tommy joked.

These punishments didn't deter the boys. They only made them hate the Temple even more.

They decided to escape. Brian would go to his mom's house. And Tommy? "Well, I didn't know where to go," he said. He thought maybe his aunt and uncle would take him in.

Since they didn't have any money for Brian's bus ticket, they swiped it from the church donation cans. They each took just two dollars a week so church staff wouldn't notice.

After a few months, when they finally had enough, they slipped out and headed over to the Greyhound bus station. Brian bought a ticket to his mother's. Then, with time to kill before the bus left, they walked over to Tommy's aunt and uncle's house.

The boys told them everything: the all-night lint picking, the catharsis sessions, their family separations. Shocked, the couple agreed to let Tommy live with them, but *only* if his mother agreed.

Once they had Edith on the phone, they explained their willingness to take Tommy in. She asked to speak to her son.

He got on the line.

Did he really want to leave the church? Edith inquired.

"I couldn't believe my ears," said Tommy. "I had a choice? I told her *yes,* it's what I wanted."

She wouldn't stand in his way, she replied. She would get his clothes and bring them right over.

"I almost cried, I was so happy," Tommy recalled. "Our plan was working."

Soon the doorbell rang.

Tommy answered.

It was his mother. Behind her stood two Temple guards.

Tommy screamed, and Brian bolted out the back door. He tried to make it to the bus station.

Guards nabbed him at the corner. They shoved both boys into the backseat of a car.

No one said a word to the teens when they returned. Guards dragged Tommy to an upstairs room and locked him in. For the next two weeks, he remained a prisoner. He saw no one except those who brought his meals. He had no idea what had happened to Brian.

Then, at last, his prison door opened. Father had made a decision.

"[I was] sent to Jonestown," said Tommy.

When Tommy arrived in Guyana in the fall of 1975, the now fifteen-year-old knew nothing about farming or building. His father taught him. Soon Tommy got so good at hammering, he could pound nails with both his right and his left hands. Sure, the work was hard, but at least he had some freedom. And he didn't have to see Jones's face every day.

Although he still missed Brian, Tommy made a new friend in Jonestown, an Amerindian boy about his age named David George. The Touchette family had taken the boy in after discovering his mother was too poor to care for him properly.

When Tommy and David had spare time—after dinner, or during the afternoon downpours that brought work to a standstill—the boys roamed the jungle. David knew all about its plants and animals, and he shared his knowledge with his American friend. The two came across anteaters, sloths, monkeys, parrots, and a giant frog. David also taught him how to tell the difference between edible and poisonous plants; how to treat snakebites by applying cassava root; and, most importantly, how to find his way through the tangled wilderness by looking past the trees to breaks in the canopy. Soon the jungle became a familiar place to Tommy. Yes, there were things to fear in the bush. But there were wonders, too.

Chapter Twenty-Four

Death and Sacrifice

IN SEPTEMBER 1975, JONES CALLED A SPECIAL PC MEETING at the San Francisco Temple. Once the members were gathered, he told them he'd brought a treat—red wine.

The group looked at one another. Father forbade drinking alcohol.

Jones assured them it was all right. The wine, he told them, was a token of his love. He poured them each a small glass.

Delighted, the members clinked glasses. They sipped and laughed, enjoying the moment.

Jones watched, an odd smile on his face, while they drank it all. "I have something to say to you," he said when the last glass stood empty. "The wine you just drank has a slow-acting poison in it. Within forty-five minutes, each of you will get very sick, and soon after that, you will die."

Jim McElvane, head of security, reacted first. He lay down on the floor at the back of the room and crossed his hands over his chest.

"What are you doing?" asked Jones. "The poison can't be affecting you that quickly."

"No, Father," McElvane replied. "I want to make myself comfortable and go quickly."

Staff member Patty Cartmell screamed. "I don't want to die. I want to get out of here right now." She ran for the door, but guards stopped her.

Jones looked around the room. "Are there any other traitors who want to try and get a doctor?"

No one else moved. They sat there waiting, fear etched on their faces.

Forty-five minutes passed slowly.

At last, Jones made an announcement. There was no poison in the wine. It had all been a loyalty test. "I now know which of you can be trusted and which of you cannot." He turned to Patty. "I hope you learned a lesson about yourself. You are too enamored with life, and until you are so tired of living that you want to die, you can never be trusted to do great things for this Cause."

He looked toward the others. He hoped they understood that dying for their beliefs was a privilege.

Death and *sacrifice.*

Jones used the words a lot in his sermons that fall. "I love socialism," he said in one, "and I'd die to bring it about. But if I did, I'd take a thousand with me."

Listeners took him to mean a thousand of the Temple's enemies. But the following week Jones added, "A good socialist does not fear death. [Death] would be the greatest reward he could receive."

Listeners began to grasp the idea that Jones meant for *them* to die.

Most weren't shocked. They saw themselves as comrades in arms in the great fight against capitalism, and it didn't take much imagination to envision dying violently at the hands of government agents, just as civil rights leaders and student protesters had. In 1973 government agents had brutally suppressed Americans at Wounded Knee (the American Indian Movement) and in 1969 at the Stonewall Inn (the gay rights movement), all while the United States continued fighting a bloody and senseless war in Vietnam. Perhaps Peoples Temple was next.

Two years after he'd first shared the term *revolutionary suicide* with the PC, Jones introduced it to the rank-and-file members. "We've got to go down in history," he told his followers. "Everyone [here] will die . . . for our belief in integration."

Stephan Jones often wondered how someone as handsome and charismatic as his father could be "so full of shit all the time." He saw clearly how his father lied, manipulated, and controlled people with fear. And he knew his father used fear to control him, too. And yet he recognized that his father could "tap into something very real, and show something very real, and was very loving especially during [the church's] early period." When his father looked at someone—including Stephan—he could "just light them up."

Stephan rebelled in little and big ways. He often sneaked into his father's room in the San Francisco Temple to steal money from his pockets. Jones never carried much cash—just a few dollars—but it was easy pickings since Jones never locked his door.

Occasionally, Stephan would find Jones with a lover. Often it was a onetime thing, some male or female member. By 1976, though, it was often twenty-three-year-old Maria Katsaris.

Maria had joined the Temple three years earlier. Back then she'd been introverted and awkward and suffered from feelings of inferiority. She'd also felt confused about her future.

By small increments Jones had built her up by giving her an ever-expanding role in the church. Slowly, she gained confidence and began to feel that her life had purpose. Recently, Jones had decided to build her self-esteem even further by sleeping with her.

Those who knew Maria were dismayed by the change in her. Now the young woman was an ultraloyalist—humorless, overbearing, and vigilant about reporting minor infractions. Like Carolyn Layton, she was part of Father's inner circle, as well as one of his regular mistresses. And like Carolyn, she would do whatever he asked.

These sexual liaisons made Stephan seethe with resentment. His feelings overtook him on a Saturday morning when the congregation headed off from the San Francisco Temple on a weekend bus trip to Redwood Valley. After he was sure the buses had pulled away, he crept into his father's room. On top of the chest of drawers sat a bottle of quaaludes. Stephan gulped down a handful. Then he sat down to wait. He slipped into unconsciousness.

That's when Jones walked back in. Seeing his son's limp body, he shouted for help. Within minutes a Temple nurse shoved a tube into Stephan's nose and pumped out his stomach. Gradually, the teen came around.

He peered at the concerned faces surrounding him. Even his father looked worried. And despite pain and wooziness, Stephan felt good. "It was torture, but it was attention," he said. For once he felt important to his father.

Marceline hurried to San Francisco. No longer would she oversee the Redwood Valley Temple. She needed to be close to her son. She didn't, however, move in with her husband. And she did not live communally. Instead, the Temple set her up in her own apartment. It even had a spare bedroom so family could stay overnight. With her nursing experience Marceline found a well-paying position at the Berkeley Department of Health. Unlike other church members, she did not turn over her salary.

Marceline recognized Stephan's misery and resolved to do anything she could to help him, even if that meant breaking church rules. When Stephan said he'd like to take acting classes, she enrolled him in the American Conservatory Theater. And when he wished for a place of his own, she rented him a studio apartment. She paid for it out of her paycheck.

Stephan still attended high school by day, but at night he worked as a valet, parking cars to help pay his living expenses. In his spare time he hung out at his apartment, watching television and eating junk food. For the first time the teenager was tasting independence. And he liked it.

His father detested the arrangement. He declared it elitist and bourgeois but allowed it if Stephan kept it secret. If anyone asked, Stephan was living with his mother.

How could Stephan not tell his friends? Soon his brothers Tim and Jimmy, and Temple buddy Johnny Cobb, turned up at Stephan's place every chance they got. Free. Unsupervised. Open to a world beyond the church.

Jones obsessed about the situation. How would it look if his son defected? And what if he took his friends with him? It would be another Gang of Eight. He couldn't let that happen. And he knew just how to prevent it: Jonestown.

Part Four

Exodus

The thing [that's] important to remember: the elements of the Temple that couldn't be found anywhere else were so attractive, so wonderful, so uplifting, that we'd do whatever we had to. . . . We'd tell ourselves whatever story we had to. . . . It was our community. . . . I know there were a lot of people who were held by that. So regardless of what got people [to Guyana], see, once you're in, it's about *way* more than loyalty to Jim Jones.

—Stephan Jones, son of Jim Jones and Peoples Temple survivor

Chapter Twenty-Five

Life in the Jungle

IN EARLY FEBRUARY 1977, MARCELINE'S TELEPHONE RANG. IT was her husband, and he didn't mince words. He was taking Stephan to Guyana in the morning.

Marceline begged him to reconsider. For Stephan's mental health, she argued, he needed to be near his mother—not forty-five hundred miles away in some godforsaken jungle.

"It won't be for long," her husband assured her. It was just a visit. The teen wouldn't be gone more than a week.

Did Marceline believe him? Probably not. But as usual, she relented.

Stephan's father wanted to speak with him. She handed him the phone.

Jones told the teen his plans.

Stephan flatly refused to leave.

Jones got Marceline back on the line. He knew their son listened to her. She had to persuade him.

Yet again, Jones coerced his wife into giving him exactly what he wanted. Marceline finally turned to Stephan and said, "I want you to go."

With no one to back him up, Stephan gave in.

He left with his father the next morning.

Less than forty-eight hours later, father and son arrived in Jonestown. It was not the Caribbean paradise Jones had promised. Fewer than fifty settlers lived there, and the few standing buildings were constructed of wooden poles and canvas roofs with crude wooden floors. Stephan looked around the primitive encampment. Thank goodness he was only staying a week.

Then Michael Touchette and his older brother, Al, turned up, filthy from work but grinning at the sight of Stephan. Michael must have recognized his buddy's shock. The structures were temporary, he explained. Now that the sawmill was built, they'd soon have plenty of lumber for constructing permanent buildings. Proudly, he pointed out the hundreds of acres of land they'd cleared and cultivated.

Michael went on about his bulldozer driving, too. It felt so satisfying, he added, to raise a town from the wilderness. He suggested Stephan stay permanently.

Not a chance, Stephan replied. No way was he going to give up his apartment, his acting lessons, and his newfound independence for *this.*

Two days later, when everyone was sitting around after dinner, Jones steered the conversation to the topic of sacrifices. What would they be willing to do for the Cause? Would they give up their former lives, stay in Jonestown, and never look back?

Everyone except Stephan agreed they would.

Jones and the others turned to him . . . waiting.

As moments slipped by, the pressure grew. If it had just been his father staring at him, Stephan felt he could have handled the situation. But it was his friends, his church family. He didn't want to appear selfish to *them.* So, he nodded.

Jones smiled. If that was Stephan's decision, then he would abide by it.

The next morning he returned to California without his son.

In those first days Stephan longed for all he'd lost. But slowly, as days became weeks and then months, he not only adapted to his new life; he embraced it. His body became muscular and bronzed from hard work in the sun. He let his black hair grow long and tied it behind his neck. He built bunk beds and laid flooring, learning as he went. In his hut he kept an anaconda and an emerald tree boa as pets. He liked to walk through the bush with one of these brightly colored creatures coiled around his neck. He felt a deep sense of purpose and accomplishment. As he strode through the settlement, he'd think, "I put every nail in that cottage" or "I knocked down the tree to cut the wood to build that house." He wasn't just building this place for Peoples Temple, he realized. "I was building a place for me, too. Jonestown was the first thing I ever worked for."

Suzanne, the Joneses' adopted daughter, had long rationalized her father's deceptions and extremism. A faithful church member, she'd served on the PC and in numerous staff and advisory positions. In 1975, at twenty-three years old, she'd married Mike Cartmell. "Together we were like Temple royalty," recalled Mike. Members expected them to one day take the reins of leadership. Jones himself had called Mike his "designated heir."

But as Jones's drug use escalated, Suzanne found herself growing more and more alienated. Her once-doting father had turned into a paranoid and cruel tyrant. She began to think about defecting.

Little did she know that Mike, too, was disillusioned with the direction the Temple had taken. "No matter the goal," he admitted, "I couldn't justify [my actions] anymore. The beatings. The lying. I hated myself for going along." Like his wife, he was contemplating quitting. Neither, however, dared breathe a word about their feelings to the other.

For Suzanne the final straw came in February 1977.

Jones approached her, wearing his sunglasses and a sideways smile she'd seen often—the one he used to charm and coerce young women. He laid a heavy hand on her shoulder. He told her how very attractive he found her.

Suzanne recoiled. She said she was going to tell her mother.

Go ahead, he responded. Marceline knew all about his desires, and it was "all right with her."

Suzanne knew that was a lie. She had to break free.

She did it slowly. As Jones's "princess," she'd long gotten away with skipping meetings. "I don't remember her ever being punished for it," said Mike Cartmell. Now Suzanne began going even less.

On February 18, Mike Cartmell shocked the congregation by defecting. "I stole away to a senior citizens' residence in Oakland, where I lived under an assumed name," he explained.

Six days later Suzanne stopped going to the Temple altogether. Jones demanded his daughter be found. Staff soon tracked her down to a small apartment in San Francisco. Talk with her, Jones ordered Marceline. Get her back.

By telephone Marceline begged her daughter to return to the church. As usual, she found excuses for Jones's terrible behavior. You're confused, she told Suzanne. You're mistaken. Speak with your father. Work things out.

Suzanne refused. She was done with Peoples Temple, as well as with her father. She did make her mother a promise, though. She wouldn't speak publicly about the church or smear Jim Jones.

Jones, however, smeared her. From his pulpit he accused her of defecting so she could live "high on the hog." He called her an "ungrateful heifer" and a "capitalist pig," and claimed she was part of the government's conspiracy against them, a CIA operative. Then he lowered his voice and said she was a "wicked, wicked woman" because she had tried to "get her own brother Lew to go to bed with her." The Temple, he concluded, was better off without her.

Followers agreed. Suzanne Jones was a traitor.

Chapter Twenty-Six

First Cracks

MARSHALL KILDUFF COVERED CITY HALL FOR THE *SAN FRANcisco Chronicle.* Included in the young reporter's beat were the city's twice-monthly Housing Authority meetings. Typically, these were boring events where tenants complained about landlords and contractors bid on maintenance projects. All that changed when Jim Jones joined the board in October 1976.

One year earlier, George Moscone, a mayoral candidate at the time, had visited Peoples Temple in hopes of winning Jones's political endorsement. The church leader controlled a bloc of thousands of voters in San Francisco, where elections were often decided by slim margins.

Always ambitious, Jones had dreamed of becoming the most politically influential religious leader in California's history and had seen Moscone's visit as a step toward that goal. He endorsed Moscone, who went on to win the election. In turn, Moscone showed his gratitude by appointing Jones chairman of the Housing Authority board.

At every meeting the leader swept through the double doors of the meeting room surrounded by hundreds of followers, who filled

Jimmy Jones, pictured here at around the age of four. Even at this young age, he wandered the streets of Lynn, Indiana, unsupervised and dependent on townspeople's kindness.

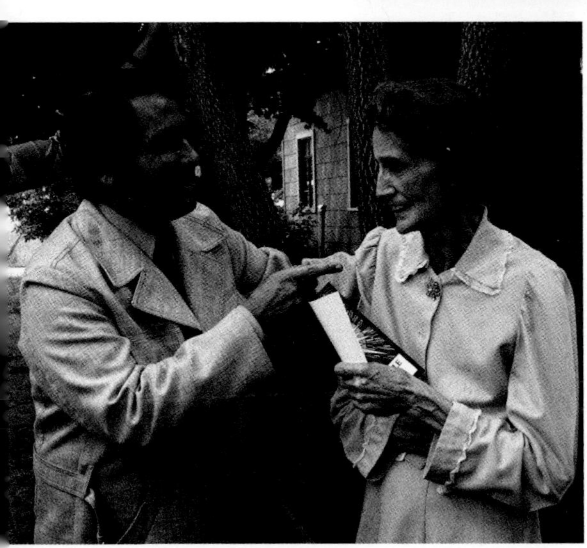

Jones's "second mother," Myrtle Kennedy, standing beside him in 1976. Jones traveled to Lynn twice after establishing Peoples Temple so he could impress her with his success as a preacher. Myrtle, who died in 1977, did not live to see how his ministry ended.

Eighteen-year-old Jim Jones and twenty-one-year-old Marceline Baldwin pictured on their wedding day in Richmond, Indiana's Trinity Methodist Church. Also married in the double ceremony was Marceline's sister Eloise Baldwin to Marion Dale Klingman.

Jim and Stephan Jones in Indiana c. 1963. Little Stephan adored his father but eventually came to recognize him as "the bogeyman."

The Redwood Valley Temple was the heart of all church activity. As this photo from 1968 shows, members have put away folding chairs and turned on the record player to dance in the same space in which they worshipped.

The "rainbow family" c. 1972. From left: Lew Jones, Suzanne Jones, Jim Jones, Jimmy Jones, Stephan Jones, and Marceline Jones. As usual, Agnes Jones is not pictured.

This photo, snapped in Redwood Valley in 1972, shows Jones surrounded by Peoples Temple children, some wearing their Sunday best. Infant John Victor Stoen sits crying on Jones's lap. The preacher later claimed to be the baby's father.

Between services, potlucks like the one in this photograph, c. 1973, were held in the Redwood Valley Temple parking lot. A pleasant event like this one turned to chaos after Jones faked his assassination and resurrection.

Moved by the spirit, an unidentified Temple member shouts out praises. A microphone is held in front of her by a church worker so that everyone can hear the rapture to which Jones's preaching has brought her.

The "pioneers" receive a visit from Father (in the hat) c. 1974. To his left stands Michael Touchette (holding the pole). Behind him in the white T-shirt and bandanna around his head is Jim Bogue.

Jim Bogue (facing the camera), Michael Touchette (at the wheel), and Jack Barrow clear jungle land c. 1974.

Tommy Bogue (back row, in the dark shirt) wears a look of boredom as he sits in the Jonestown school. His Amerindian pal, David George, sits to his right. To his left is an equally bored Vincent Lopez, with Marrian Griffith to his far left. The focused student is Kevin Grubb, son of teacher Tom Grubb.

Brian Davis, Tommy Bogue's best friend and "comrade in mischief."

To water plants, residents formed a bucket brigade, passing a full pail from person to person. Jones's adopted son Tim Tupper Jones is the second person in the line on the right.

Marceline and Stephan Jones during a visit to Jonestown in 1974.

Stanley Clayton (second from right) worked on one of th settlement's many kitchen crews. On th night of November 18, 1978, he managed to escape from the pavilion an hide in the jungle.

Arrivals traveled from Port Kaituma to Jonestown on a tractor-pulled trailer. Here Jim and Stephan Jones, as well as the Temple's pet chimpanzee, Mr. Muggs, lead the way in 1974.

the public seating. Jones took his chair in front without removing his sunglasses. His guards positioned themselves near him, glowering from behind their own shades. Because this was a public event, they came unarmed. Still, they looked intimidating. Every so often a woman, obviously an aide, scurried over to hand Jones a note or whisper in his ear. Whenever he spoke, his followers leaped to their feet, clapping and shouting for several loud minutes.

Marshall Kilduff found it all weird. He had to know more about Jim Jones. And so, on a Sunday morning in February 1977, after having called ahead, he walked into the Geary Boulevard Temple. A member met him at the front door, where the reporter joined a tour with ten others. The group was shown the whirlpool for arthritic seniors, the kitchen that churned out thousands of meals daily, the day care for working parents, and more. The other visitors asked lots of leading questions about the Temple's good works. Kilduff quickly saw through them. They were plants—other members placed there to make the church look good.

At last, they headed into the sanctuary, where Kilduff was given a front-row seat. He estimated two thousand people were there. For the next couple of hours, the reporter took in the singing, the shouts, and the hallelujahs. He heard a long and mostly nonsensical sermon from Jones. He witnessed several healings. Everyone was warm and welcoming, seemingly full of happiness. Still, the reporter sensed that something was off. It was *too* perfect.

The reporter left more curious than ever. He yearned to write an investigative piece about Jones and Peoples Temple. The next day at work, he pitched the idea to his boss, Steve Gavin, but the editor said no. The *Chronicle* had done a piece about Jones already, a positive one, about a year back.

Next Kilduff pitched his idea to a small magazine called *New West.* The editor there *was* interested . . . until he got a call from Jim Jones. Somehow Jones had gotten wind of the proposal and convinced *New West*'s editor to forget about doing the article, insisting it would jeopardize the church's good works. The article was killed.

From then on, Kilduff noticed Jones's aides sitting close to him at Housing Authority meetings. They peeked at his notes and blatantly eavesdropped on his conversations with other reporters. What Kilduff didn't know was that staff repeatedly sifted through his trash, looking for clues to what he was writing. They followed him around town, noting where he went and to whom he spoke. They reported everything to Jones.

Even without a publisher for the piece, Kilduff began investigating. He talked with San Francisco pastors who decried the adulation Jones demanded from his members. He spoke with community leaders who praised the Temple's charitable efforts. He interviewed people who'd attended services but had decided against joining. Some spoke highly of the Temple. Others voiced concerns. But none wanted to be quoted using their real names. Things just seemed to be getting weirder and weirder.

In March the reporter's luck changed. *New West* hired a new editor, Rosalie Wright, and she, too, thought something fishy was going on behind the Temple's closed doors. She accepted Kilduff's pitch and assigned one of *New West*'s reporters, Phil Tracy, to work with him. Dig deep, she told them.

At the next Housing Authority meeting, a photographer from the magazine turned up and took pictures of Jones, his guards, and his followers—much to the leader's frustration.

Hours later Wright's work phone began ringing, and the calls continued over the following days. At first, these calls were pleasant enough: Did Wright realize all the good Jim Jones did in the world? Was she really going to smear this godly man just to make money? But as time passed, they grew more menacing. Some callers demanded she kill the story, or else. Others discredited Kilduff, claiming they had explosive information about the reporter that would destroy his career, and the magazine along with it. Others said nothing—they simply breathed eerily on the other end.

When her home phone began ringing, Wright grew so worried, she moved her family to a safe house. She'd heard the threat loud and clear: They knew where she lived.

Kilduff and Tracy got phone calls, too. Some came from folks telling them how Jones had cured their cancer, or paid their rent, or gotten them off drugs. Others were from people who threatened to hurt them if they hurt Jim Jones.

Hearing about these calls, a reporter for the *San Francisco Examiner* wrote a piece about them. What, he asked readers, did the Temple have to hide if Jones's followers would go to these lengths?

After the story ran, Kilduff and Tracy began getting a different kind of phone call. These came from church defectors. Some gave their names, while others remained anonymous, but all wanted to talk about what they'd endured in Peoples Temple. Until now they'd believed the press would never go up against Jones, but the *Examiner* piece had convinced them to come forward. "And it broke [the story] wide open for us," said Phil Tracy.

One of those defectors was Jim Cobb from the Gang of Eight. Jim had returned to dental school and now lived in Berkeley. He invited the reporters, along with seven or eight other former members, including his old buddy Wayne Pietila, to his home. Nervous at first, the defectors slowly opened up. "They started to tell us what was going on," recalled Tracy. What they detailed was so awful that he "didn't want to hear it."

Catharsis sessions. Beatings. Sexual coercion. Blackmail.

At the end of the night, as the reporters drove back to San Francisco, Kilduff asked Tracy, "Do you believe them?"

Tracy replied, "What are you talking about? Will anyone believe *us*?"

Chapter Twenty-Seven

Going to the Promised Land

THE AIR WAS SOUPY AND DIESEL-SCENTED. JIM JONES breathed it in—Guyana. Then he shuffled down the airplane's metal stairs toward the fluorescent lights of the airport terminal. It was late April 1977, and he had come with a scheme he'd yet to share with anyone. Soon, however, the entire Temple would know what he was thinking.

Paula Adams, a member of the Temple's public relations staff, greeted him. After leading him to the Temple van, she drove through the streets of Georgetown. It was past midnight, and everything—including the flaking colonial buildings and dingy factories—was dark. At last, they rounded a corner. Ahead, a two-story, cream-colored villa blazed with light—Lamaha Gardens. Just weeks earlier, the Temple had purchased the residence. Jones believed it was vital that he have constant access to Guyanese leaders, and he envisioned the place as the Peoples Temple embassy in Georgetown.

With its telephones, typewriters, and taping equipment, the villa's main-floor office crackled with activity. So did the radio room, which housed one of three shortwave radios operated by the Temple. (The other two were in San Francisco and Jonestown.) Because all church communication funneled through Lamaha Gardens, the radio was staffed around the clock, usually by someone from the five-member public relations team that permanently lived in the villa. On the second floor were the living quarters—kitchen, living room, bathroom. As was the Temple way, every available space was jammed with bunks, cots, and sleeping bags for members en route to Jonestown, or for the semipermanent administrative staff that would rotate in and out from the settlement every few months. It wasn't unusual for there to be as many as seventy people in the house at any one time.

Michael Touchette's father, Charlie, as well as Stephan and some others, waited for Jones in the villa's wood-paneled living room. They'd been ordered to Georgetown because Father wanted to speak to them in person.

Jones strode into the room. Fueled by amphetamines, he paced and cursed. He was being spied on, he cried. He was being harassed. With the help of reporters Kilduff and Tracy, Temple enemies were spreading lies and discrediting him. It was the first step toward a government roundup. They'd all be put in concentration camps.

He turned to Charlie Touchette. "What do you think about moving a lot of people down here quickly?"

"It's impossible," said Charlie.

Jones thought a moment. "How many people can we accommodate now?"

"About one hundred fifty to two hundred," replied Charlie, but even that number was optimistic. The pioneers hadn't yet built enough cottages and dormitories to adequately house that many people. And the water and sewage facilities couldn't accommodate so much use. Neither could their tiny kitchen—no way could it possibly produce three meals a day for hundreds of people. Besides, how would they feed everyone? Yes, the tiny community was closing in on self-sufficiency. They were successfully growing cassavas, pineapples, bananas, and sweet potatoes. It wouldn't be long before they'd be able to sustain themselves. But they couldn't possibly harvest enough for *hundreds* of people. Food would have to be shipped in from Georgetown, an expensive proposition.

How many followers was Jones thinking? Charlie asked.

All of them, he replied, almost two thousand. And he wanted to do it over the course of the next few months, rather than the ten years originally planned.

Charlie was stunned, but he couldn't argue with Father.

The time for the exodus had come.

As Jonestown settlers stepped up construction, Jones decided to make a promotional film (the first of several), one that would show the wonders of the Promised Land to members back in California.

Using a Super 8 camera, Temple public relations man Mike Prokes panned over fields of cassava plants. Smiling workers leaned on their hoes and waved before the camera focused on Jones standing in front of a cozy-looking, pastel-colored cottage, its wooden walkways lined with blooming hibiscus. Everyone would stay in places like these, he said to the camera. He pointed across the compound. There was the nursery, with its pink walls. Oh, the children were going to love it here. And look at the schoolhouse, complete with a blackboard and shelves of books. Over there was the playground and the health clinic. "Jonestown has turned into an absolute village," he said. "Really, you have a heaven across the sea waiting."

All of it was a lie. Only a few cottages and walkways had been built. The fields weren't producing as reported, and the pigs kept dying of jungle diseases.

Now Jones toured the supply warehouse. As he pointed at the full shelves, he rattled off each item's name. "Rice and black-eyed peas, cookies and fruit drinks." He lifted the lid from a box. "Kool-Aid," he said. Then he looked directly into the camera. "When fascist terror brings concentration camps, you have a home."

The order came down from Father: All members must get a passport. A committee of seventy special aides was created to help people with the process. If a member didn't have a birth certificate (needed to obtain a passport), committee members wrote away for it. They filled out the forms. They snapped the required photos. And they accompanied members to the passport office and paid the fee.

Members began departing from California in May 1977—just weeks after the meeting at Lamaha Gardens—in groups of forty or fifty so as not to draw attention. Secrecy veiled their every move. Jones's aides worried that outsiders might try to stop the exodus, especially the taking of children. Some of these youngsters, wards of the State of California, were in foster care and had been placed by officials in the homes of several members. Other children (some as young as two and three) were taken there by noncustodial adults. Legally, permission should have been sought before any of these children were relocated. Instead, on Jones's orders, they were hustled out of the country.

He hustled his other sons out, too. Twenty-one-year-old Lew arrived on March 29 with his pregnant wife, Terry. She would give birth to their son, Chaeoke, just six days later, making him the first Temple child born in Guyana. Eighteen-year-old Tim and his wife, Sandra (Jim Cobb's sister), soon followed, as did seventeen-year-old Jimmy and his girlfriend, Yvette Muldrow. (They would eventually be married in Georgetown.) Agnes and her family joined them, too.

In San Francisco, Temple aides went through the membership rolls, deciding when people would be sent to Jonestown. Those with skills—nursing, carpentry, farming—went first. So did members Jones considered troublemakers.

Meanwhile, key people—Marceline Jones, Carolyn Layton, and others—stayed in the United States to hold the organization together and present a business-as-usual facade. But ultimately, they, too, would make the trip. Jones's aides calculated that by sending one hundred members down a month, they could fully relocate by February 1978.

The exodus was planned down to the last detail. When a member's departure was imminent, special aides submitted a change-of-address form to the post office on the person's behalf. They made sure keys were returned to any landlords that weren't part of the Temple. Outstanding bills were paid, and any car titles were transferred to the church. Since families often traveled separately, and months apart, Jones required parents to give the Temple power of attorney over their children. Aides wrote resignation letters for those working outside the church. They also helped members arrange with Social Security to have their monthly payments mailed to Temple headquarters in San Francisco.

One never knew when Father would call them to the Promised Land. Without warning, four aides would appear at a member's home or workplace and cheerfully inform the person that it was time to go. Immediately. That day. That minute. While one aide helped the member pack, a second watched the phone to prevent them from making any calls, and a third aide comforted those being left behind. The fourth aide was there to deal with anyone who didn't want to go. Some members were eager to move to Guyana. But many balked at going—they didn't want to move away forever. Aides told them they could just go for a visit. Stay a few weeks, they said. If you don't like it, you can come back.

This was a lie, of course. No one would be allowed to return.

Once the member was packed, aides drove them to the Temple and put them directly onto a bus, where they joined dozens of others. A supervisor held all their passports, as well as their Temple-purchased plane tickets.

Under the cover of darkness, the buses moved out of the parking lot and traveled across the country. Some went to airports in New York, others to Miami, Atlanta, or Philadelphia. This, too, was meant to disguise what was happening. Large groups of exiting Temple members at the San Francisco and Los Angeles airports were bound to draw unwanted attention. Only the oldest and frailest members boarded flights from these cities. In this way, members simply disappeared without a word to relatives on the outside.

Nonmember Fred Lewis came home from work one day to find his wife, Doris, and their seven children, ranging in age from seven to sixteen, gone. The apartment they'd shared for seventeen years had been stripped. Lewis later learned that his furniture and kitchen articles had been sold by the Temple. "She left me one mattress and no note," said Fred. Frantic with worry and hoping for answers, he pounded on the locked front door of the Geary Boulevard Temple. No one answered. It was months before he received a letter from Doris telling him where his family had gone. He never saw them again.

Followers who remained were encouraged to be extra loud at

services so no one outside would suspect the congregation was shrinking.

Throughout June, July, and August 1977, the exodus intensified. By September, four hundred members had been relocated to Jonestown.

Their leader stole away, too. In the middle of a June night, just a few weeks before the *New West* story hit the newsstands, Jim Jones boarded a plane bound for Guyana. Once at the settlement he alternated between drugging himself into indifference and raving hysterically: What would the *New West* article say?

Chapter Twenty-Eight

"Inside Peoples Temple"

"INSIDE PEOPLES TEMPLE," READ THE BOLD-LETTERED TITLE of the article published in *New West*'s August 1977 issue. Beneath it ran an ominous subheading: "Jim Jones is one [of] the state's most politically potent leaders. But who is he? And what's going on behind his church's locked doors?"

The story covered Jones's commitment to integration and his rainbow family. It chronicled the Temple's beginnings and its ties to San Francisco politicians, as well as credited its current work in the poverty-stricken neighborhoods of Los Angeles and San Francisco. Nothing written was damaging . . . until page three. That's where the defectors' interviews began. Twelve people shared their experiences. They told about the all-night planning commission meetings and the catharsis sessions. They revealed the beatings and the boxing matches, and the Temple's demand for followers' real estate, paychecks, bank accounts, and pensions.

Gang of Eight member Wayne Pietila detailed the fake assassination attempts. And more recent defectors Deanna and Elmer Mertle told how their daughter Linda was "beaten so severely that . . . her butt looked like hamburger."

Grace Stoen, a former member of Jones's inner circle whose ex-husband, Tim, had once been one of the Temple's top attorneys, also spoke out. She spilled details about the church's financial dealings—how she kept "a kind of log of documents that she [notarized] . . . including power-of-attorney statements, deeds of trust, guardianship papers, and so on, signed by temple members and officials." She also discussed her defection a year earlier in 1976. "I packed my things and left [without telling Tim]. I couldn't trust him. He'd tell Jim." She drove to Lake Tahoe, where she lay on the beach and tried to relax. "But every time I turned over, I looked around to see if any of the church members had tracked me down."

The article's final section was titled "Why Jim Jones Should Be Investigated." When Kilduff and Tracy had examined the properties gifted to the church in the Mendocino County recorder's office, they discovered that many had been notarized illegally. "An investigation of the 'care homes' run by the temple or temple members in Redwood Valley may also be in order," the reporters pointed out. Defectors claimed that money paid by the state for those living in the homes actually went to the Temple.

Most notably, however, they wrote about the 130 foster children that had been sent to Guyana. These children had been placed in Temple homes by "federal courts, state courts, probation departments" because they were seen as "disturbed or incorrigible." The state considered Peoples Temple a last resort for them. But was the Temple allowed to take them out of the country without telling state authorities? If they were already gone, how would the state get them back? And were they being beaten, as the defectors claimed? State authorities had a duty to guarantee the safety of these children, the reporters concluded.

The article ended in a way that let readers know there were more revelations to come. "The story of Jim Jones and his Peoples Temple is not over," wrote Kilduff and Tracy. "In fact, it has only begun to be told."

The article created a sensation in the Bay Area, and other news outlets across the country picked it up. On behalf of the Temple, PR man Mike Prokes, who'd returned to the United States, denied everything. No, there was no coercion or physical abuse of members. No, the church didn't force people to donate their property or homes. No, followers were *not* planning to relocate to Guyana anytime soon. And no, reporters could not speak with Jones. He was out of the country and unavailable.

Other articles quickly followed. The *Examiner* as well as the *Chronicle* now pursued the story. More defectors came forward, emboldened by the *New West* piece. Other terrible incidents were revealed: A child was forced to eat his own vomit. . . . A woman was stripped and ridiculed. . . . A teenager was unknowingly drugged so Jones could fake raising him from the dead. . . . A critically ill twelve-year-old died because church members tried to treat him by putting a picture of Jones over his heart.

Mayor Moscone worried about the stories. Was Jones really the man the articles portrayed? Would he be a political liability as chairman of the San Francisco Housing Authority board? Moscone telephoned Temple representatives in San Francisco and demanded to know how long Jones would be in Guyana. Representatives assured the mayor that Jones would be coming back soon.

He wasn't. On August 2, Jones dictated his resignation from the board over the settlement's shortwave radio to Marceline, who was heading the San Francisco Temple in his absence. In his terse letter he didn't mention the allegations. Instead, it gave his reason for leaving as church business in Guyana.

Chapter Twenty-Nine

Father in Jonestown

WAVES OF PEOPLE POURED INTO JONESTOWN—TODDLERS, teens, pregnant women, schoolchildren, babies, the elderly and infirm. "I was shocked at the people being sent to Guyana," recalled member Tim Carter. "They had no business being there, and I don't mean that in a judgmental sense, but [Jonestown] was not an easy life. It was just not done carefully, and it was a mistake."

Housing was the most immediate problem. Settlers had built only a half dozen cottages, each meant to sleep six people at the most. But with the influx of hundreds, housing construction had been accelerated. Stephan and the others gave up on the idea of cozy cottages and knocked together dorms that could house dozens.

The outhouse situation presented problems, too. There was just one twelve-foot structure dug over a deep pit and divided in half. Each side seated as many as sixteen people, side by side. There was no privacy in these open toilet facilities, not even between the sexes. (Jones's cottage had a private single facility with real toilet paper rather than the leaves and magazine pages rationed to residents.) There was always a long line at the outhouse door. Obviously, more toilet facilities were needed. But how would the pioneers find time to build these when they couldn't even keep up with housing?

And then there was the matter of water. There was plenty for drinking, but what about showering? They couldn't collect rainwater because standing water became a breeding ground for mosquitoes that spread diseases like malaria. Instead, members hauled water from a creek to a closed container above the group shower facilities. That hadn't been a problem when there'd been just fifty workers. But now there were so many more people, filthy from fifteen hours of labor in the blazing sun. There was nothing to be done but limit showers to two minutes. Residents were warned to keep their mouths closed since the water was contaminated.

Despite these primitive conditions, the new arrivals settled in. While Jonestown certainly disappointed them (this was *not* the tropical paradise Father had promised), many believed they'd be going home in a few months, and so they made the best of it. They worked hard but also enjoyed their time together. At day's end they gathered in the pavilion to chat, laugh, and sing. Stephan often pointed the newly installed loudspeaker system toward the group and played current music from Earth, Wind & Fire or the O'Jays. Then they did the bump or the hustle, sharing in one another's fellowship without insults and beatings.

Then Father arrived.

"Everything changed," said Stephan.

From the moment he landed in Guyana, Jones completely dropped the veneer of Christianity. He never again mentioned Jesus Christ or performed a healing. While some residents, especially elders, continued believing in the leader's deity, most now regarded Peoples Temple only as a radical political organization, and Jones as one of history's great socialist leaders. He no longer bothered with religion.

Deliberately located beyond the reach of law enforcement, the press, and outside families of members, Jones could now say and do as he pleased.

Over the coming months, admitted Stephan, "we absolutely enabled my father." Those in his inner circle, particularly, allowed Jones to believe he was in complete control. But most of the time he was too "whacked out on drugs," said Stephan, to handle the thousands of administrative duties required to run Jonestown. And so, Carolyn Layton and Maria Katsaris, who'd both arrived in Jonestown, oversaw the day-to-day operations. They were helped by others in the inner circle—Mike Prokes, Annie Moore, and Marceline Jones among them. They dealt with Temple finances, made public relations decisions, determined housing assignments, and oversaw the organization of labor and the school curriculum. They involved themselves in agricultural matters, too, making decisions about clearing land, raising livestock, and using insecticides.

Departments were set up to oversee important community operations—agriculture, livestock, carpentry, health care, and so on. The housing department supervised the communal raising of the settlement's babies and children; the relationships department approved marriages, divorces, couplings, and pregnancies. A leader with specialized knowledge headed each department and was given lots of leeway. Working in relative freedom, each could implement new ideas without constantly needing Jones's permission. Although required to report back on their progress, they typically met with Carolyn or others in the inner circle.

The inner circle still carried out Jones's orders; he was still their leader. But *how* his demands were met was entirely up to them.

Occasionally tiny cracks appeared in their devotion, especially if Jones's order went against their own judgment. Harriet Tropp, part of the settlement's inner circle and the settlement's spokesperson, went so far as to write a memo to Jones stating: "I think the essence of the problem [when it comes to decision-making] is that no one is willing to oppose your opinion in certain matters. And I frankly think that sometimes you are wrong, and no one is willing to say so." Tropp knew this was "a volatile statement," but as a committed foot soldier to the Cause, she also knew Jones relied on her. She didn't think he would punish her. And he didn't.

Other times the women surrounding Jones *countermanded* his orders. One time when Jones insisted guards "shoot to kill" anyone on the road from Port Kaituma, Carolyn changed this extreme order to the more reasonable "stop them." This, said Stephan, "became a pattern of Dad's leadership. An order would be given, then rescinded or modified. [We] soon learned to overlook . . . [Dad's] more histrionic statements."

One of Jones's earliest worries was the mail. He worried incessantly about letters arriving from concerned families and friends back in the United States. Most simply wanted to know their loved ones were well; they wanted to stay in touch. But Jones was paranoid about the content of the letters. What if they criticized him or the settlement or, worse, offered to pay a member's return flight? Jones demanded that all mail be censored. And his inner circle got it done. They created a committee that opened and read every incoming letter. If it included anything that could be construed as anti-Temple, it was filed away, never to be delivered.

The committee read all outgoing mail, too, as a way of controlling public opinion back in the States. There could be no suggestion that Jonestown was less than idyllic. If the letter did not meet Temple-approved standards, the committee members returned it to the writer with specific suggestions scribbled in the margins. Censors suggested generic phrases that praised Jonestown's beauty, as well as Father's goodness. Teenager Patricia Houston revised a letter to her relatives in California three times before it finally met censor approval. When it arrived in the United States, it read: "Jonestown is too beautiful to show in pictures, write on letters, etc. You have to be here and get the beautiful feeling of being where you are free. I am glad Father has provided this place for us." The wording left family members suspicious. It sounded nothing like her stepdaughter. Still, the censoring of mail worked well. Not a critical word about Jonestown was ever leaked to the outside world . . . at least by its residents.

Jones obsessed about happenings *inside* the settlement, too, and so he turned to his security force. In California guards had looked for enemies beyond the Temple's walls, but in Jonestown they looked inward. Two dozen of Jones's most trusted followers—male and female—roamed the settlement armed with shotguns or pistols. Acting as Jonestown's police, they enforced Father's rules through violence and intimidation. Members were beaten for not working hard enough, for grumbling about the food, or for complaining about the heat. On Father's orders guards kept a close eye on those regarded as negatives—members who'd been previously called to the front, or who were suspected of wanting to leave. They also patrolled the settlement's perimeter, monitored the front gate, and surveilled residents' movements from a forty-foot-tall guard tower near the cottages. But perhaps most importantly, they acted as Jones's bodyguards. Everywhere Jones went, two members of the security force accompanied him. They stood at attention onstage whenever Father spoke, and they guarded his cottage day and night.

According to Father, he had a *secret* security force, too. "I have people put there among you," he warned followers. "Nobody knows who they are, but they are my superspies."

It was a lie, but an effective one. It made people even more afraid to talk to one another, compare experiences, or share opinions. They didn't dare complain about living conditions or express concerns about leadership. Most were terrified of being called to the front. In Jonestown, Father was crueler than ever.

Troublemaker Tommy Bogue had learned this firsthand when, weeks earlier, he'd planted watermelon seeds in the corner of a field. He didn't hide what he was doing. He didn't think it was against Temple rules to grow his own fruit.

But someone spotted him and tattled to Father.

Jones called the teenager to the floor. Onstage, from the green lawn chair he always sat in, he accused the boy of being an elitist. Everything in socialism should be shared, he hollered. There was no *mine* or *yours.* This wasn't some fat-cat capitalist community where individuals decided what to grow. If they wanted watermelons, they planted and tended them *together.*

Father's face became red from heat and fury. Behind him a hand-painted sign tacked onto a pavilion pillar read "LOVE ONE ANOTHER." He turned to the group. What did they think? Should they let Tommy keep on being the stupid little boy he'd always been?

Shouts and curses erupted from the followers. They hollered out suggestions for punishment. As a relative, Tommy's father, Jim, knew he was expected to show anger. He shook his fists and called his son foul names.

Tommy apologized, but it didn't matter.

Jones asked for a plate of hot peppers. "Here's something you can [have] all by yourself," he said after they arrived. He ordered the boy to start chewing.

Tommy put the first pepper—what the Guyanese appropriately called a "Ball of Fire"—into his mouth.

"Keep chewing until I say swallow," commanded Jones.

Tommy chewed. The first bite wasn't too bad, but by the fifth his nose and throat flamed and his eyes streamed. He suddenly felt furious. He wanted to spit the mess out at Jones and shout "Hell, no!" but who knew what torture that might lead to?

He managed to choke down the plateful. His tongue felt swollen, his throat blistered. He got out the words "Thank you, Father" and stumbled back to his seat. He hated Jonestown. He despised Jim Jones. He had to get out.

Chapter Thirty

God's Nurse and a Surprise for Tommy

THE JUNGLE COMMUNITY HAD ITS SECRETS, AND ONE OF them lurked in Jonestown's medical dispensary. Only a handful of people, including nurse Annie Moore, had access to the locked room. Besides the cases of ordinary, frequently used medicines like penicillin, insulin, and blood-pressure pills, there was also an alarming number of behavior-altering drugs that caused hallucination, confusion, blurred vision, and speech disturbance. Among them were ten thousand injectable doses and one thousand tablets of Thorazine, an antipsychotic; twenty thousand doses of the painkiller Demerol; five thousand doses of the tranquilizer Valium; two hundred vials of injectable morphine; and thousands of other doses of powerful drugs like quaaludes, Vistaril (for anxiety), and Noludar (a sleeping aid). It was enough to subdue Jonestown's eventual population of almost one thousand people more than forty times over.

Jonestown's doctor, Larry Schacht, had ordered them all, procuring them through separate purchases made from different distributors. In the United States a physician placing multiple orders of narcotics would have raised alarms. But Guyanese officials, eager to please the Americans, turned a blind eye. Schacht's stockpile grew.

Ten years earlier Schact had arrived at the Redwood Valley Temple with injection marks scarring his forearms. The Temple sent him first to their drug rehab program and then to medical school. He'd graduated with honors, but just five weeks into his internship, Jones called him to Guyana. Now, at twenty-nine, he was the community's only doctor, treating everything from athlete's foot (the warm, humid climate and communal showers made it a common problem) to lung cancer. Often, during patient visits, he was forced to flip through the pages of medical reference books for answers.

Jim Jones's health was rapidly deteriorating. He swung between insomnia and long hours of sleep. When awake, he could be accusatory, raging, incoherent, and wheedling by turns. He had spikes in body temperature and experienced episodes of rapid heartbeat. Some days he forgot to eat. Other days he gobbled everything in his well-stocked private refrigerator. He claimed to be in constant pain. He also claimed to have a slew of serious ailments: cancer, a heart condition, fungus in his lungs. But those in his inner circle knew the truth—it was drugs. Still, no one, not even Schacht, tried to sober him up. As Stephan explained, "You don't tell God he has a drug problem."

Annie Moore, who'd graduated from nursing school in 1975, became his private caregiver. With loving dedication she took his temperature, listened to his heart and lungs, and administered his medications—uppers and downers, painkillers and sleeping pills. Jones had been a user for so long that he'd developed a tolerance to most of the drugs, and time and again she increased his dosage. As Annie injected him, she must have worried about overdose. But Jones insisted he needed relief, and she provided it without question.

She tried to buoy his spirits, too, by drawing bright, cheerful pictures that she taped to his bed's headboard—a get-well card featuring a farmer with a menagerie of animals, a picture of the jungle against a bright orange sky. She sat by his bedside, sometimes reading aloud to him, other times just watching him sleep. One day she left him a note that read, in part: "I just wanted you to know that I do not mind being your nurse and there's nothing more I would rather be. You should not feel guilty for having me watch you. I would rather be around you than anyone else in the world."

The tractor rumbled into the Promised Land one May evening in 1977 with forty more arrivals. It had been an arduous trip, first by plane to Georgetown and then along the coast aboard a rusty shrimp trawler, the *Cudjoe,* owned by the Temple. The boat trip took twenty-five hours. The last six miles had been in the Temple trailer, bumping over the dirt road, deeper and deeper into the jungle.

From the pavilion Tommy Bogue watched the newcomers arrive. He knew what would happen. The newcomers' expressions would light up with a moment of excitement, followed almost immediately by confusion, then dismay and anxiety. It somehow made Tommy feel better. Seeing the truth written on their faces validated his own feelings. Jonestown really *wasn't* paradise. They were all just play-acting. It *was* all bullshit.

Aides hustled the group through the arrival process. They collected everyone's passports for "safekeeping," then opened their luggage and took out any useful items—a spare pair of jeans, a set of sheets, a bottle of aspirin, extra underwear. These would be either redistributed among the residents or sold by the Temple in the open-air market in Georgetown. Then, left clutching the remnants of their belongings, newcomers received both their housing and job assignments. The most able-bodied ended up in the fields or on building crews. Those with special skills, like typing or welding, were placed where their abilities could best be used. Small children were given the task of collecting leaves to use for toilet paper. Seniors, if able, were put on toy duty, making dolls or painting wooden cars made by the carpentry shop. These, too, were sold in the Georgetown market.

By this point realization had usually dawned on most new arrivals that Jonestown was *not* the land of milk and honey. But as had earlier residents, they forced smiles onto their faces, expressed happiness at being there, and thanked Father for bringing them to the Promised Land.

From his spot Tommy noticed a familiar face.

Brian! Tommy shouted out his friend's name.

Brian Davis turned and grinned. It had been more than a year since the two mischief-makers had seen each other. "However, within an hour, it was as though we had never been separated," Tommy would say later.

That first day, Tommy showed his buddy around the compound before taking him into the jungle to explore. Over the next weeks Tommy shared all he'd learned from his Amerindian friend, David. He taught Brian how to mark a trail and squeeze fresh water from a vine. Tommy felt completely comfortable in the bush, and soon so did Brian. It became a haven for the teenagers. They could slip away into the tangled darkness without fear of being followed. For a few minutes, at least, they felt free.

But, of course, they weren't. Every weekday after early-morning chores (weeding for Tommy, dishwashing for Brian), they headed to Jonestown's school.

Kids of all grade levels sat in the same class as their teacher, Tom Grubbs, droned on about equality and socialism. Tommy and Brian were bored out of their minds.

Hoping to liven up the classroom, the friends created a game they called Advanced Vocabulary. "We took a dictionary and started learning all the big words, you know, the ones few people know the meanings to," explained Tommy.

At first, Grubbs was impressed, even amused, by their vocabularies. But when they began to use words he didn't know, he grew annoyed. He demanded they speak in plain English, but they ignored him.

Finally, one morning Brian used a word with six syllables.

What was the word? Recounting the story later, Tommy couldn't remember, but when Brian said it, Grubbs "popped his cork."

The teacher pointed a shaking finger at the boys. "You, you, you don't even know what those words mean!" he shouted.

"So we defined them," Tommy said, "complete with proper use in a sentence."

The other students laughed.

And Tommy and Brian gloated in triumph. They'd outsmarted the teacher.

But Grubbs got the last laugh. He expelled them from school. From then on the boys had to work twelve hours a day.

"We didn't feel so smart anymore," admitted Tommy. "And to top it off, just to provide us with some additional needed intelligence, they shaved our heads."

While Tommy labored in the fields, Brian toiled in the kitchen, helping to prepare enough rice and gravy for hundreds of people. By the end of the workday, both boys were exhausted. "We hated it there," said Tommy.

As they had two years earlier, the boys decided to escape. And this time they were determined to succeed.

Part Five

Jonestown

You were faced with suicide, you know, drinking the potion. And you can sit here and say, "I'd never do it, no way," or "I would stop somebody from doing it, I would stop everybody from doing it," or "I'd go through the crowd and spill it over!" But when you're there, you might have those thoughts, but you don't act on them. . . . You didn't have a choice. You had to stand up and be representing the cause, be about the cause, because [your friends] are willing to give it all up. . . .

—Eugene Smith, Peoples Temple survivor

Chapter Thirty-One

Hyacinth in the Promised Land

IN JULY 1977, HYACINTH AND ZIP BOARDED A PLANE IN OAKland, California, bound for New York City. The women weren't allowed by Temple aides to carry their own passports or plane tickets until they'd been escorted to the gate. No one else from the Temple flew with them, either.

As the plane took off, Hyacinth opened her passport. Jones himself had helped her apply for it weeks earlier, but this was the first time she'd held it in her hands. She rubbed her finger over her name. A passport to travel the world. She never could have imagined it. She wished she felt better about the trip. She worried about traveling at her age—seventy-five—especially with her bad leg.

When aides had arrived at their door earlier that day and said it was time to go, Zip had yelped with joy and started packing. But Hyacinth had resisted—she wasn't fit enough to live in the jungle. The aides had reassured her. The sisters didn't have to go forever, they lied. They could sign on for any amount of time they chose. After a bit of back-and-forth, Hyacinth and Zip agreed to a year in Jonestown. Aides promised that if it didn't work out, Father would send them home early.

In New York City the sisters switched planes. They flew to Georgetown and, like everyone else, traveled on to Jonestown by boat, then by a flatbed pulled by a tractor. Aides assigned them to a tiny one-room cottage that they shared with two other senior women. Made of plywood and painted pink, it didn't look anything like the cottages in Jones's movies. Where were the pretty little fences and flower gardens?

According to Hyacinth, four beds had been crammed into a space built for two. (Jonestown records actually show that at one time as many as thirteen people were squeezed into the residence.) The shuttered windows did not have glass or screens. When it rained, which was almost daily, Hyacinth had to close the shutters so water didn't pool on the crooked floor. But without a breeze the cottage quickly turned as hot and humid as a sauna. When she opened the shutters after a rain, swarms of insects flew in. "Most of my day's work was swatting flies," she said. The best thing about her new home was its corrugated metal roof. It sounded nice when rain fell on it. Problem was, it also made the cottage oven-hot during the day.

From her front step Hyacinth could look down onto Jones's cottage. Unlike other residences, his place had screens and glass. It had a window air conditioner and, she'd heard, a refrigerator stocked with soda and chocolate, cheese and lunch meat. If she shaded her eyes, she could even see into his bedroom, where he had a soft double bed that he shared with either Carolyn or Maria. (Marceline had her own cottage.) Both women lived with him, as did Carolyn and Jones's son, two-year-old Kimo, and a five-year-old named John Victor Stoen, who was mothered in Guyana by Maria.

Through the window she could see Carolyn and Maria waiting on Jones, sometimes wearing nothing but their bras and panties. Adultery! Hyacinth now knew with certainty what she'd long suspected—God had taken away Jones's healing powers because he was an unrepentant sinner.

Hyacinth tried to make the best of her situation. With Zip's help, she sewed slipcovers for the rough-hewn chairs built by the Temple carpenters and made a bright rag rug for the wood-plank floor. Finally, she put her worn but well-loved biography of Abraham Lincoln on her bedside table. Things felt better, even though she knew the truth. They weren't ever going home.

She established a daily schedule. That made her feel better, too. Rising around seven a.m., she straightened up the cottage and washed out her clothes. Workers brought her breakfast on a tray because she couldn't stand in line for food. Afterward, she headed to the pavilion for a seniors' exercise class, where she bent and stretched under the supervision of a Temple nurse. Then it was time for work. Hyacinth's job was making cloth dolls. Called Jonestown Dolls, they were all different races and were sold in Georgetown's markets for twenty-five dollars each. At noon, her workday done, she went back to her cottage for lunch. In the afternoons, she sat around and read or studied African history. Jones had started a senior class on the subject. "It was just something to keep [my mind] occupied," she said, to keep her from dwelling on her predicament. Even so, she couldn't help but find herself repeatedly asking, "Jesus, what have I got myself into?"

Despite Jones's constant threats about the jungle's dangers—venomous snakes, quicksand, and man-eating pumas—Hyacinth had "double feelings" about the thick, forbidding bush that surrounded the compound. "There were times when I was ready to walk through the jungles to escape; then I'd get resigned to dying [in Jonestown]."

People *did* try to escape, but only one managed to thrash through the jungle to safety. The others were placed in the Extended Care Unit. It sounded like a nice place, but Hyacinth and the other residents knew what happened in the ECU: Troublemakers were drugged senseless with barbiturates for weeks. When they emerged, they looked blank and had difficulty holding a conversation. That's what happened to one of the Temple's lawyers, Gene Chaikin. After Jones learned of Gene's plans to defect, he sent him to the Extended Care Unit, where he went from being a fiery attorney to a shambling ghost. Even after he was released, Jones continued to drug him. Maria Katsaris buried the pills in the cheese sandwiches she made him as a special treat. Gene never left.

Daily life in Jonestown was grinding. Unlike Hyacinth, most residents worked in fields that were as much as a mile and a half away from the cottages, toiling in temperatures that often rose to well above one hundred degrees. Lunch was brought out to them. Usually, it consisted of a bowl of rice soup, since the settlement's thin soil couldn't produce nearly enough to feed the growing community. Shipped in from Georgetown, the rice was supplemented by cassavas; wild greens like amaranth, with its edible leaves; and occasionally shark meat. (Guyanese fishermen considered the fish an inferior catch and so sold it at a bargain price.) Workers got thirty minutes to sit and eat before returning to the weeds, the heat, and the snakes that slithered among the crops.

"Work went from a means of production to a means of control," explained Stephan Jones. "And when you got off, your time was *his* time."

Suffering from the effects of drugs, Jones slept in most days. Carolyn let it be known that residents shouldn't disturb him because he was doing important work for the Cause. By the time his followers ended their days at six p.m., Jones, at last, was awake.

At seven-forty-five p.m., the PA system began blasting the day's "news." Read by Jones, it was a blend of fact and fiction meant to convince followers that whatever hardship they were enduring was nothing compared to the misery of the United States. Since most residents were African American, Jones focused on atrocities being committed back home against Black people. Black children, he told them, were being castrated in the streets of Chicago, and eight major cities had been destroyed by race riots. He claimed that scientists had engineered a way to kill off minorities by poisoning the water systems of inner cities and that the Supreme Court had banned nonwhites from attending college.

Without access to any other means of information, many residents believed these reports.

These news broadcasts took up any time residents might have had to socialize after their two-minute showers and during their meager rice-and-greens dinners. (On Sundays, as a special treat, every follower got a single cookie. Jones handed them out as if bestowing blessings.) After all, when Jones spoke, everyone else was expected to stop everything and listen.

The timing of these broadcasts was intentional. "Hitler did his indoctrination speeches around six to seven p.m. when workers were home eating and their resistance to change was low," one inner-circle member had written to Jones in a memo. It was an idea the Führer-admiring Jones seized on.

Eleven p.m. was bedtime—*unless* there were discipline problems that required the group's attention. And in a community that boasted almost five hundred people by August 1977, there were *always* discipline problems. Then Jones sat onstage in his lawn chair doing his best not to appear stoned while guards described all sorts of violations—resting on the job, flirting, grumbling about food.

Jones dealt harshly with food complaints. After one resident pointed out the maggots in his rice, Jones called him to the front and shouted at him. Didn't he know that the inferior rice was the CIA's fault? Agents couldn't allow an interracial social experiment to flourish, so they'd tainted Jonestown's food stores. To complain about food was to fall into the CIA's hands. Worse, it was to be in league with them—a traitor. And traitors were beaten with a leather strap.

These beatings grew so severe that many residents ended up in the infirmary afterward. Sometimes victims lay unconscious on the pavilion's hard-packed dirt floor for several minutes while the other followers sat, seemingly unmoved. But beneath their blank expressions, many recognized the wrongness of these punishments. Some tried to distance themselves by intellectualizing them. "All rebels suffered for their beliefs," senior citizen Edith Rollins told herself. "Why should we in Peoples Temple be any different?"

Others didn't act because no one else did. "It's like you had to prove you were really with us . . . by putting [Father], or putting the Temple, or putting the movements ahead of your own . . . code of ethics," explained member Jean Clancey.

And some, like Hyacinth Thrash, simply refused to look. "I just sat at the back [of the pavilion] and held my head down with my hand," she said.

These discipline meetings often lasted until three a.m. Then the undernourished, exhausted followers stumbled to bed. But even then they couldn't escape Father. Every night his voice droned on over the

PA system. Sitting in front of the microphone, conveniently located in his cottage, Jones read aloud textbooks on communism and guerrilla warfare, biographies of revolutionaries, or whatever else he felt like. If his words became too slurred from drugs, Carolyn or Maria put on a tape of an old lecture. He claimed he did this so his followers could learn in their sleep.

Not everyone believed this. Outspoken Harriet Tropp wrote a note to him: "I have entertained the thought that you are deliberately using a known psychological technique of interrupting people's thought processes with specific information, so as to keep them in a kind of disjointed state—a state that makes them both more receptive to information fed to them, and less able to do concentrated (and often treasonous) things." Harriet didn't disapprove of the technique. If it worked, particularly with rank-and-file members, she was all for it. But it was, she added, "driving me nuts."

Pioneer Michael Touchette agreed. "It would just be hour after hour after hour." Sometimes, unable to take it anymore, he and a couple of his buddies would climb onto the bulldozer and ride out into the jungle, clearing a path as they went, until all they could hear was birdsong and the buzzing of insects. "It was relief and rebellion," admitted Michael.

Hyacinth Thrash didn't need to flee into the jungle to escape Jones's endless harangue. She took it in stride. "With me, it went in one ear and out the other."

Chapter Thirty-Two

The Stoens and the Six-Day Siege

FIVE-YEAR-OLD JOHN VICTOR STOEN SHOOK HIS SMALL FIST at Pop Jackson, shocking the old man. But Pop knew better than to reprimand John Victor. He was Jonestown's "child prince," Father's son and future heir to the Promised Land. Lest any resident forget this, John Victor's guardian, Maria Katsaris, dressed him like Jones and styled his hair in the same way Father wore his. The boy had even been trained to mimic Jones's mannerisms. Sometimes he even used the same rhetoric as Jones. "Father was terribly proud of him," recalled one member.

John Victor had been born in 1972 to Temple members Grace and Tim Stoen. Pillars of the Temple, both had worked ceaselessly for the church, Tim as an attorney and Grace as an accountant. The birth of their son on January 25, 1972, had thrilled them. But twelve days later Tim signed a peculiar document. It stated that Jim Jones was really John Victor's biological father; that Tim had begged Jones to sire a child with Grace because he'd been unable to; that he wanted his child to be fathered by "the most compassionate, honest, and courageous human being the world contains."

Tim later claimed the document had been a loyalty test. Like so many other members who'd signed self-incriminating but entirely false affidavits, he'd assumed the document would be filed away, never to be seen again.

No one will ever know who John Victor's biological father really was. Grace refused to admit or deny any physical relationship with Jones, and DNA testing was not yet available. Certainly, John Victor, with his brown eyes and thick black hair, looked like Jones. But he could also have inherited these features from either Grace or Tim, who both had dark hair and dark eyes.

By 1976, Grace had grown disillusioned with the Temple. Her marriage was unraveling, and her son had been taken away to be raised communally. She hated the berating and the punishments, as well as the fraud and fleecing she saw as a Temple accountant. And so, over the Fourth of July weekend, she climbed into her car and drove away. She went without John Victor because she was unable to retrieve him from the family he lived with. She believed he was safe, though. After all, Tim was still a devoted member of the church, and the community loved the little boy. How could she have known that within months of her leaving, Tim would sign yet another document, this one handing over his parental rights to the Temple? Church leaders whisked John Victor to Guyana.

In November 1976, Grace telephoned the San Francisco Temple in hopes of speaking with her son. That's when she discovered he was gone. She sobbed for days before pulling herself together. She would fight for John Victor.

In February 1977 she contacted Tim. She was filing for divorce, she told him. She was also seeking custody of their son.

Not long after this conversation, Tim flew to Guyana for a monthslong visit. He was looking forward to being with John Victor. But Jones was suspicious. Could Tim be planning to steal the boy away? Was he planning to win back Grace's affection by returning her son? Jones ordered Jonestown guards to rummage through Tim's belongings. Under no circumstances, he told them, was Tim allowed to take John Victor out of the settlement.

Tim was infuriated by Jones's actions. He'd been a loyal follower for seven years. He'd given up a luxurious Berkeley apartment, a fancy sports car, and a lucrative private law practice to work as a Temple attorney. He'd given everything to the Cause—even his family—and all he'd gotten in return was paranoia. In June 1977 he defected by going on a business trip from which he never returned. Unable to smuggle John Victor out from under Maria Katsaris's watchful eye, Tim left without his son. He hoped that once back in the United States, he could regain his son through legal channels.

In August, Tim and Grace put aside their differences and began working together for the return of their son. Later that same month a California judge invalidated the Temple's guardianship papers and granted custody of the boy to his mother. Soon after, their attorney, Jeffrey Haas, headed to Guyana. He arrived in Georgetown on September 4 carrying the judge's order compelling Jones to hand over the boy. Haas hoped to reunite mother and son by the end of the month, but first he needed to convince the Guyanese magistrate to honor the California order.

Haas's lawsuit, as well as his presence in Guyana, rattled Jim Jones. The Temple retained guardianship of almost every child in the community. Signing over one's parental rights was not only a loyalty test but also an essential part of communalism because it allowed church leaders to legally move children from home to home. But Jones feared that the California judge's invalidation of the Temple's guardianship of John Victor would open the doors for other custody battles. What if he was forced to return even more of the children?

As Haas worked his way through the Guyanese legal system with some success, Jones raged, paced, and popped pills. He absolutely could *not* release John Victor. He'd publicly claimed the boy as his son—how would it look if he just handed over John Victor? He would lose all credibility as his people's protector. What should he do?

There was something bigger at stake, too. Jones saw the custody battle as an effort to destroy Peoples Temple and thought that letting John Victor go would be the first step toward the group's annihilation. "The way to get to Jim Jones is through his son," he told his followers. "They think that will suck me back [to the United States] or cause me to die before I give him up. And that's what we'll do. We'll die."

To Jones, John Victor wasn't simply a child he had to protect. John Victor was a child *all* of Jonestown had to protect, even if it meant giving up their lives to do so, a powerful symbol of the community's life-and-death struggle against the tyranny of the outside world. Suddenly, retaining custody of the precocious and spoiled, often sweet, occasionally naughty child was "a matter of life and death," member Bonnie Yates later wrote. "Not just for him, not just for John Victor, but for 918 people."

On the night of September 5, Jones called his son Jimmy to his cottage and explained that the people needed a common enemy they could rally against. They needed to believe they were under attack. Would Jimmy help him with that?

Just after eleven p.m. Jimmy crept into the bush carrying a rifle. Most of the residents were already asleep. There had been no discipline meeting that night, and the PA system was curiously yet mercifully quiet for a change. When Jimmy was completely hidden, he turned and aimed at his father's cottage. He squeezed the trigger again and again.

The shots exploded into the darkness. Terrified residents screamed and struggled out of their bunks. Stephan Jones, as well as members of the security force, raced toward Jones's cottage. They found him lying on the floor. He acted disoriented and told them he'd had a premonition and bent down. The bullets had whizzed over his head, barely missing him.

He got to his feet. Those shots meant just one thing, he cried. The CIA's mercenary army had arrived. They had the settlement surrounded. Grabbing up the PA system's microphone, he shouted into it. "Alert! Alert! We are under attack." He ordered everyone to the pavilion.

Thus began Jonestown's first and longest "white night," a term Jones created to describe an acute community emergency. Many fake attacks would follow, manufactured to keep his followers fearful and obedient. White nights conditioned residents to believe that they were locked in a struggle for their collective survival, that there was a vast right-wing conspiracy against them. In this way, *everything* could be (and was) blamed on their enemies—malaria (agents had switched out their preventatives with sugar pills), the death of the chickens (poisoned grain).

Residents streamed from their cottages, screaming, crying, pressing terrified children to their chests.

Jones, surrounded by armed guards, stood onstage, ranting and semicoherent. There would be no surrendering, he shouted. Anyone caught trying to desert would be "hacked to death with a cutlass."

The bedlam increased. Guards handed out weapons—knives, shovels, pitchforks, even big sticks. All the while, Jones screamed insanely about the well-armed adversaries who had just tried to assassinate him. They were out there in the jungle right now. They'd come for John Victor, but they wouldn't stop there. They'd take *all* the children away. But have no fear, he cried, his voice rising hysterically.

"I've got a hell of a lot of weapons to fight. I've got my claws. I've got my cutlass. I've got guns. . . . And I'll fight. And I'll fight."

He ordered the residents to form a line around the compound's perimeter, facing the jungle. No one was exempt—not children or seniors. Hyacinth found herself clutching a shovel. As she crouched in the bush beside Zip, her bad leg throbbing, she felt terrified . . . but not of mercenaries. "Folks were getting more scared of Jim than the enemy," she admitted.

Stephan Jones had been ordered to watch the front gate as well as the road leading into Jonestown. As he huddled behind a makeshift barricade of rubber tires, he pondered events. He knew his dad had staged attacks in the past—but could he have staged something this extreme?

Meanwhile, buddies Brian and Tommy clutched machetes and stared into the shadows. Every rustling tree branch, every twig snap seized their attention. They stood guard for hours, eating the rations of rice and water carried along the line by fellow members. They tried to grab a few minutes of sleep.

But Jones kept up a steady verbal barrage of fear and drama. By now he'd returned to his cottage, where he'd closeted himself with Carolyn and Maria. They did nothing to stop him as he screamed hysterically, "I'm hit. I'm hit. I'm hit. I'm hit." Minutes later he fabricated an outlandish tale of negotiation with the enemies. "Keep calm," he told his followers over the PA. "Whatever you do, don't take offensive action. We want peace. We want asylum somewhere . . . so don't do anything rash, I beg you." He also shouted to imaginary enemies in the jungle, "We have fired no weapons! We have fired no weapons!" Then to his followers he said softly, "So keep calm and keep down. Do you copy? Let me hear you."

From their jungle stations, they cheered.

The "siege" continued. Time blurred. Night turned to day, then back to night. Jones's followers still held their defensive line but with less zealotry. They were exhausted both physically and emotionally. Still, according to Stephan Jones, most didn't doubt Father. If he said the jungle was full of paid assassins and kidnappers, then it was.

On the second night, Jones changed tactics. Members were going to leave, he announced. Under cover of darkness they would drive to Port Kaituma, climb aboard the *Cudjoe,* and sail away to communist Cuba. He didn't explain how everyone—there were now seven hundred people in Jonestown—would fit on the old shrimp trawler meant for seventy passengers. Nor did he explain why the mercenary army would allow them to simply drive out of the settlement.

Fifty seniors, along with Jones, John Victor Stoen, and Maria Katsaris, left in the first group. Hyacinth and Zip were among them. As the truck bumped along the dirt road, Hyacinth wondered if her aching, arthritic body could hold out much longer.

At Port Kaituma the seniors shuffled up the *Cudjoe*'s narrow gangplank. In the darkness someone slipped, setting off a domino effect. There were shouts and cries as the elders scrambled to get their footing. Hyacinth's cane splashed into the water as the woman behind her tumbled off the gangplank. She came up out of the muddy water shrieking. It would turn out that she'd fractured her pelvis.

None of it mattered to Jones. He had the injured woman hauled aboard, then handed out machetes to the seniors. While the injured woman moaned at their feet, he told them to defend the boat.

Hours passed, but no one else from the settlement joined them. Hyacinth stood clutching the weapon in one hand and her cane, recovered from the water, in the other. Where was everyone else? Had they been killed by the mercenaries?

Finally, Jones made an announcement. He'd been in contact with Cuba, he said. "They'll let me and my family in and a few leaders, but no one else. The rivers are blocked to the rest of us. I say to hell with it. I wouldn't be a leader worth tinker's shit if I just went. Those miserable SOBs [in Cuba] are afraid to stand up to the United States."

"Thank you, Father," a dozen or so voices called out.

"My God," Jones went on, "if they won't let us all go, none of us go. . . . I won't go without you."

"Thank you, Father," more people cried.

"If I'm the only socialist alive, then I'll die a socialist," he declared.

The seniors cheered.

For Hyacinth it meant nothing but relief. She climbed stiffly back into the tractor trailer. It was dawn by the time she limped to her cottage and eased into bed. As she closed her eyes, she hoped Jones wouldn't start hollering again.

The "siege" continued. By September 8, three days after the first shots rang out, Stephan was past suspicious. If the enemy was out there, why didn't they just attack? Surely, cutthroat mercenaries weren't afraid of a community—many of them old people and children—waving farm implements and sticks. Besides, his father had sent people back to work during the day.

Stephan recognized the truth: The "siege" was nothing but an elaborate and terrible stunt.

By the fifth night Jones had upped the ante. Leaving just a few followers to defend the perimeter, he called the others to the pavilion for an all-night rally. He asked that everyone turn toward the jungle and shout, "Come and get us!"

Then, words slurring, he said that he'd "rather die than return to the United States. Wouldn't you?"

He'd "rather die than give up a single one of his people to those fascists. Wouldn't you?"

He'd "rather die than endure this endless harassment. Wouldn't you?"

He looked around the pavilion. "Who wants to commit revolutionary suicide?" he asked. Only two people raised their hands—Maria Katsaris and Harriet Tropp.

The next night Jones asked the same question during yet another rally. This time three people raised their hands—Maria, Harriet, and Carolyn Layton.

Everyone else wanted to fight. They'd come to the Promised Land to create a better world. Not to die.

Meanwhile, in Georgetown, attorney Jeffrey Haas felt pleased by the progress he'd made in the Guyanese courts. Not only had the magistrate honored the California custody papers, but he'd also issued an order for John Victor's immediate removal from the Temple community. From Lamaha Gardens ultraloyalist Sharon Amos, the newly appointed head of the public relations team, read the order to Jones over the radio.

The next morning Jones radioed Marceline in San Francisco. His followers would commit suicide at five-thirty that afternoon unless the custody process was stopped, he told her. She should contact Guyana's deputy prime minister, Ptolemy Reid, for his help. Reid, who wanted the settlement to succeed in order to stave off Venezuelan territory claims, had already done the community a big favor by loosening his government's immigration and customs regulations. Now Jones wanted another—for Reid to stop the custody suit.

While Marceline and others at the Geary Boulevard Temple frantically tried to track Reid down, Jones asked Harriet Tropp's brother, Dick, to compose a letter explaining to the world why they'd committed revolutionary suicide. Dick sobbed as he wrote it.

Marceline couldn't reach Reid. But she did manage to contact his wife, Ruth, who assured her that John Victor would not be taken away. Marceline relayed these words to her husband.

Jones called off the mass suicide.

Days later Jeffrey Haas returned to the Guyanese court. The custody process, he learned, had ground to a halt. Suddenly, no one there could help him. Haas flew home without John Victor.

Chapter Thirty-Three

Gone Boys

BY NOVEMBER 1977 BEST FRIENDS TOMMY BOGUE AND BRIAN Davis had decided on an escape plan. They would hike thirty-five miles through the jungle to Matthews Ridge. With skills learned from their Amerindian friend, David, they believed they could survive in the bush. When they got to the town, they'd ask to be escorted to the American embassy in Georgetown. The hike, Tommy estimated, would take a couple of days. "Then we'd be home free," he said. The teens began dreaming of "succulent Big Macs."

On the day they left, they hid two machetes in the burlap bags used for collecting firewood and headed to the bush line. After plunging into the thick foliage, they waited to see if they'd been followed. Coast clear, they pulled out their machetes, dropped the bags, and began hacking their way toward Matthews Ridge.

They made good time until night fell. "Once it gets dark in the jungle, you cannot see your hand in front of your face—literally," said Tommy. They had a choice: Wait in the pitch-dark jungle with jaguars and anacondas, or head toward the single road connecting Port Kaituma and Matthews Ridge. They chose the road.

Starlight illuminated their route. They were miles from Jonestown now. As they walked, they talked about what they would do when they got back to the United States. Brian couldn't wait to see his mother, and Tommy looked forward to hugging his aunt and uncle. "It was going to be great," he thought.

Brian stopped walking. "Do you hear that?"

Both boys listened.

"A tractor's coming!" cried Tommy.

The two darted off the road and scrambled behind a small rise.

Minutes later the Jonestown tractor rumbled into view, several armed guards clinging to its sides. The teenagers didn't breathe. The tractor drove past their hiding place.

The boys released their breath. They hadn't been seen. Still, they remained crouching for several long minutes. Maybe, Brian suggested, they should just go back into the jungle.

Tommy agreed.

Too late, they realized that a group of shadowy figures surrounded them. Not only had they been spotted, but they'd also been outmaneuvered.

Tommy and Brian leaped to their feet, machetes raised. They weren't going back.

The guards pointed their guns. Don't make us shoot, they said.

The teens dropped their weapons. Rough hands grabbed them and marched them to the tractor.

Tommy felt sick with disappointment. They'd come so close. And now . . . he was heading back. He could see the pavilion blazing with light and packed with people. Jones was sitting in his chair. Disappointment turned to fear.

As the guards pushed him into the meeting, Tommy could feel

the crowd's fury. They'd been dragged out of bed because of the boys' actions. They would want revenge. And so would Jones.

The guards shoved the boys to the front.

Jones demanded to know what they'd planned. Where were they headed? How far did they think they could get?

Tommy told him.

"You know about the [jungle dangers]?" shouted Jones. "The puma? The leopard? The ocelot? 'Bout fifty kinds of different, uh, poisonous reptiles? Are you aware of all this? Any of this? How long you been around here?"

"Fourteen months, Father," said Tommy, his voice thick with fear.

"The anaconda?" Jones went on.

"I'm aware of all this—" Tommy began.

Jones cut him off. "Thirty-six feet long? Can crush a horse in seconds?"

"Yes, Father," said Tommy.

"What kind of story were you going to tell?" Jones shouted. "What was going to be your story about this place?"

As Jones spoke, the followers grew angrier and angrier. Their leader was whipping them into a frenzy.

Brian spoke up. "I was going to say that I chose to . . . uh . . . go on my own and that I was given the choice, so I took it."

Jones laughed nastily and looked toward his followers. "Do you believe this?"

"No!" came an angry chorus.

"Anybody got any questions to ask these assholes?" growled Jones.

It was his followers' cue to go on the attack.

"Shameful bastards!"

"Goddamn white fascist bigots!"

"Vile filth!"

Tommy's mother, Edith, rushed to the front and slapped her son's face again and again until Jones hollered, "Enough!"

But the followers shouted over their leader. They seemed to blaze with hatred for the boys. The fury grew more and more frightening.

Edith screamed at them. "Neither of you deserve any pity. . . . I want to be allowed to use the machete on both of you. 'Cause I'll cut both of your heads off, 'cause both of you deserve it. . . . I feel I should be allowed to kill you tonight, and if nothing else, kill myself, to keep the church from getting in trouble."

"That's very honorable," replied Jones, "but, uh, we wouldn't dream of sacrificing you for these vermin." He asked his followers what they should do with the boys.

"Tie them to the trees!"

"Put them up against a wall and shoot them."

A man ran up and tackled Brian to the dirt floor. Climbing onto the skinny teenager's chest, he wrapped his strong hands around the boy's neck and throttled him, all the while spewing insults. Brian's face turned red.

Jones watched for a few moments. Then he called the man off and turned to Tommy. What did the teen suggest Jones do with them?

Tommy bowed his head. "I don't really deserve to live," he said.

"That's right, you don't," a woman shouted.

"I don't—I don't think I deserve to live, either," added Brian.

That's when someone came up with the idea of shackling the boys together.

Jones approved.

Guards dragged Tommy and Brian to the machine shop, where makeshift shackles were made from thick chains and metal bands. A worker welded one end of the shackles onto each of the teen's ankles. The hot metal burned their skin before their feet were thrust into buckets of water.

"[Jones] thought it was great, burns and all," said Tommy.

Then the guards shoved the two into their dorm. They fell exhausted onto their cots. But just two hours later, before the sun had even risen, guards shook them awake. "Get moving," they ordered.

After being handed axes, the teens were marched across the compound to a field. An eighty-foot log (the equivalent of an eight-story building) lay on the ground. Three feet in diameter, it was hardwood and difficult to cut. The guards ordered the boys to chop it into two-foot lengths.

Tommy and Brian worked from four a.m. to eight p.m. for weeks, until at last the job was done. Each night when they returned to the compound, they headed to the showers. "We discovered something," said Tommy. "That you can't take your pants off with shackles on, so you and your pants were washed at the same time."

They learned to run in sync, too, since the guards made them sprint wherever they went, dragging the heavy chain along with them. They were also prohibited from speaking to each other, or to anyone else except for their guards.

By the time Tommy and Brian finished chopping the log, big sores had formed on their ankles. Over the next few days, the wounds grew infected and oozed green pus. No one cared.

At Jones's insistence they continued their forced labor. They were made to carry the chopped pieces across the compound to the kitchen. If either dropped one, or didn't move fast enough, or took too long to sharpen their axe, the guards hit them alongside their heads. By week three the boys felt numb with exhaustion. "We were at the point [where] we didn't care," admitted Tommy.

When all the pieces had been carried to the kitchen, guards gave them a wood splitter and ordered them to break each piece into even smaller pieces. After three days of this, Brian put his palm on the splitting wedge and told Tommy to hit it with the sledgehammer.

"No," Tommy whispered back, "it'll break your hand."

"Then just hit my thumb." Brian was desperate. He couldn't take any more. "We'll [get sent] to the infirmary," he said.

But Tommy couldn't do it. "No!"

"Just do it," begged Brian. "I have to have a break."

Tommy lifted the sledgehammer. He took a deep breath and brought it down.

"My thumb, my thumb!" screamed Brian.

As Brian had hoped, the teens went to the infirmary.

The nurse on duty examined the thumb. To Brian's disappointment, it wasn't broken. She did, however, notice their ankles. The infection had gotten so bad that it was eating away the skin. She bustled off. Minutes later she returned with Marceline.

Marceline, who'd remained in charge of the San Francisco Temple until October, when she'd moved permanently to Jonestown, examined the teens. The infection shocked her, but so did their overall physical condition. Thin, exhausted, and dehydrated, they were on the edge of collapse.

Marceline hurried away. When she returned, she brought orders from Father: Unshackle the boys. Once they were freed, she sent them to the showers, where they peeled off the clothes they'd worn for more than three weeks. Their wounds oozed pus. As ordered, they returned to the infirmary for treatment.

But their punishment wasn't over. The next day they landed on the "learning crew"—work duty created for disciplinary problems and those needing correction. Residents assigned to it worked twelve hours at a time. They were prohibited from speaking with anyone and were forced to run everywhere. The guards treated them with brutality. "Side kick to the stomach, sweep kick to the ground," explained Tommy, "that [would] teach [those on the crew]."

Three weeks later Jones finally released the boys with one stipulation: They were never to speak to each other or be seen together again.

Chapter Thirty-Four

Death and Secrets

LYNETTA JONES, A HEAVY SMOKER FOR FIFTY YEARS, WAS IN the last stages of emphysema when she followed her son to Jonestown in September 1977. She had looked forward to the adventure of living in the jungle, but the boat trip from Georgetown had destroyed her already fragile health. Once in Jonestown she never left the private cottage that had been built for her. In early December she suffered a stroke. As Jones sat beside her, she gasped for breath, unable to talk or even move her eyes. She died on December 9.

A tearful Jones announced her death that same day and invited those who'd known Lynetta to view her body. Life had been difficult for his mother, he said, but in death she looked "very well, very well indeed."

The next morning, with little ceremony, she was buried in a fenced-in grave near the settlement.

The women surrounding Jones greeted 1978 with pessimism. Leading the community had become a grinding around-the-clock slog.

Neither Jones nor the other residents seemed to appreciate their long hours and dedication. Carolyn and Maria, especially, felt tired and dispirited. Just maintaining the status quo had become difficult. Foremost, there was Jones's deteriorating condition. Increasingly out of control, he sometimes staggered about in front of residents or urinated off the wooden sidewalks in front of them. Carolyn didn't know how much longer the inner circle could keep his drug abuse a secret. So far, they'd explained away his slurred speech and grogginess as low blood sugar. But the residents weren't fools. If they didn't already suspect the truth, they soon would.

Added to this was mounting pressure from back in the States. The press was demanding investigations into Jonestown for human rights violations and child abuse.

And then there was the failing settlement itself. It was nowhere near self-sufficient. Residents were tired and hungry, stressed and traumatized. Carolyn couldn't see any way forward, nor could other members of the inner circle. The dream was unraveling.

On a February night residents gathered yet again in the pavilion. Ticks scuttled across the dirt floor, drawn by the body heat. On the corrugated tin ceiling above, a pinktoe tarantula stalked a small lizard.

"How many of you plan your deaths?" Jones asked.

A murmur ran through the pavilion.

"Do you ever plan your death?" he snapped impatiently. "You're gonna die. Don't you think you should plan such an important event?"

An eight-year-old girl named Maya Ijames raised her hand. "What does planning your death mean?" she asked.

Replied Jones, "I think a healthy person has to think through his death, or he may sell out."

By "sell out," Jones meant betray him. He hated the idea that after he died, followers might talk to the press about him and Jonestown.

"I want you to be so principled that you're ready to die at the snap of a finger," he went on. "That's what I want to build in you. That kind of character."

An uncomfortable quiet settled over the residents.

The silence irritated Jones. "Some of you people get so . . . nervous every time I talk about death!" He pretended to take his last gasping breath, causing some in the pavilion to laugh. Then he pointed at one of the seniors. "You're going to die someday, honey," he shouted. "You old bitch, you're going to die!"

A few months later Jones asked a handful of ultraloyalists—Carolyn Layton, Annie Moore, Harriet Tropp, Marceline Jones, Maria Katsaris, Larry Schacht, and Phyllis Chaikin, director of the infirmary (and wife of the secretly drugged lawyer, Gene Chaikin)—to research ways to kill *all* of Jonestown's residents. "Be creative," Jones told them. "And thorough."

Annie Moore rose to the challenge. "It would be terrorizing for some people if we . . . started chopping heads off or whatever," she wrote in a memo. Instead, she recommended poisoning the community's food or water. Or even better, maybe they could corral everyone into a tightly confined space and release carbon monoxide fumes into the air. She also offered to kill the children "because I think I could be as compassionate as the next person about it."

Phyllis Chaikin suggested they gather everyone in the pavilion. Then, one by one, followers would be "escorted to a place of dying," where they would be shot in the head by a guard. "If Larry [Schacht] does not find the person definitely dead, their throat is slit with a scalpel." The corpse would then be thrown into a ditch so the sight of it wouldn't terrify the next victim.

Marceline Jones had a different idea. Instead of killing everyone, why not let each adult decide their fate? Anyone younger than eighteen would be spared. "For many years I have lived for just one reason, to safeguard the lives of children." The Temple should find an asylum for the little ones, especially toddlers and babies. "They could," she said, "be saved for socialism." She added that she would gladly help kill the willing adults. Her nursing skills would guarantee that it would be quick and humane.

Larry Schacht had an idea, too, although he wasn't yet ready to reveal it. He was still researching. At night when the patient load in the infirmary eased, he pulled out the medical books he'd ordered from the States and did the calculations. How much cyanide would they need?

Chapter Thirty-Five

The Jonestown Team

STEPHAN COULDN'T BELIEVE IT. SOMEHOW A BASKETBALL had arrived in a shipment of supplies. The eighteen-year-old dribbled. The ball felt good in his hands, and it inspired an idea. He would use the wooden floor of a roofless, unfinished building as a half-court. With help from brothers Jimmy and Tim, he put up a homemade basket, as well as a floodlight so they could play at night. Then the Jones boys (except for Lew) and a handful of friends formed a team. They even enlisted one of the security guards, Lee Ingram, to be their coach, and Michael Touchette agreed to be their athletic trainer.

In their limited free time, they played boisterous games. Basketball allowed them some escape from the madness, a diversion that made their lives feel a little bit normal. It was also a tool for agency and rebellion. They hadn't asked Jones's permission to play. Every time Stephan swept leaves off the court and went at it, he felt as if he were "thrusting a middle finger" at his dad.

As soon as he found out, Jones wanted the court dismantled . . . immediately! "What a folly!" he cried. "What a waste of time when the world's in shambles and we need to be changing it."

Then Marceline spoke up. Why not use the team to inspire pride in the residents? she said. In fact, maybe they should invest in uniforms and play against Guyanese teams. It would promote goodwill, she argued, as well as give the illusion that the Temple wanted to interact with the outside world.

Jones, surprisingly, went along with it.

It wasn't long before the team had become hometown heroes. Residents gathered at practices to whistle and clap as the team dunked and scrimmaged. And when the team's blue-and-white uniforms arrived, a handful of senior women lovingly sewed on the numbers. To residents, it was about so much more than basketball. The players provided a ray of hope and positivity in their dark, exhausting days.

Shanda James, a former girlfriend of Jones's adopted son Tim, lived in Jonestown. She was pretty and joyful, and Tim still cared for her a lot. In October 1978 she became an object of interest to Jones. Despite all the leader's talk about color blindness, he'd never been sexually involved with a Black woman before, and he wanted the lively, appealing nineteen-year-old.

She resisted his overtures at first but inevitably gave in. She had no other choice.

Tim knew what was happening between Shanda and Jones, and he hated it. And yet Tim blamed *her.* She was *making* Father do it, he claimed.

It wasn't long before Shanda wanted out. She wrote Jones a note. "Thank you for our time together," it read, "but there's a young man I'm interested in."

That same day Jones ordered her to the Extended Care Unit,

explaining to his followers that Shanda had tried to kill herself. Nurses drugged her with the powerful antipsychotic drug Thorazine. Late that same night guards dragged a zombielike Shanda from the ECU to their leader's cottage. Tim, who was on watch outside his father's door, knew what was happening inside. His father was raping his friend.

At that moment it all came tumbling down—Tim's faith in his father, his blind devotion. He felt revulsion at Jones's corruption and cruelty.

Stephan, who was sitting alone in the pavilion with the lights off, heard his brother storming past. He called Tim over.

Tim told Stephan what had happened. "We gotta kill him," hissed Tim. "We gotta have a revolution. We gotta throw this son of a bitch out."

Stephan, too, had once considered killing his father. But though he'd known for years that Jones was a charlatan and a madman, he shook his head. Think of how the people in Jonestown would react, he said. "The only way you can take care of Jim Jones is to hope he dies naturally or gradually phase him out. That's the only way you're gonna do it. I'm sorry."

The brothers sat silently in the dark together, brooding.

The next day Stephan encountered his father on the path to the pavilion.

"Walk with me," said a weaving, obviously stoned Jones. He waved away the two bodyguards who were with him.

Stephan took his dad's arm. "What's really up with Shanda?" he demanded. "You put her in [the ECU] because she wants to leave you, didn't you?"

Jones feigned insult. "I can't believe you're saying that."

Enraged, Stephan cursed at his father.

Jones cursed back.

Nearby followers turned to stare. Father and son rarely displayed their disagreements in public.

Stephan stormed off.

When Jones got back to his cottage, he called for Tim. "Shadow [your brother]," he ordered. He wanted to know everything Stephan got up to.

Tim nodded, then immediately went in search of Stephan. But instead of spying on his brother, he tattled on their dad. "I'm supposed to be watching you." The brothers laughed and headed over to the basketball court.

Tim never reported anything to Jones.

Soon afterward, Stephan believed he, too, was being drugged. Some mornings he could barely get out of bed. He had bouts of hives. Twice, his body swelled up so badly, he felt as though he was suffocating, and he needed medical treatment to breathe.

Stephan noticed the sly expression on Jones's face whenever they were together. The teen recognized that look—Dad was up to no good. However, he could never prove his suspicions.

Around the same time, Tim got called to the front during a meeting for using too much lip protector. The blond, fair-skinned teenager had problems with sun exposure, and his uncovered face often burned, even blistered. For this minor infraction followers railed and insulted him for hours. Of course, Tim knew his father had planned this beforehand. No one would dare assail a Jones boy without the leader's prior approval. Tim also knew it had nothing to do with ChapStick. It was about refusing to spy on Stephan.

Tim didn't act contrite or apologize. "I ain't got nothing to say. Whatever you want to do with me, go ahead on. . . . Three-fourths of it is bullshit."

"Don't give me no stuff," Jones snapped. "That's arrogant. . . . That's totally wrong."

"That's right!" came the cries from the crowd.

"You know what it sounds like to me?" Tim snapped back. "Someone's not getting his ass kissed."

The congregation was agog; no one ever spoke back to Father. Even more astonishing was that nothing happened to Tim as a result. Jones just waved the teen away.

Tim dropped back into his seat and stared at his dad. Jones looked terrible—bloated and pasty, his skin tinged yellow. He'd been taking amphetamines and Percodan alternately, and Jimmy Jones believed he was also injecting heroin, although he could never prove it. Stephan, Tim, and Jimmy now viewed these drugs as their allies. Someday the drugs would kill their dad. They hoped it would be soon.

Back in the United States, a group of people related to Jonestown's residents began meeting in the Berkeley home of defectors Elmer and Deanna Mertle (who now used the names Al and Jeannie Mills for fear of Temple reprisals). Calling themselves the Concerned Relatives the group included Grace and Tim Stoen, Steve Katsaris (father of ultraloyalist Maria Katsaris), and Jim Cobb Jr., who had escaped as part of the Gang of Eight. He didn't think he could convince his mother, Christine, to leave Jonestown, but he hoped to bring his youngest siblings—fifteen-year-old Brenda and thirteen-year-old Joel—back to the United States.

And then there were Howard and Beverly Oliver. They'd permitted their sons, nineteen-year-old Bruce and seventeen-year-old Billy, to go to Jonestown for a brief vacation, but when weeks turned to months with no sign of their return, the Olivers became desperate. Jones, the couple believed, was holding their boys against their will.

The Concerned Relatives felt frustrated and frantic. Those who'd heard Jones preach about revolutionary suicide feared he'd go through with it. All that summer of 1978, they worked to enlist the help of U.S. officials, writing senators, members of Congress, ambassadors, the State Department, the FBI, even President Jimmy Carter. But authorities repeatedly said they couldn't do anything. They claimed to be constrained by the First Amendment's religious freedom guarantee. They also pointed out that Jonestown was subject to Guyanese rather than American law.

The Concerned Relatives considered drastic measures. Should they hire mercenaries to kidnap their relatives from Jonestown? Was that even possible? There had to be some way.

Father took suicide votes at every meeting now. It became obvious to followers that voting against death was not an option. No one wanted to anger Father. No one wanted to be publicly humiliated, called a traitor, or beaten. Besides, raising one's hand was easier than listening to his long, incoherent harangues. All anyone really wanted to do was go to bed. So, when Jones asked who among them would die a revolutionary death, everyone dutifully raised their hands and voted yes.

Chapter Thirty-Six

Exit Plans

HAROLD CORDELL HAD MANAGED TO SNEAK IN A SMALL transistor radio when he moved to Jonestown. His family had followed Jones from Indianapolis, and now he had twenty-four family members living in the settlement, including his five children, his estranged wife, and his mother. At night in his bunk, he pressed the radio to his ear and listened to Voice of America. With creeping horror he realized Jones was lying to the community about events back in the States. Socialists weren't being rounded up and killed, as the leader had said. And the U.S. government hadn't invented a mind-control device that transmitted messages of hate and racism.

Obviously, Jones's bleak and hopeless picture was meant to stop followers from longing for home. But Cordell believed there was an even darker reason for the lies: to make death look more appealing than life.

Someone had shipped a carton of Gideon Bibles to the community. Jones had them passed out. Use the pages for toilet paper, he said.

Hyacinth refused. Wipe herself on God's word? she complained to Zip.

Her sister turned on her. "What did Jesus ever do for us anyway? It was Jim who did for us."

Hyacinth felt something crumble inside. With whom could she share her faith if not her sister? It was hard not to say the word *God* out loud, but she managed it. Instead, she prayed, ceaselessly and silently in her head for God to release her from her nightmare.

For months now, Michael Touchette had been eating better than most everyone else. His mother, Joyce, was Jones's personal cook, and as such, she prepared all of Father's special food—meats, salads, rolls, milkshakes, iced tea. Whenever she could, she made extras, then sneaked them to Michael. He, in turn, shared with a small group of trusted friends, including his brother, Al, as well as Stephan Jones. But not the other Jones boys, Michael admitted later, because "Tim and Jimmy acted like they didn't stink."

One day Joyce cooked up a bunch of hamburgers for Jones . . . and her sons. Michael alerted Al and the others to come and eat by using the group's secret signal: rubbing his nose. The young men met in a secret spot. "We ate good," admitted Michael, "real good."

Did any of them feel guilty about eating hamburgers while others subsisted largely on rice and gravy? Did they recognize their privilege as the antithesis of the egalitarianism they were striving to create?

Larry Schacht, Jonestown's doctor, had finally figured it out. "Cyanide is one of the most rapidly acting poisons," he wrote Jones in a memo. He'd experimented on a pig and been happy with the result. While it had been a painful death, it had also been quick. From his reading of the medical literature, Schacht knew the lethal dose for adults. After receiving Jones's approval, the doctor placed an order for one pound of cyanide—enough to kill eighteen hundred people. It cost $8.85.

Back in the States, the Concerned Relatives were making progress at last. In August 1978, Congressman Leo Ryan agreed to look into the conditions in Jonestown. A Democrat from San Mateo, California, Ryan represented the 11th Congressional District, which included San Francisco. He was brash and tenacious, with a reputation for throwing himself into the thick of things. To investigate prison corruption, he'd had himself anonymously incarcerated in Folsom State Prison. To save baby seals, he'd hiked across the frozen wilderness and personally put himself between the infant animals and their would-be hunters. After race riots in Los Angeles, he'd posed as a substitute teacher in Watts, a poor neighborhood, to see for himself the condition in which families lived. And now he had decided to head into the remote jungle to visit Jonestown.

A few details needed to be hammered out first. His fact-finding mission would have to be cleared with both the State Department and the House Foreign Affairs Committee. He also wanted to put together a group with which to travel, including members of the press and his own staff. He hoped to take along some of the Concerned Relatives, too.

In Jonestown, Tommy and Brian hung out in secret. They met each other at night in the bathroom or under cottages. Despite the possibility of being caught, they couldn't let go of each other. Their friendship was the single glimmer of goodness each had.

One night in late summer, as Tommy walked past the warehouse, he found a box containing two dark green capes. He took them and gave one to Brian. Now when night fell, they donned what they called their "cloaks of darkness."

"We pretty much felt we were invisible," said Tommy.

And they *did* blend into the shadows. Slipping across the compound and into the jungle, they talked and laughed for hours.

Jim Bogue admired his son's rebel spirit, but he desperately needed Tommy to stop breaking the rules. One day while the two worked together in the fields, he explained why Tommy *had* to keep his nose clean: Jim was hatching an escape plan.

For weeks Jim and his buddy Al Simon had been hacking a trail through the jungle. They'd told Jones they were out prospecting for gold, and surprisingly leadership hadn't thought to send a guard with them. The men would disappear for the entire day, and no one would be the wiser.

Tommy's older sisters, twenty-two-year-old Teena and twenty-one-year-old Juanita, already knew about the plan. But Jim hadn't said anything to his ex-wife, Edith, or his current wife, Luna. He didn't trust either of them.

Al Simon hadn't told his wife, Bonnie, either. She was a true believer, as well as a Jonestown guard. When the time came to escape, Al planned on grabbing his three kids and his father before slipping away.

Both men had other family members in the settlement—nieces, nephews, cousins, stepchildren, and in-laws. Jim and Al felt guilty about not including them, but they had to protect their children first. They knew they'd get only one chance at escape. They couldn't mess it up.

That's why Tommy had to stop making trouble. It would be impossible to retrieve him if he was on the learning crew under armed guard.

Understood, said Tommy. When would they go?

Jim couldn't say, but Tommy needed to be ready at a moment's notice.

What about Brian? Tommy asked.

Tommy could go fetch his friend when the time was right. "But . . . tell him nothing until then," said Jim.

In early November 1978, Harold Cordell noticed a metal drum aboard the *Cudjoe*. It contained chemicals, newly arrived from the United States. Cordell's job was to inventory every item arriving in Jonestown. Strangely, this container wasn't on his inventory list. Even stranger, none of the other workers knew who'd ordered it.

A guy on the loading dock peeled back a label on the drum, revealing a skull and crossbones, the universal warning for poison.

Harold went cold. Was Jones going to kill them all by poisoning the water system? He watched as the metal drum was loaded onto the truck and then driven to Jonestown's warehouse.

That night Harold took a chance and told his partner, Edith Bogue, about the poison. He confessed his fear.

Edith was terrified, too.

The couple clung together, whispering. They needed to escape. They needed to save their kids. Between them they had nine children in Jonestown. They agreed not to say a word to any of them in case someone snitched. Instead, they planned in secret.

How many others lay in their bunks at night longing for escape? How many others had made plans? These numbers are unknown.

Chapter Thirty-Seven

The Congressman's Visit

ON NOVEMBER 1, CONGRESSMAN RYAN WROTE JONES. HE explained that at the request of the Concerned Relatives, some of whom were his constituents, he planned on visiting Guyana. "I do so as part of my assigned responsibilities as a member of the House Committee on International Relations," he continued. "It goes without saying that I am most interested in a visit to Jonestown and would appreciate whatever courtesies you can extend to our congressional delegation."

Jones did not want to extend *any* courtesies. Why should he have to open his doors to those "fascists"? No, he would forbid the congressman access to Jonestown. He thought the Guyanese government should deny the congressman, too. He demanded that Deputy Prime Minister Ptolemy Reid put a stop to Ryan's visit. Reid, however, refused to side against the United States government. His aides told Jones his decision. They suggested Jones acquiesce to the congressman. In return Jones threatened them. "We prefer death to this kind of [harassing] treatment," he said. If the congressman and his committee were allowed into the country, it would be "a grave mistake."

His threat went unheeded.

The inner circle gathered in Jones's cottage along with Peoples Temple attorney Mark Lane. Father demanded Lane write the congressman and tell him not to come, that he would not be allowed into the community.

Mark Lane advised against it. Let Ryan's party come, he said. Transparency was in the Temple's best interest. If he didn't, he'd end up with "congressional hearings and all that stuff," the attorney said.

Marceline's argument was simpler. They had nothing to hide. If a couple of followers wanted to return to America, so what? She was sure that what they'd built would impress the congressman.

Carolyn Layton had an entirely different opinion. She felt that all hope for Jonestown was lost. From here on out they would be constantly harassed by lawsuits and investigations. The Temple's finances would be drained trying to fend off legal threats. *That's* how the government would destroy them—if mercenary soldiers didn't get there first.

Later, in the privacy of their bedroom, Carolyn asked Jones a different question. It appeared his mind was made up about committing suicide if things went badly during the congressman's visit. But was it really the only solution? She worried that history would not see their act as a noble and courageous one. "I know we can't worry about how [our actions] are interpreted," she said. "I just hate to see it all go for naught."

On the morning of November 6, Stephan, Tim, and six other basketball players (including Jim Cobb's younger brother Johnny), as well as coach Lee Ingram and athletic trainer Michael Touchette, climbed into the truck that would take them to the *Cudjoe.* The Jonestown team was headed to Georgetown to play a series of exhibition games against the Guyanese national team. (Jimmy, who played center, was already in the capital on a Temple assignment.) Jones, of course, hadn't wanted them to accept the Guyanese invitation, but Marceline had stepped in again. Now the whole town, except Jones, turned out to see them off. Residents hugged the boys and shook their hands. A few even cried.

After hurrying the players into the truck because she feared Jones might suddenly change his mind and call them back, Marceline went over to Michael Touchette. "No matter what happens, please take care of my sons for me," she said.

Michael promised he would.

That night during the evening meeting, Jones lolled in his green lawn chair. Unable to cope with mounting pressure, he had upped his drug use. He could no longer walk without the help of two guards and had a hard time focusing or holding a thought. Between bursts of rambling speech, his chin dropped to his chest. At one point he tried to spell a simple word that he didn't want the children to hear. After several attempts he gave up in frustration.

Finally, he broke the news he'd known for days. "I heard some congressman wants to come here."

His words were met with cries of fear. Many saw this as their worst nightmare about to come true—the arrival of CIA agents and mercenary soldiers in Jonestown, and the forcible seizure of their children by the U.S. government.

But not Jim Bogue. He realized that a congressional visit would divert attention. All eyes—the guards', the inner circle's, Jones's—would be trained on the guests. It would be the perfect time to escape.

Harold Cordell had the same thought. Ryan's visit might be the last chance he and his partner, Edith, would have to round up their kids and head into the jungle.

In Georgetown the Jonestown team finally got to practice on a full-size court with a polished wooden floor and acrylic backboards. Stephan played power forward, Jimmy played center, and Tim was a guard. The squad felt faster here, more skilled, and aggressive. Free.

After practice the players rode around Georgetown in the Temple van. Using money Stephan had swiped from his dad, they ate in restaurants and went to movies. "We were enjoying the outside world with our inside brothers," said Stephan.

On November 13 they played their first game against the Guyanese. The Jonestown team played hard, but just as Stephan had feared, they were outrun and outmuscled. They lost by thirty points.

The following morning the squad went into a frenzy of training. Hoping to salvage some self-respect in the second game, they drilled and scrimmaged until late afternoon. Then they returned to Lamaha Gardens, where they were staying.

That night, Jones radioed his sons. He wanted the entire team back in Jonestown immediately.

Stephan argued. "You want to make good PR? Well, we're doing it. We've got another game tomorrow—"

Jones cut him off. "I told you that I want you back tomorrow."

"No," Stephan pushed back, "we're doing too much good here."

Furious, Jones wheeled on Marceline. Get on the radio and make your disobedient sons return home, he told her.

She did as he demanded. Maybe they should listen to Father, she told him.

"You don't have to talk for him," replied Stephan.

His comment sent Jones into a rage.

Stephan reveled in his dad's reaction. Not one member of the team cared what Jones thought anymore. Away from Jonestown they had begun to share their true feelings about the settlement and its leadership. "It was time to stop waiting—waiting for the right reason, the right moment to rise against him; waiting for him to get too sick, too strung out to lead; waiting for him to die." The team had committed themselves to "taking him off the throne" as soon as they returned, said Stephan. "My father's days were numbered."

Twenty-four hours later, on November 15, Congressman Ryan arrived in Georgetown with his entourage—two staffers, two reporters from the *San Francisco Examiner,* one reporter from the *San Francisco Chronicle,* a four-man NBC TV crew, a freelance writer, and fourteen members of the Concerned Relatives, including Grace and Tim Stoen, Jim Cobb, Beverly Oliver, Steve Katsaris, and Steve's adult son, Anthony.

After some rest the congressman headed over to Lamaha Gardens. Sharon Amos, head of the Temple's PR team in Guyana, answered his knock. Ryan smiled disarmingly. "I'm the bad guy," he said. "Does anyone want to talk?"

Sharon looked at him suspiciously.

Ryan explained he was on a fact-finding mission—that was all. He assured her he had an open mind.

She let him into the living room to speak with the Jones boys.

Ryan asked how they liked living in Jonestown.

"We're making a statement," said Jimmy. "We're trying to build a new country for people who have been oppressed because of their race or sex."

Despite their concerns about Jones's leadership, none of the teens trusted Ryan with the truth. For too long it had been drilled into them that the U.S. government was the enemy. Still, they found Ryan not only pleasant but also willing to listen. Stephan wondered if he should radio Jonestown and tell his dad that. But there wasn't time. The team was due on the basketball court.

In that second game Jonestown's players performed better. They still lost, this time by twenty points, but they felt more cohesive out there. Passing. Shooting. Rebounding. And they were having *fun.*

On Thursday night, November 16, Marceline made an announcement. After negotiations between Temple lawyer Mark Lane and Congressman Leo Ryan, terms for a visit to Jonestown had been agreed upon. The congressman and his entourage would be arriving the next day. They would spend the night and depart on Saturday after completing interviews with family members of the Concerned Relatives.

Jones added a garbled, rambling warning: "I want to remind you again that there is quicksand [out in the jungle]. . . . I can't imply to you what a tiger can do with one blow of his leg. One blow can break your neck. Not to mention, of course, he can eat you. Caiman, larger than crocodile, the most fierce in the world, can swallow you in one gulp."

He's insane, thought thirty-year-old Dale Parks, a respiratory therapist in the settlement's infirmary. Dale's family traced its Temple roots all the way back to the Indianapolis church. But secretly, Parks hated everything about Jonestown—the constant talk of death, the regimentation, the lies, and the cruel punishments. Most of all, he hated the lunatic that Jim Jones had become. Weeks earlier he, too, had made the decision to get out.

Dale had spoken with his family, tentatively at first. He came to learn that they shared his feelings. And so, while pretending to be good followers, they'd secretly made escape plans. They'd hidden some belongings at the piggery, where Dale's father, Jerry, worked, and now they waited for the best day to slip into the jungle and hike to Port Kaituma.

Chapter Thirty-Eight

Friday, November 17

THAT MORNING JONES MADE A RARE APPEARANCE DURING breakfast. "It looks like they're coming," he told residents. The congressman and his party were already en route from Georgetown. He added, "Please listen to what I'm saying. I'm trying to save our babies. . . . These [government] people are trying to set you up. And as far as your relatives coming up to you, be civil, but don't get engaged in any long conversation; don't fall for their sweetness. They know how to play a game, and you've got to be extremely careful, extremely careful. Everybody understand that?" Then he stumbled back to his cottage for a "vitamin" injection.

That afternoon Ryan's plane flew over Jonestown. Residents shaded their eyes and looked skyward. It carried representatives of the three groups they'd been conditioned to distrust most: the U.S. government, the American press, and Temple defectors. The plane disappeared, heading toward Port Kaituma. It was just a matter of time before the enemy arrived.

Not everyone who'd flown to Georgetown with Congressman Ryan went on to Port Kaituma. Knowing the community's deep anger toward them, Tim and Grace Stoen remained behind. So did Steve Katsaris, who believed his daughter, Maria, would be more receptive to a visit from her brother, Anthony. Eight other relatives also stayed, mostly because there were not enough seats for them on the plane Ryan had chartered. The congressman also left behind one of his staffers.

At Port Kaituma the plane eased down, bumped over the dirt runway, and came to a stop. The passengers made their way down the plane's stairs and toward a group of angry young men from Jonestown who awaited them. Congressman Ryan and staffer Jackie Speier climbed into the back of the Jonestown dump truck, and Temple attorneys Mark Lane and Charles Garry got in after them. Everyone else remained standing on the airstrip.

What about the press and the family members? asked Ryan.

"We'll try to get them in tomorrow," said Lane. He turned to the remaining group. "But don't try to come to Jonestown on your own."

Obviously, Jones had changed his mind about letting everyone in. As the truck rumbled away, the reporters and Concerned Relatives—Jim Cobb Jr., Anthony Katsaris, and others—sat down in the shade to wait.

An hour later Marceline welcomed Ryan and the others to Jonestown with smiles and iced tea. She would take them on a tour, she said.

But Ryan insisted on speaking with Jones. He wanted to settle the matter of those left behind at the airstrip.

It took the leader half an hour to appear, wearing a red polo shirt and his sunglasses. Lane and Garry stood beside him.

Ryan didn't mince words. He'd come because Jones was accused of holding people against their will. Why not invite the press and family members in? Wouldn't that be the best way to silence critics? Let the world see what he had created here and that he had nothing to hide.

Jones was prepared to argue, but Lane pulled him aside. "I am imploring you to open it to the world and let them come in," he said.

Jones relented. As the dump truck headed back into Port Kaituma for the rest of the group, he muttered, "I hope to God I have done the right thing."

The sun had dipped by the time the truck returned to the settlement. Residents packed the pavilion. They stared as reporters made their way to the table where Jones sat and immediately peppered him with questions.

Meanwhile, the Concerned Relatives sought out their families. Beverly Oliver found her two sons and hugged them. Had they gotten the letters she'd sent to Jonestown?

No, they replied.

Why hadn't they ever written? she asked.

Because they'd been told she was a CIA agent, and that the other Concerned Relatives wanted to kill everyone in Jonestown.

Beverly tried to steady her emotions. She steered the conversation to her sons' lives. How did they spend their days? What did they do for fun?

The three talked, settling on a bench together. Neither son said a negative word about Jonestown, and they warned their mother not to say anything bad, either. Beverly basked in their protectiveness. It was clear they still loved her.

In the back of the pavilion, Anthony Katsaris tried to talk with his sister, Maria. But she remained cold and aloof, refusing to return his hug or look him in the eye. He'd barely gotten started before Jim McElvane, former head of security, sat down with them. Intimidated, Anthony fell silent.

Across the pavilion twenty-eight-year-old Jim Cobb Jr.'s entire family (except for his brother Johnny, who was playing basketball in Georgetown) surrounded him. His mother, Christine, kept patting his arm. Tears dripped down her face. Jim begged her to let him take his siblings back to the States. She begged him to return to the community. He changed the subject. Pulling out a camera, he snapped pictures of his family. They mugged for the lens. Jim promised to send them copies once he'd had them developed.

While all this was happening, Ryan and Speier had gotten to work. They didn't know what to expect. "The State Department was telling us there wasn't a story [here]," recalled Speier, "that there really wasn't anything to talk about." And yet they had a long list of people who, according to their relatives back home, were being imprisoned. She and Ryan needed to interview each of them. Seated at a table set off to the side of the pavilion, they began speaking to residents one at a time. Because they'd been warned that Jonestown might be bugged, they'd brought a printed card that instructed anyone who wanted to leave to simply nod their head.

No one did.

Ryan had also brought a stack of letters from family and friends. After finishing the last interview for the evening, he handed them out. The inner circle had suspected this might happen. Earlier, Maria had instructed residents to hand over any mail to Temple censors without opening it. Most residents would comply. The censors, in turn, would then toss the mail into a file labeled "Letters brought in by Ryan." Recipients would never read them.

A special meal was served that night—barbecued pork, biscuits, collard greens, and fruit punch. Residents knew it was for show, meant to prove to Ryan's party that the settlement ate well. Still, a full belly was pure joy. It also felt good to get together in the pavilion for music and dancing instead of suicide votes and catharsis meetings.

A program had also been planned in the visitors' honor. The Jonestown band played while couples danced and laughing children chased one another through the crowd. The residents appeared healthy and happy. They'd been given better clothing—and the bright colors of their dresses and shirts added to the celebratory atmosphere.

Neither Carolyn Layton nor Annie Moore had much fun, though. The two kept their eyes on Jones as he continued to talk with reporters. Even from her spot across the pavilion, Annie could see his tongue lolling as he careened from one topic to the next.

Bob Brown, the NBC TV cameraman, captured the entire interview on film:

"I feel like a dying man," Jones states abruptly, having mentioned death several times already.

One of Ryan's reporters asks him about his mass-suicide talk.

Jones pretends to be insulted. "I only said it was better that we commit suicide than kill," he said. He adds that he'd rather die than give John Victor Stoen back to his mother.

On cue Carolyn trots out the six-year-old. See how much the two look alike? Jones says. He even pries open the child's mouth so reporters can see their similar dental structure.

Recalled one reporter later: "I felt embarrassment and pity for Jones as he stumbled and sometimes slurred words. I wondered if he was drugged by fever, or by medication, or was mentally ill. And an uneasy feeling came over me."

Back in Georgetown, Stephan and his teammates took to the basketball court for their last game of the exhibition series. They'd resolved to redeem themselves in this final matchup. For the first time they felt like they were playing fluidly, as a team. Dribble. Pass. Shoot. Rebound.

The Guyanese players were surprised. They finally had some competition. The game was on!

In the second half the Jonestown team tired. Still, they gave their all. They lost by a respectable ten points.

Giddy at their level of play, they returned to Lamaha Gardens. They couldn't wait to radio the community and share the exhilaration of the game.

Back in Jonestown someone shouted over the music, "Our basketball team just beat the national team by ten points!"

This lie was greeted by thunderous applause.

Jones grinned at the reporters. "Now that's a coup," he joked, then claimed the victory made the Temple team the best in the Caribbean.

Onstage, the talent show began. Teenager Poncho Johnson sang "The Greatest Love of All," a Temple favorite. On this night did the last lines of that song resonate with residents?

And if, by chance, that special place
That you've been dreaming of
Leads you to a lonely place
Find your strength in love

Lew Jones also sang, which prompted his father to talk with reporters about his rainbow family. Others performed, too.

Then Marceline called Congressman Ryan to the front. A consummate politician, he cozied up to the crowd by mentioning that he'd run into a former student from his teaching days here in the community, as well as an old classmate of his daughter's. It just went to show, he said, that they weren't total strangers after all. Then he grew serious. "I think you all know that I'm here to find out more about questions that have been raised about your operation here, but I can tell you right now, that from the few conversations I've had with some of the folks here already this evening, that whatever the comments are, there are some people who believe this is the best thing that ever happened to them in their whole life."

An explosion of whistling, stomping, shouting, and clapping reverberated through the pavilion. Ryan grinned and tried to silence them, but residents kept up the ecstatic noise. The band's drummer banged out a jubilant beat. It went on for minutes.

"See?" Jones told a reporter. "There's no barbed wire here. We don't have three, let alone three hundred, who want to leave."

Around this time twenty-five-year-old Vernon Gosney sidled up to NBC reporter Don Harris. Vernon hated Jonestown, and he and his eighteen-year-old friend, Monica Bagby, had decided to defect. Surreptitiously, Vernon handed Harris a note.

Startled, Harris dropped it.

Quickly scooping it up off the pavilion floor, Vernon handed it to Harris again. "Oh, you dropped something," he said.

A little boy saw it all. "He passed him a note," the kid sang out. He pointed at Vernon. "He passed him a note."

Harris opened it and read it to himself: "Vernon Gosney and Monica Bagby. Help us get out of Jonestown."

At the same time, people began crowding in on Vernon and asking him questions. Vernon was terrified.

Seeing the commotion, Congressman Ryan made his way over. Harris handed him the note. Ryan silently read it. "You're the first one to ask to leave," he said.

Vernon looked around at the angry followers. "You're in great danger," he told Ryan. "You need to leave now."

Ryan answered calmly, "We have no transportation."

Vernon, however, persisted. "You're in danger."

Ryan patted his arm reassuringly. "We can't leave until tomorrow, but don't worry. You have the congressional shield of protection around you. Nothing will happen."

Unconvinced, Vernon returned to his cottage. His friend Monica Bagby and the other residents also turned in. The only thing that seemed to be protecting the "traitors" was the presence of Congressman Ryan. As had been agreed on earlier, he and Jackie Speier were spending the night in Jonestown.

Meanwhile, the reporters and Concerned Relatives boarded the dump truck for the forty-five-minute ride back to a guesthouse in Port Kaituma. Their driver brusquely said he'd be back for them in the morning.

Chapter Thirty-Nine

Saturday Morning, November 18

THE GROUP FROM PORT KAITUMA ARRIVED BACK IN JONES-town around ten-thirty a.m. By that time Ryan and Speier had already begun interviewing residents. Jones was still in bed, sleeping off his tranquilizers, but Marceline was there to meet them. Today, she insisted, she would show them around.

Most of the reporters followed her to the hospital, the nursery, the kitchen, and the school. It was a canned tour, meant to use up their time in Jonestown. Only reporter Don Harris stayed back at the pavilion. "I'll whistle when something happens," he told them.

Today was the day, Dale Parks decided. Because of Ryan's visit, it was a free day, and no one had to report to work. With guests in the compound, Jones's attention, as well as that of the security guards', was directed elsewhere. It was the perfect chance to escape.

Seven members of the Parks family met at the piggery. Dale went over to the place where he'd hidden plastic bags of food and clothing.

Everything was gone.

Had he and his family been found out?

Jones finally emerged from his cottage. He wore the same sunglasses and red shirt from the night before. He looked sweaty and ashen.

The press broke away from Marceline to cluster around him.

Reporter Don Harris asked about the accusations of mistreatment and imprisonment.

"People play games, friend," said Jones. His voice sounded weary. "They'll lie. They'll lie. What can I do about liars? Are you people gonna leave us? I beg you. Please leave us."

Harris handed him the note from Vernon Gosney. Jones read it. He looked at the reporter. "If it's so damn bad, why is [Vernon] leaving his [four-year-old] son [Mark] here?" he asked Harris. "Can you give me a good reason for that? I'd take my son with me."

The Parks family walked into the pavilion. With their escape through the jungle foiled, they'd decided to leave with the congressman. Shoulders back, the white-haired matriarch of the family, Edith, approached Jackie Speier. "We want to leave," she said. "All seven of us."

Jones heard. He stumbled to his feet and headed over to them. "Please don't go," he begged. "Wait a week or two, and I'll give you . . . five thousand dollars."

Jerry Parks shook his head. "You held us here as slaves, and now we're getting out."

Tommy Bogue saw this exchange. He raced to tell his father, who called an emergency meeting. Members of their escape party met at the sawmill. Jim Bogue argued for leaving *now.* He had no doubt that the Parks' defection would push Jones over the edge.

Jim's buddy Al Simon agreed—but he had to find his six-year-old son, Alvin, first. "I'm going to go get him, and I'll be right back."

Jim urged him to hurry.

Minutes later Jim's ex-wife, Edith, came up the path with her partner, Harold Cordell.

Jim didn't trust Edith or Harold. He felt sure they'd come to spy.

Edith pulled her daughter Teena aside and told her about the container of poison Harold had seen being unloaded.

"Mom, so help me if this is a trick—" Teena began.

Edith cut her off. "It's not a trick. I'm afraid for our lives."

Both of them began crying. Then Teena turned to the others. "Mom is with us," she said. Harold was, too.

That's when nineteen-year-old Marilee Bogue arrived, responding to her father's summons. She looked at them suspiciously.

The group clammed up. Everyone knew Marilee couldn't be trusted. She was a true believer who'd often turned in her own family members. Jim planned to jump his daughter when the time was right and carry her out. He wanted to go *now.* Where was Al?

Two guards strode up. Had they seen Joe Wilson's wife and son? they asked the group. Wilson was looking for them.

The mention of Wilson, Jonestown's tough, swaggering security chief, must have unnerved them. Wilson would do *anything* Father asked, even murder.

The group said no, and the guards moved on.

But the encounter spurred them to action. They couldn't wait any longer. Jim weighed the options: Run into the jungle, or go with the congressman? He turned toward the others. He believed casting their lot with Ryan was a better bet than hiking the thirty-five miles to Matthews Ridge, even if that meant their defection would be public. Jim believed the congressman's position in the U.S. government would protect them. What did the others think? Should they go with Ryan?

All but Marilee agreed.

The Bogues and Harold Cordell headed for the pavilion, where Jones sat on a bench, surrounded by a small knot of his closest aides.

Jim Bogue walked straight past him. He approached Congressman Ryan and said that his family wanted to leave, too.

Edith went up to Jones. "We're gonna go back," she told him with difficulty.

Jones stood, walked over to Jim, and put his arm around him. "You don't have to go," he said. "And if you do go, you'll be welcomed back anytime. Even some of those who have lied about us have come back."

Bogue didn't reply. He had nothing more to say to Jim Jones.

For the next hour both Jones and Marceline tried to persuade the families to stay. The leader tested their resolve, proclaimed his love for them, offered solutions to their problems. He summoned all his warmth and charm. He reminded them that Jonestown's residents were their family, too.

Please stay, Marceline chimed in. Things would be different. "We're going to have a lot of reforms."

Nothing changed their minds.

Other residents, having heard about the defections, hurried to the pavilion. They huddled in groups, eyes wide, looking worried or bewildered. Some wore expressions of longing and indecision. Did they want to go, too? Were they too afraid to step forward?

Congressman Ryan believed so. "They're coming out of the

woodwork," he told one reporter. It was obvious he felt vindicated. No one could say this mission had been a witch hunt. Twenty people in all had come forward—and he'd ordered an additional plane over the Temple radio.

Ryan's staff member Jackie Speier and a couple of reporters accompanied the defectors, who feared harassment, to their quarters to pack. Jones watched them go. Reported one journalist: "In his emotion and pain, he sucked in his cheeks, then inflated them, then licked his dry lips, repeating the actions again and again. This once-eloquent man appeared lost for words, his lips seemingly cemented together, even as he spoke."

Jones grabbed his chest as if in pain. "A pill," he said to Marceline. She just patted his arm.

The press circled the couple. They fired questions at Jones about beatings and other forms of abuse. He denied them all.

Don Harris asked him if there were any guns in the compound.

"I have strictly prohibited guns," Jones lied. He placed an imaginary gun in Harris's hand, then added, "You don't have to shoot me. The media smear does it."

At that moment, like a bad omen, the clouds turned black. A blast of wind tore through the pavilion, ripping away the handmade posters and toppling chairs. Seconds later a heavy rain beat down. It bowed trees and formed streams of muddy water that coursed along the pathways.

Then, as suddenly as it had come, the rain stopped.

Ready to depart, Jim Bogue looked frantically around for his daughter. Marilee had been with him when they'd first returned to the pavilion, but now she was gone. Hiding, he figured. The painful truth struck him. He'd have to leave her.

Meanwhile, Jones bent to hug twelve-year-old Tracy Parks goodbye.

He turned to Dale and tried to whisper something in his ear, but Dale pulled away. The Parks family followed the Bogues to the dump truck, where Monica Bagby and Vernon Gosney already sat. Inexplicably, Vernon had packed his clothes but left his son.

Tommy hung back, scanning the crowd. At last, he found the face he'd been searching for—Brian's. His friend stood beside his father, watching it all.

"Come on," said Tommy. "Go with me."

Brian shook his head. He was only sixteen, and his father refused to let him leave.

Tommy couldn't believe it. This was *it.* Girls, hamburgers, *life* were almost within reach. "Come on!"

Brian looked miserable. "I want to go with you," he said, "but they won't let me."

What more could Tommy do? Without his best friend, he climbed into the truck.

Al Simon, along with his father and three kids, also headed for the truck.

His wife, Bonnie, ran after them. "I'll kill you! I'll kill you!" she screamed hysterically. "You bring those kids back! Don't touch my kids!"

Al and his family kept moving.

Bonnie turned to Marceline for help.

Marceline gathered the woman in her arms. No one would take her children, she assured her.

Temple lawyer Mark Lane stepped in front of Al's group. Al had no legal right to take the children, Lane told him.

Al didn't see any other options. He couldn't leave without his children. He turned back.

Believing he could work something out between Al and Bonnie,

Congressman Ryan decided to stay behind, too. A plane could come for him in the morning. He felt sure that by then even more residents would decide to leave, too.

It was the middle of the afternoon now. Jones stood on the playground away from the residents as the truck rumbled to life. Carolyn held an umbrella over his head. She whispered to him, and he waved goodbye.

At that moment Larry Layton, Carolyn's ex-husband and a fervent devotee of Jones, hopped into the truck. He wore a rain poncho but carried no luggage. He claimed he just wanted out.

The other defectors glared at him. They didn't trust Layton. He was a hard-core loyalist. He would never leave Jones.

Dale Parks whispered to the reporters. "I sense danger."

But there wasn't time to sort out the matter. They needed to get to the airstrip, where planes would be waiting for them.

The dump truck lurched forward, then ground to a stop in the thick mud created by the storm. A bulldozer would have to push it out.

Meanwhile, in the pavilion, Congressman Ryan strategized with the Temple lawyers. He'd need them to help get everyone out who wanted out. Additionally, he'd need to spend another night in Jonestown. Could they arrange that with Jones?

Ryan didn't see it coming. Member Don Sly grabbed him from behind and put a knife to his neck. "You're going to die!" he hissed.

But Sly hesitated—and in that second the attorneys tackled him. They knocked the knife from Ryan's windpipe. In the struggle the attacker was cut, and blood splattered across Ryan's white shirt.

All around people were screaming and crying as the security guards dragged the attacker away.

Jones pushed his way through the crowd. "Does this change things?" he asked the shaken congressman.

"It doesn't change everything, but it changes some things," Ryan managed to reply.

Those close to Jones knew he'd asked the man to kill the congressman. Followers would never do something so drastic without Father's orders.

Ryan now wanted to leave with the others. His face gray, he hurried down the wooden path, briefcase in hand and blood-splattered shirt open to his belt. He climbed into the front seat of the truck, which had just been freed from the mud. The group headed toward the Port Kaituma airstrip.

Chapter Forty

Saturday Afternoon, November 18

IN GEORGETOWN EVERYONE ON THE BASKETBALL TEAM EXcept Jimmy went to the movies. He stayed back at Lamaha Gardens. But not long after the players left, he heard Sharon Amos talking with Jones on the radio. His father's voice sounded breathless and excited.

Jimmy moved to stand in the office doorway. "I've sent my avenging angels after [Ryan]," Jones was saying to Sharon.

Sharon noticed the teen standing there. "Jimmy's here," she told Jones.

Jones told her to put him on.

"Dad?" said Jimmy.

"Where are your brothers?" demanded Jones.

Jimmy told him.

Jones insisted they return to Lamaha Gardens immediately.

The urgency in his voice scared Jimmy. He sent a message to the movie theater. Then he and Sharon sat by the radio, waiting. Jones had said he'd tell them more when everyone was back.

The truck carrying the congressman's party made it only as far as the settlement's front gate before being stopped. Security chief Joe Wilson, pistol tucked into his belt, hopped onto the running board and ordered the passengers to crowd to the sides of the truck. "Let me see who you got in here," he snapped. Supposedly, he was still searching for his wife and child. But even after determining they weren't in the truck, he remained on the running board and headed to the airstrip with the others.

His presence, as well as Larry Layton's, worried Jim Bogue. If anything went down, he whispered to his son, Tommy should grab his sisters Juanita and Teena and head into the jungle.

The truck arrived at the airstrip just minutes before the two planes: a six-seater Cessna and a Guyana Airways Twin Otter that could seat twenty. Within minutes both were ready for boarding. Despite Ryan's request, there still weren't enough seats to accommodate all the passengers. Nine people would have to stay behind and wait for another plane. Jackie Speier suggested it be the journalists. They grumbled. They had deadlines to meet. Huddling together, they debated who would stay. Meanwhile, Speier assigned seats to the others. Most of the defectors would fly back on the bigger plane, but a few would join Ryan on the Cessna.

At that moment a tractor pulling a flatbed trailer with a dozen armed Jonestown men drove onto the airstrip. It parked about two hundred feet from the airplanes, just to the side of the runway. The driver of the dump truck put his vehicle into gear and joined them. The men glared at the departing party.

"I think we've got trouble," Don Harris said to his fellow reporters.

Speier waved the group toward the planes. "Come on," she said. "Let's get on."

As defectors and Concerned Relatives scuttled up the gangways,

Joe Wilson broke away from the idling vehicles and sauntered toward the boarding area. He pulled Larry Layton aside, and the two spoke privately for a few moments. Then, after shaking hands under Larry's rain poncho, Joe headed back to the tractor trailer.

And Larry scrambled aboard the Cessna. He took a seat behind Monica Bagby, Vernon Gosney, and Dale and Tracy Parks.

At the door of the larger plane, passengers shoved suitcases and bags up the stairs before climbing aboard themselves. Tommy and Teena Bogue took their seats, eager to get moving. Jim Bogue followed, as well as his daughter Juanita, Harold Cordell, and some others.

Only the journalists, as well as Ryan, Speier, and a few Concerned Relatives, were still standing on the tarmac when they heard the tractor trailer begin moving down the runway toward them. It stopped about thirty feet from them, parallel to the planes. Leaping from the vehicles, the Jonestown men opened fire, shooting out the Otter's front tire before training their guns on the people.

Aboard the Cessna, Layton yanked out from under his poncho the pistol Wilson had handed him and began shooting. He wounded both Vernon and Monica before Dale Parks wrestled it away. Dale turned the gun on Layton and pulled the trigger. But the gun didn't fire. He punched Layton in the face. Layton fell back, knocked unconscious.

Aboard the Otter, Harold Cordell shouted, "Duck down!" But Patricia Parks, Dale and Tracy's mother, wasn't fast enough. A bullet whizzed through the plane's open door and struck her in the back of the head, killing her instantly.

Tommy lunged for the plane's door. As bullets ricocheted around him, he tried to close it, but it was too heavy. Teena helped. Together they heaved it shut before flinging themselves to the floor, panting and trembling. That's when Tommy noticed he'd been shot in the left leg. But he wasn't in pain. Terror overwhelmed all his senses.

Most aboard the planes were luckier than those on the runway. The gunmen killed NBC cameraman Bob Brown, reporter Don Harris, and photographer Greg Robinson. They also killed Leo Ryan.

The congressman, hit in the neck during the initial barrage of gunfire, had managed to get behind the Cessna's front tire, trying to shield himself from the bullets. One of the Jonestown men approached and shot him point-blank in the head. Leo Ryan became the only congressman to be assassinated while in office.

The men didn't bother to finish off the other wounded victims. They'd done what they'd been sent to do. They'd killed the congressman. Climbing back onto the vehicles, they drove away, grinning and making victory signs.

When the shooting had begun, some on the tarmac had raced for cover in the jungle. One of those was Jim Cobb. As bullets whizzed by his head, he'd zigzagged toward the brush. Diving into the foliage, he crawled as fast as he could through vines and thorny growth. The needle-sharp plants punctured his knees and shredded his hands, but Jim kept his head down and kept moving. Finally, scratched and bloody, he stood. Still, he went deeper, the mud on the jungle floor sucking at his shoes. When the deep shade of the canopy approached total darkness, he shinnied up a tree and settled into its branches. "I was absolutely incredulous at what was happening because . . . last week I was in dental school and here I am—in the jungle hiding out in the top of a tree where they will shoot me or I'll be eaten by a jungle cat," he later said. Jim stayed in the tree all night.

Back on the tarmac Vernon Gosney—shot in the back and wheezing from a collapsed lung—stumbled out of the Cessna. He, too, made for the jungle's edge, where he dropped into a rise of grassy brush. Were their hunters really gone? Vernon couldn't be sure. He lay there, stifling his moans of pain. He wondered about Monica and hoped she wasn't dead.

Dale Parks climbed out of the Cessna, too. He kept a tight grip on Larry Layton as he dragged the assassin out into the open. Dale's sister, Tracy, sobbing uncontrollably, followed them. She didn't yet know her mother was dead. Dazed, she took in the carnage on the tarmac. Bodies and blood were everywhere.

Behind her the Cessna roared to life. "The pilot poured on the throttle," recalled one survivor, "until it seemed the buzz would tear directly into us. Then white metal flashed overhead." Monica Bagby, badly wounded, lay on the floor—the only passenger to leave the airstrip that day. Also aboard was the pilot of the Otter. Once the shooting had stopped, he'd dashed from his bullet-ridden and inoperable Otter into the smaller plane. Now, as it headed for Georgetown, the two pilots frantically radioed ahead. Their reports of a bloody massacre were almost incoherent.

Back at the airstrip minutes passed. The humid air filled with the cries and moans of the wounded. Cautiously, survivors emerged from the bush. Tommy, shocked and in pain, lowered the Otter's door and stumbled down the gangway.

Slowly, the survivors regrouped. Jackie Speier moaned. Her injuries were severe. Not only had she taken shots to her arm and pelvis, but a hole the size of a dinner plate had also been gouged out of her thigh. Anthony Katsaris had been shot in both his chest and his back, while photographer Steve Sung's arm and shoulder had been blown almost completely off. Blood soaked their clothing, and they shivered from shock. No one knew what to do for such terrible injuries. Others had also been shot. Though their injuries were not as severe, they, too, needed medical attention. And then there was the question of the dead. What should be done with them?

There was movement at the side of the runway.

"They're coming back!" someone shouted.

Tommy, remembering what he'd promised his father, grabbed Teena. That's when he noticed that she'd been shot, too. Blood dripped down her calf. Despite their wounds, however, they sprinted for the jungle. Frozen with terror, Juanita found herself unable to follow. But Tracy and eighteen-year-old Brenda Parks, along with Brenda's boyfriend, raced after them. Panicked, they ran deep into the tangled wilderness. Before long they were lost.

Back in Georgetown, Stephan and Tim hurried to Lamaha Gardens. They joined Jimmy in the radio room. Jones was transmitting again, his words slurred, his voice wheedling. The "avenging angels" had done their work, he told them. Congressman Ryan was dead.

"We're going to see Mr. Frazier," Jones said. It was code for committing revolutionary suicide. He asked if they had any poison in the house.

Sharon Amos told him no.

Jones suggested other methods: piano strings, knives.

"Is this real?" Jimmy kept asking. "Is this real?"

Sharon Amos turned to one of her daughters, twenty-one-year-old Liane Harris. "We might have to die," she said.

"Okay, fine," replied Liane.

"Let's wait a minute," Stephan pleaded. "We need a plan or we won't accomplish anything."

It was very possible his dad was lying. "I believed Dad was too much of a coward to carry out [revolutionary suicide]," admitted Stephan. Besides, Carolyn or Maria would surely countermand the order if he was serious . . . wouldn't they?

He decided to go over to the Pegasus Hotel, where the few Concerned Relatives who hadn't gone to Jonestown were staying. Maybe they had more information. Before he left, however, he turned to coach Lee Ingram and asked him to telephone the San Francisco office. "Tell them . . . not to do anything until they heard from me."

Lee agreed. He picked up the phone receiver.

Stephan, along with his brother Tim and basketball player Johnny Cobb, hurried to the hotel, where they spoke with Tim and Grace Stoen, as well as Steve Katsaris. No one had heard anything. Alarmed, they all headed to the American embassy.

Marine security guards refused to let them in.

Stephan demanded to know why.

After several tense minutes a low-level official arrived at the door. He told them the news: There'd been a shooting at the airstrip. Details remained sketchy, but it appeared some people had been wounded.

It all seemed unreal to Stephan. A nightmare.

On his way back to Lamaha Gardens, he noticed a small plane flying overhead. He hoped it was Congressman Ryan and his group. "Please be them," he prayed.

As Stephan approached the house, a woman ran toward him. "Sharon killed herself and her children," she cried.

"Where are they?" shouted Stephan.

Someone pointed upstairs to the closed bathroom door.

After taking the steps two at a time, he shoved open the door.

Sharon and her three children—Liane, eleven-year-old Christa, and eight-year-old Martin—lay on the tiled floor. Guyanese authorities would later conclude that Sharon had slit the smaller children's throats first. Then Liane had killed her mother before turning the knife on herself.

"My memory of the rest of that night is kaleidoscopic," said Stephan. The police arrived. They interrogated everyone and searched the house for evidence. "Faces loom and then fade, as did my mind." He desperately wanted to get back to Jonestown. "I knew that Jim Jones's worst was upon us," said Stephan. "I felt like I might be the *last* person who could reason with Dad." He begged the police to take him to Jonestown.

"All that can be done is being done," an officer replied.

Later, after authorities removed the bodies, Stephan lay in a downstairs bedroom, staring up as blood from the bathroom above seeped through the plastered ceiling and dripped onto the floor. "I was dizzy with the dark possibilities that whirlpooled my head."

At the Port Kaituma airstrip, the terrified survivors realized it had been a false alarm. Temple gunmen had not returned to finish them off.

During the shooting residents of the tiny village had remained safe inside their homes, but now they emerged. All around them were moaning and crying and the awful stillness of the dead. Dale Parks, who'd still been holding tight to Larry Layton, finally released him to local policemen, who took the assassin to the town jail. Authorities had already summoned planes from Georgetown to evacuate the wounded. But, explained one police officer, it was past dusk, and since the airstrip didn't have lights, it would be impossible for a plane to land. Help would not arrive until morning. Until then, all they could do was cover the bodies and shelter the badly wounded.

Town residents erected an army tent near the ruined Otter. Using bedsprings as stretchers, they carried the four worst cases—Jackie Speier, Anthony Katsaris, Steve Sung, and Vernon Gosney—inside. Survivors took shifts caring for them. All but Sung were awake and in excruciating pain. Jackie Speier asked a reporter to tape-record a final message to her parents.

Tommy and his group remained missing. Jim Bogue tried to quell his fears. His son was too jungle-savvy to have been caught by the Jonestown men . . . wasn't he?

The hours passed slowly. Every unfamiliar sound caused survivors to hit the ground. Some survivors took refuge in a darkened room in the back of a Port Kaituma bar. Reporters and defectors sat in anxious silence.

Chapter Forty-One

The End

IN JONESTOWN AT AROUND FOUR THAT SAME SATURDAY afternoon, Lew Jones came on the loudspeaker and called everyone to the pavilion.

Zip Edwards, who had watched the day's events unfold, hurried to her cottage to grab a sweater. She found her sister, Hyacinth, sitting on the edge of her bed.

Zip told her about the defectors.

"That so?" replied Hyacinth. She'd secretly been planning to escape to the American embassy during her next doctor's appointment in Georgetown. Had she known about Ryan's offer, she might have gone with him.

Zip handed Hyacinth her cane.

But Hyacinth stubbornly crossed her arms. She wasn't going.

Zip frowned at her. "Jim's going to be awful mad at you if you don't come down to the pavilion."

"He'll just have to come and drag me down," retorted Hyacinth. "'Cause I ain't going on my own!"

Zip changed the subject. "I believe I'll wear my red sweater tonight."

The statement gave Hyacinth pause. Since when did her sister talk about fashion?

Their roommate, Esther, patted Hyacinth's hand. "We'll tell you [what the meeting was about] tonight when we get back," she said.

The two headed for the pavilion.

The community assembled inside. Parents held small children on their laps; teenagers sat with their friends; seniors waved to one another.

Their leader, meanwhile, was in a meeting with Marceline, as well as Harriet Tropp and her brother, Dick. Huddled together just feet from the pavilion, they talked in fervent whispers.

Dick was arguing. "There must be another way."

"Tell me what it is," responded Jones.

Harriet interrupted. "Dick, stop being a pain in the ass. You're just afraid to die."

Maria Katsaris approached the group. She whispered in Jones's ear.

"Is there a way to make it taste less bitter?" he asked her.

Maria shook her head.

"Is it quick?" he asked.

"Yeah, it's really quick, and it's not supposed to be painful at all," she replied.

Jones thought a moment. "Okay, do what you can to make it taste better." He turned and walked onstage.

Guards carrying guns and crossbows followed him. They spread out and began patrolling the pavilion's perimeter.

As usual, a tape recorder was running. Jones sat in his green chair and woefully shook his head. "How very much I have tried to give you a good life."

He told his followers that a catastrophe was about to happen on Ryan's airplane. One of the defectors was going to shoot the pilot, causing the congressman's plane to plummet into the jungle. That action, he told them, would result in an invasion of Jonestown. Their enemies would soon be parachuting in on them.

"So, my opinion is," he went on, voice weary, "that we be kind to our children and kind to our seniors and take the potion . . . and step over quietly, because we are not committing suicide. It's a revolutionary act. We can't go back. They won't let us alone. . . . And there's no way, no way we can survive."

Sixty-year-old Christine Miller got to her feet. A gutsy member, she knew her mind and spoke it now.

"Well, I don't see it like that," she said to Jones. "I mean, I feel like—as long as there's life, there's hope. That's my faith."

"Someday everybody dies," replied Jones. "And I'd like to choose my own kind of death—I'm tired of being tormented to hell, that's what I'm tired of." He paused before adding, "Tired of it."

Some in the crowd applauded.

But others started to speak. What were they saying? No one knows. Jones reached over and turned the tape recorder off, censoring voices and responses he didn't want taped for posterity. He would do this twenty more times in the course of the forty-four-minute recording.

When he turned the recorder back on, he was saying, "I'm going to tell you, Christine, life has no meaning."

There was more applause.

"I'm not ready to die," insisted Christine.

"I don't think you are," interrupted Jones. "I don't think you are."

Christine pressed on. "I look at the babies, and I think they deserve to live, you know?"

"They also deserve more," countered Jones. "They deserve peace."

"Right!" shouted someone.

Christine wouldn't give up. "We all came here for peace."

"And . . . have we had it?" Jones asked.

"No," she said.

"I tried to give you peace," he said. "I've laid down my life practically. I practically died every day to give you peace."

A woman in the crowd expressed confusion. Were they all going somewhere?

Jones corrected her. "It's suicide. Plenty have done it."

Christine continued to fight. "When we destroy ourselves, we're defeated. We let them, the enemies, defeat us."

"We win when we go down," he countered. "We win."

"I have a right to say what I think, what I feel," Christine continued. "And I think we all have a right to choose our own destiny as individuals. . . . And I think I have a right to choose mine, and everybody else has a right to choose theirs. . . . You know?"

"That's what twenty people said today," Jones shot back, referring to those who'd defected.

Christine would not let it go. "I think I still have a right to my opinion."

Another woman, Ruby Carroll, stood. But the moment she started speaking, Jones turned off the machine. When it came back on, he was warning her that she'd regret not dying that day. Had Ruby also declared her resistance to suicide?

Another woman stood. "You must prepare to die," she told Christine.

Christine snapped, "I'm not talking to you." She turned to Jones. "Would you make her sit down and let me talk while I'm on the floor?"

Jones ignored her. "The best testimony we can make is to leave this goddamn world," he argued.

Many in the crowd applauded.

Jim McElvane rose. "Christine, you're only standing here because [Jim Jones] was here in the first place. So I don't know what you're talking about, having an individual life."

A woman chimed in, "[Father] has saved so many people."

"You want to see John [Victor] die?" Christine suddenly said.

"What's that?" asked Jones.

"You mean you want to see John, the little one, who's keep—"

Noise from the crowd prevented the rest of her words from being recorded.

"Do you actually, do you think I would put John's life above others?" replied Jones.

"He's young," Christine reminded him. "They're young."

"I know, but he's no different to me than any of these children here. He's just one of my children. I don't prefer one above another."

Christine had hoped that by mentioning John Victor, Jones would back down. She understood how important the boy was to the leader. But Jones knew something she didn't—Congressman Ryan was dead, and soldiers would soon be on their way to Jonestown. The time had come to die.

"That's all I have to say," Christine concluded. She sat back down.

With Christine silenced, Jones changed the tone of his voice. Now he used the cadences of a Pentecostal preacher. He quoted from the Bible, appealing to those who'd grown up in the church, as he had so many years earlier in Indiana. "I'm going to lay down my burden. Down by the riverside."

"You mean you want us to die?" cried a woman.

Jones talked over her. "Peace, peace, peace, peace, peace, peace, peace, peace, peace, peace." His voice was pleading.

A man spoke up. He was weeping. "If you tell us we have to give our lives now, we're ready—at least the rest of the brothers and sisters are with me."

Several in the crowd raised their voices.

And Jones snapped off the tape recorder. Were others contradicting the weeping man? Were they declaring that they *weren't* ready?

When the recorder came back on, it was to the roar of the tractor trailer returning to the settlement. One of the shooters jumped out and ran to the stage. He whispered in Father's ear.

Jones turned to his followers. "It's all over, all over," he told them. "The congressman's dead."

How did the crowd react? Once again, no one knows. Jones turned off the recorder.

When he restarted it, he was saying to an aide, "Please get us some medication. It's simple. It's simple. There's no convulsions with it. It's just simple. Just please get it. Before it's too late. The GDF [Guyana Defence Force] will be here, I tell you. Get movin'. Get movin'. Get movin'."

Aides carried out a steel vat from the kitchen. The liquid inside was dark purple—grape-flavored—mixed with cyanide, Valium, and chloral hydrate (a sedative used for insomnia). Someone brought out stacks of paper cups and set them beside the vat. Temple nurses clutching bundles of syringes, with and without needles, moved to the front.

Jones called for the children to die first. As the nurses filled syringes from the vat, the guards trained their weapons on the residents. No one would be allowed to choose between living and dying. The only decision left to them was death by poison or by gunshot.

In Jones's cottage Carolyn Layton and PR man Mike Prokes typed letters while Marilee Bogue entertained John Victor Stoen and Kimo, and Annie Moore went through stacks of papers. The group worked calmly, as if it were an ordinary day.

Maria Katsaris, meanwhile, headed down to the pavilion, where she began giving orders. "You've got to move," she said. "Everybody, get back behind the table and back this way, okay? There's nothing to worry about. Everybody, keep calm and keep your children calm."

Mothers were asked to bring their babies forward.

First in line was Ruletta Paul and her year-old son, Robert. She appeared calm and deliberate as she picked up a needleless syringe from the table and squirted a few drops of poison into her baby's mouth. She squirted the rest into her own. Then, following directions, she walked out of the pavilion and sat down in a nearby muddy field with the baby in her lap. Soon Robert frothed at the mouth. He convulsed and fought for breath. Ruletta rocked him until she, too, was overcome by the effects of the cyanide. Within minutes, both were dead.

Some mothers followed Ruletta's example by calmly surrendering both their infants and themselves. But many others clutched their little ones to their chests. Temple nurses soon gave up trying to convince them to voluntarily kill their children and instead had guards pry the little ones away. The nurses squirted the poison into the babies' mouths themselves. Their numb and grieving mothers followed suit. Like Ruletta, they stumbled out into the field and waited for the cyanide to do its work.

Followers were weeping now, screaming and struggling, many hysterical.

Thirty-three babies had been born in Jonestown. Within minutes, all were dead.

It was time for the older children to come forward.

"I don't want to die!" shrieked one little boy.

"No!" cried another.

Twelve-year-old Julie Ann Runnels fought hard. She refused to swallow, repeatedly spitting out the poison. Finally, Temple nurses grabbed her braids and yanked her head back. They poured the potion into her mouth, then covered her mouth and nose, forcing her to swallow it. A nurse escorted the sobbing child to the field.

Most parents drank from paper cups filled by the nurses before walking away to join the dead and dying. They watched their children die before succumbing themselves.

Back in the pavilion Maria Katsaris reassured the remaining parents.

"[The children] are not crying from pain," she lied. "It's just a little bitter-tasting."

An older woman admonished the other followers. "I'm looking at so many people crying. I wish you would not cry. And just thank Father."

Others joined in thanks.

"Please," groaned Jones, "for God's sake let's get on with it. . . . Let's just be done with it. Let's be done with the agony of it."

A young mother began screaming. "You can't do this!"

"Mother, Mother, Mother, Mother, please," said Jones. "Mother, please, please, please. Don't do this. Don't do this. Lay down your life with your children, but don't do this."

The woman wasn't heard again.

By six-forty-five p.m., nearly three hundred children, and many of their parents, were dead. Jones instructed the rest of the community to line up. "Where's the vat with the green *C* on it?" he called to aides. "Bring the vat with the green *C* in . . . here so the adults can begin."

His words were met with tears, pleading, and shouts of defiance.

"Lay down your life with dignity. Stop the hysterics. This is not the way for people who are socialists or communists to die," he scolded.

By nine o'clock only about a hundred of the more than nine hundred residents still lived. Jones taped a final lie for posterity. "We didn't commit suicide; we committed an act of revolutionary suicide protesting the conditions of an inhuman world."

The tape ended.

Hyacinth waited in her cottage for Zip and Esther to come back. Then she heard shooting, and somebody calling for Rheaviana Beam. She figured her friend had skipped the meeting, too. Had guards fired their guns into the air to scare Rheaviana into going? Would they shoot at her next? She decided to hide.

"My bed was behind the door, and I had a wide bedspread that hung down to the floor on both sides," she said. With difficulty, she crawled under the bed and scrunched into a far corner.

She heard more shooting.

"Maybe the mercenaries *have* come," she thought.

She lay there a long while. Outside the settlement fell silent. No more gunshots. No voices, either.

Hyacinth crawled out and got into bed. She pulled up the covers. Zip could tell her about the meeting in the morning. She closed her eyes and fell asleep.

Jones had gotten out of his chair and was pushing stragglers toward the vat. Marceline hugged those still standing. "I'll see you in your next life," she said.

The final residents didn't want to die. Nurses walked among them, plunging syringes into their upper arms. One woman fought the guards as they tried to drag her to the vat. She was held down and injected, too. A sobbing senior citizen repeatedly walked up to the table and then walked back to his seat. An impatient nurse, wanting to get the dying done, jabbed a syringe into his arm. He convulsed and fell to the floor.

By ten-forty-five p.m., almost everyone was dead. Their bodies fanned out around the pavilion. Most fell face down, arms around their loved ones. Larry Schacht made the rounds with his stethoscope, checking to be sure no one had a heartbeat. When he was finished, he downed a cupful of the deadly mixture he'd created.

Meanwhile, nurses went through the senior cottages, the medical clinic, and the ECU, injecting all those who couldn't make it to the meeting. Then they, too, took the poison. Only the guards remained. Jones told them all to hug goodbye. They did. Then they dipped their cups and drank.

Member Stanley Clayton saw it all. He'd worked his way toward the jungle by pretending to check the bodies for survivors. Once he got close enough, he made a break for it, diving into the bush. He hid there in the pitch-blackness of the jungle for hours. Later, he would say that the eventual silence coming from Jonestown was more terrifying than the dark jungle. After a while, he got up and ran down the muddy road that led out of Jonestown.

Most likely, Marceline was one of the last to kill herself. She would have stayed to embrace and comfort the others. Unlike Carolyn Layton, Lew Jones, and Dick and Harriet Tropp, who sequestered themselves in Jones's cottage, Marceline put herself in the heart-wrenching middle of it all. She was there for the people as they died. And then when it was finished, she chose to go with them, dropping to the floor at the head of the pavilion.

Jim Jones sat alone in his green chair. He'd watched and listened as more than nine hundred of his followers died. All that remained now was silence. Peoples Temple was no more.

This hadn't been revolutionary suicide—no matter how Jones justified it in his drug-addled mind. It was not blind loyalty, or the ultimate test of devotion. Certainly, the children didn't commit suicide. Two hundred forty youngsters were murdered that day. So were more than one hundred eighty seniors over sixty-five. Unable to defend themselves, they, too, should be considered murder victims.

As for the remaining able-bodied adults, based on the discoveries of injection sites that appeared to have been made by force, pathologists estimated that around one hundred twenty-five of them were unwillingly injected with the poison. These people, too, were murder victims.

And what about those who felt they had no choice: Drink the poison, or be killed anyway?

Some *did* drink the poison voluntarily. They did it based on Jones's lies. He told them that their children would be taken away, and perhaps tortured, that enemies were coming any minute. Could they have seen through those lies, or had years of suicide votes, sleep deprivation, and fake crises clouded their judgment? Survivor Tim Carter put it best: "If one commits 'revolutionary suicide' based on years of experience, without the knowledge that the experiences themselves were [fabricated] by the leader, is that suicide? I assert it is murder."

Stephan Jones believes many adults took the poison "because everyone else was." He adds, "I don't know what I would have done [had I been] there. I was so caught up in the opinion of my community, so afraid of looking like a coward, that in the instant it would have taken to pop something into my mouth, I might have done it. Not out of loyalty to Jim Jones, but loyalty to those in the community." If many had already died, how could one betray their deaths by refusing to give one's own? Still, he continues, "I don't think there was a genuine suicide there . . . except maybe my father. But even then, he had someone else shoot him."

Stephan thinks that the someone was Annie Moore. She would have picked her way toward Jones, around overturned benches and crumpled paper cups. The vat of cyanide would still have sat on the table, surrounded by syringes.

From his hiding place in the bush, Stanley Clayton heard a gunshot.

Later, Jones would be found slumped, shot in the right temple with a .38 Smith & Wesson revolver.

Why hadn't he taken poison like his people had?

"Knowing my father, he didn't like how he saw everyone else dying," said Stephan. "And since he couldn't bring himself to do it, he had someone do it for him."

Only Annie remained. Making her way through the carnage, she returned to the cottage she'd shared with Jones and the others. Carolyn, lifeless, lay sprawled across the bed with Kimo in her arms. Maria Katsaris and John Victor Stoen were dead, too, as was Lew Jones and his wife, Terry, and their one-year-old son, Chaeoke.

Annie sat. In her spiral notebook with its red cover, she wrote her suicide note. "I am 24 years of age right now and don't expect to live through the end of this book. I thought I should at least make some attempt to let the world know what Jim Jones and the Peoples Temple is or was all about. It seems that some people and perhaps the majority of people would like to destroy the best thing that ever happened to the 1200 or so of us who have followed Jim. I am at a point right now so embittered against the world that I don't know why I am writing this."

She praised Jonestown: "It seems that everything good that happens to the world is under constant attack." And she wrote of her adoration for Jim Jones: "His love for humans was unsurmountable and it was many whom he put his love and trust in and they left him and spit in his face."

The letter ended wistfully: "What a beautiful place this was. The children loved the jungle, learned about animals and plants. There were no cars to run over them; no child molesters to molest them; nobody to hurt them. They were the freest, most intelligent children I had ever known. . . . Seniors were treated with respect, something they never had in the United States. A rare few were sick and when they were, they were given the best medical care."

The last line was written in different-colored ink: "We died because you would not let us live in peace!"

How long did she sit there after finishing the note? In the dark, with the dead surrounding her, Annie Moore drank the poison that had killed so many she loved. Then she picked up a gun. She pointed it at her head and pulled the trigger.

Part Six

After

In my mind they're at rest. They're beautiful, dressed in white. They're across the river in a beautiful green meadow, just beautiful. . . . In my own mind, they're at peace.

—Jean Clancey, Peoples Temple survivor

Chapter Forty-Two

The Days After

HYACINTH WOKE ON SUNDAY MORNING AND LOOKED around her cottage. “That’s funny,” she thought. “The girls haven’t come back yet.”

She dressed, then hobbled along the wooden walkway to one of the dormitories for elders. From the door she could see her friend Birdy Johnson sitting in a chair, draped in a sheet.

“Birdy?” she called.

Birdy didn’t move.

“Birdy, what’s wrong?”

Hyacinth stepped inside. She touched her friend’s arm.

Birdy was dead.

Hyacinth limped along the dorm’s row of beds.

Everyone was dead.

“Oh, my God, they came and killed them all,” she shrieked. Then the horrible truth struck. “I’s the onliest one alive!”

Hyacinth started screaming. She cried. She shook all over. Another thought came—that Zip must be dead, too.

She fell to her knees and cried even harder. Later, she claimed that was when she heard a voice in her head: “Fear not; I am with you." Hyacinth took this to be the voice of God. She lowered her hands from her face, and fear left her. She went back to her cottage and sat in a chair by the front door. Eventually, she went inside and mixed a glass of powdered milk. She lay on her bed, listening to the birds. Finally, she nodded off.

Just after dawn on Sunday morning, the medical evacuation planes landed at Port Kaituma. Incredibly, the badly wounded had survived the night, although Anthony Katsaris's breathing was labored and Jackie Speier already had gangrene in her leg. They were immediately medevacked to a U.S. naval station in Puerto Rico, where they would recover.

The press and many of the Concerned Relatives also flew to Georgetown, including Jim Cobb Jr., who'd finally come down from the tree and found his way back to the airstrip. Temple lawyers Mark Lane and Charles Garry flew out, too. Locked in a cottage during the massacre, they'd escaped into the jungle, where they'd hidden before following the road to Port Kaituma. And the reporters were transported to Georgetown, as well. They had a story to write—a big one.

What had happened to Tommy and his group? After running, panicked, into the jungle, they'd gotten lost. Tommy had believed he could rely on the survival he learned from the Amerindians. But fear and pain clouded his judgment. His leg felt angry and swollen, and he was bleeding a lot. Time and again he led the group toward a light in the distance, thinking it was a way out, only to discover it was nothing but a break in the jungle's canopy.

Saturday night fell, and the group had huddled beneath a tree in the blackness. They tried not to think about what or who might be lurking nearby. No one slept.

On Sunday, as soon as the sun rose, they continued, stumbling through the thick tangle and splashing across streams. Tommy felt feverish and faint from blood loss. By night his wound began to smell. Infection had set in.

Dawn broke on Monday—their second morning in the bush. Tommy had his bearings now, or at least he thought he did. Port Kaituma was just a few hours' walk away. But he couldn't manage it. Weak and unable to put any weight on his injured leg, he sank down alongside a river. His sister Teena, who was also feverish and in pain, stayed with him. Tommy pointed out the direction to the others. Go, he told them. Send back help.

Hours passed. Tommy floated in and out of consciousness. When awake, he worried. Were his friends still lost? Or worse, had Jonestown guards caught them?

Miraculously, he heard someone calling his name. A group of Amerindians in dugouts paddled down the river toward him. Despite his pain, Tommy grinned. His friends Brenda, Tracy, and Chris were not only safe, they'd sent back help. Tommy waved at his rescuers.

Hours later he and Teena were back in Port Kaituma. Jim Bogue gathered them in his arms and wept.

The three flew to Georgetown the following morning, where both Teena and Tommy received medical treatment. Tommy would spend the next month in the hospital there, and another month's hospitalization in San Francisco. This, as well as extensive physical therapy, eventually allowed him to fully recover.

The first contingent of Guyanese soldiers didn't arrive in Jonestown until late on Sunday, November 19. They'd come on foot, their progress slowed by heavy rain and thick mud, as well as extreme cautiousness. Commanding officers had worried about the possibility of marching into an armed camp. Instead, they discovered a horrific scene—piles upon piles of bodies dressed in bright colors: reds and greens and blues, happy colors. Already, because of heat and humidity, the bodies were badly decomposed.

Battered by the smell, the soldiers tied handkerchiefs over their noses and mouths. The troop leader, Captain Desmond Roberts, sent back alarming reports. They needed more help. "All we can see is death," he said.

Early Monday morning, Hyacinth hobbled out of her cottage.

"Lady, what are you doing here?" a soldier cried out in surprise.

They carried her to the pavilion so she could see what had happened.

"It was like a battlefield," said Hyacinth, "bodies strewn all over."

Captain Roberts asked her to help identify them. She couldn't do it. It was too awful a task. She did identify Zip, though, from a distance. "She was laying on her back . . . just outside the pavilion on the dirt floor," said Hyacinth, who recognized her sister's red sweater.

Hyacinth asked a soldier to pin Zip's name to her dress. He did.

Roberts begged her to identify Jones.

She refused. She never wanted to lay eyes on him again.

Soldiers took her to the schoolhouse, where they gave her food and water. To her surprise, seventy-nine-year-old Grover Smith was there. She asked how he'd survived.

When the poisoning started, he told her, he'd walked up to a perimeter guard.

"Where do you think you're going?" the guard had asked.

"I don't want to die," Grover had replied.

The guard had moved aside. "Have a nice life," he'd said. He'd watched as Grover walked to the edge of the settlement and hid in a ditch.

"Hyacinth," the old man now warned, "don't say nothing 'bout Jim." He still feared the leader's powers.

Hyacinth didn't fear Jones, but she didn't want to talk about him, either. When reporters arrived and asked her questions, she answered with "No comment."

All Hyacinth really wanted was to be alone. She couldn't stop thinking about Zip's death. Had she taken the poison willingly?

She agonized over the children, too. "Those little babies laying dead out there. Toddlers, so cute." She remembered how the nursery workers had paraded the littlest ones past her cottage dressed in sunsuits and paper hats. Added Hyacinth, "It's enough to make you scream your lungs out, thinking of those babies dead."

Late Monday afternoon the Jones boys, as well as Michael Touchette and Johnny Cobb, crowded into the radio room at Lamaha Gardens, waiting for news of Jonestown. The first reports from the Guyanese government were vague. Bodies were everywhere. An initial count estimated the number at four hundred.

Stephan felt a flicker of hope. Hundreds of others must have fled into the jungle. He begged authorities to let him go to Jonestown in search of survivors.

Officials refused. After the gruesome discovery, they'd placed everyone at Lamaha Gardens under house arrest. This included not only the thirteen members of the basketball team but also the thirty-nine other people who either worked at or were visiting the villa. Authorities simply had no clear idea about what had happened in Jonestown, or if those in Georgetown had had some part in the deaths.

And so Stephan and the others sat glued to the radio, taking turns around the clock. Maybe their loved ones *were* still alive.

The Jones boys knew their father was dead. His body had been found onstage in his recognizable red polo shirt, identified by a Jonestown resident who had been in Georgetown at the time of the massacre. Stephan, however, held out hope for his mother, as well as for his brother Lew and his family and for his little half brother, Kimo, and John Victor Stoen.

They waited four days.

On the fifth day, needing help with identification of the bodies, authorities took Tim Jones and Johnny Cobb to Jonestown. While they were gone, Guyanese Prime Minister Forbes Burnham gave a radio speech about the massacre. He spoke of the death of nine hundred people.

"Did he say nine hundred?" asked Stephan incredulously.

Soon a list of the dead was being read: Brian Davis; Al Simon; Mark Gosney; Agnes Jones; Shanda James; Christine Miller; David George; Marilee Bogue; Joe Wilson; Billy and Bruce Oliver; Charlie, Joyce, and Al Touchette; Christine Cobb and her children Ava,

Sandy, Joel, and Brenda; Harriet and Dick Tropp; Patty and Trisha Cartmell; Jack and Rheaviana Beam . . .

The names kept coming.

The awful, unbearable truth slammed into Stephan. Nearly everyone he knew was dead. His community was gone.

Hours later Tim and Johnny returned to Lamaha Gardens. What they'd seen at Jonestown had left them mute. They couldn't speak. Not a word. They couldn't stop the tears from rolling down their faces.

Chapter Forty-Three

Aftermath

ON A SLOPING GREEN HILLSIDE IN OAKLAND'S EVERGREEN Cemetery lies a mass grave where more than four hundred victims of the massacre in Jonestown are buried. Most of them are children. Here lies six-year-old John Victor Stoen and his three-year-old playmate Kimo Prokes. Here, too, is one-year-old Chaeoke Jones, six-year-old Alvin Simon Jr., seventeen-year-old David George, and so many more. Unrecognizable in death, without fingerprints or dental records to help identify them, few of the children's bodies were ever identified. But their names have not been forgotten.

In those first days after the massacre, the U.S. State Department pressured the Guyanese to bury all the bodies in situ. A mass grave in Jonestown seemed the most expedient way of dealing with the situation, claimed American officials. But the Guyanese flatly refused. It was up to the U.S. government, they said, to "clean up the mess."

The *mess.* How quickly authorities reduced 909 people who died in the jungle that day to a single, dehumanizing word.

Grudgingly, the U.S government collected the remains. Consigning two or three bodies to each casket, they flew them to an air force mortuary in Dover, Delaware. The first bodies arrived on Thanksgiving Day. No one marked their return home with prayers or tributes or makeshift memorials. Instead, the public responded with distance, outrage, even blame. Many Americans expressed anger about tax dollars being spent on "cultists" and their deranged behavior.

By far the worst reaction, however, was the way in which the tragedy became a jokey catchphrase. Most news outlets correctly reported that Jonestown residents had died after ingesting a mixture of cyanide and Flavor Aid, a brand of soft-drink mix similar to Kool-Aid. But some reports mistakenly said Kool-Aid, and the more familiar product stuck in the public's imagination. "Drinking the Kool-Aid" entered the lexicon. It quickly became a common expression used to describe self-deception, voluntary indoctrination, and blind obedience to a group identity. Said one survivor who lost her four children at Jonestown: "I hated that people laughed when they said it, like what happened was somehow funny."

Additionally, the media published dozens of photographs of the massacre. Mike Cartmell opened his *Newsweek* magazine one day to find a close-up photo of his mother, Patty, and sister, Trisha, lying dead. He hadn't laid eyes on them since he'd defected twenty-one months earlier. Now he was staring at their bloated bodies in a national publication. "It was the last time I saw them," he recalled.

At the time of the massacre, Peoples Temple still had hundreds of members in the United States—people who hadn't yet been called to Jonestown and were holding down the Temples in San Francisco, Redwood Valley, and Los Angeles. Crowds gathered daily outside the San Francisco building to picket. "Baby killers!" they shouted. Inside the Temple, members felt heartbroken and bewildered. Where had it all gone wrong?

Just two weeks after the massacre, papers were filed to have Peoples Temple formally dissolved. Soon afterward, the U.S. government managed to freeze the church's overseas accounts. Survivors must have been shocked to learn that Jones had stashed away $7.3 million. The government claimed it all as reimbursement for airlifting the bodies from Guyana to Dover Air Force Base.

Within the Black community African American members of Peoples Temple were stigmatized as having been duped by a white man. But as feminist author Sikivu Hutchinson notes, "It is inadequate to say that Blacks were . . . hoodwinked or even 'brainwashed' into staying in Peoples Temple's 'cult' of the white savior." Not only does that denigrate Black members, Hutchinson claims, but dilutes "the interplay of passion and desire and revolutionary longing that informed their involvement and ultimate migration" first to California and then Guyana.

Black women in particular longed for a safe and separate place for themselves and their children, away from racist America. And their decision to go to Guyana can be traced to several traditions of Black thought, says Russell Rickford, associate professor of history at Cornell University, especially the "promise of agrarianism." Blacks in America long believed that they would get a piece of the land they'd worked for generations. In fact, after the Civil War, they were promised it, but it never happened. Throughout the course of the twentieth century, the majority of African Americans went from being a rural people to an urban people. "But they never fully surrendered that dream, that desire for a piece of land where they could be self-sufficient, where they could reconstitute their communities and survive beyond the reach of white supremacy," notes Rickford. It was entirely reasonable for them to go to Jonestown. The settlement represented that promise. "They were drawing on deeply legitimate yearnings."

Mr. Muggs snuggles with Joyce Touchette c. 1974. Purchased by Jones in the United States, Mr. Muggs became one of the earliest and most unusual residents of Jonestown. He had an elaborate cage built by the pioneers, and by all accounts was well loved. He, too, died on November 18, 1978.

Agnes Jones, the often forgotten adopted daughter of Jim and Marceline, moved to Jonestown in August 1977, where she joined her husband, Forrest Ray Jones, as well as her four children.

A classroom in the Jonestown school c. 1977. Standing is teacher Shanda James, who received much unwanted attention from Jones. The boy turned toward the camera is Martin Amos, son of Sharon Amos, head of the Temple's public relations team in Georgetown.

Zipporah Edwards, Jones devotee and younger sister of Hyacinth Thrash, as pictured on her Peoples Temple membership card.

With balloons and beach balls, the Jonestown preschoolers happily parade around the compound in 1978. None of them would survive the massacre.

Jonestown as seen from the air. The pavilion sits in the center. Beside it are the two long school tents. To the left are five large dormitories that housed anywhere from thirty to fifty people. The rectangle to the left of the road running through the group of cottages at the top of the photo is the basketball court. Fields of crops and cleared land give way to thick jungle, a strong deterrent to anyone thinking of fleeing. Jones's cottage is not pictured but was located off to the right.

Stephan Jones dunks a basketball on the half-court he and some other teens built c. 1978.

Annie Moore leans against the door of the medical dispensary, where Jonestown's vast stores of drugs were kept, in May 1978.

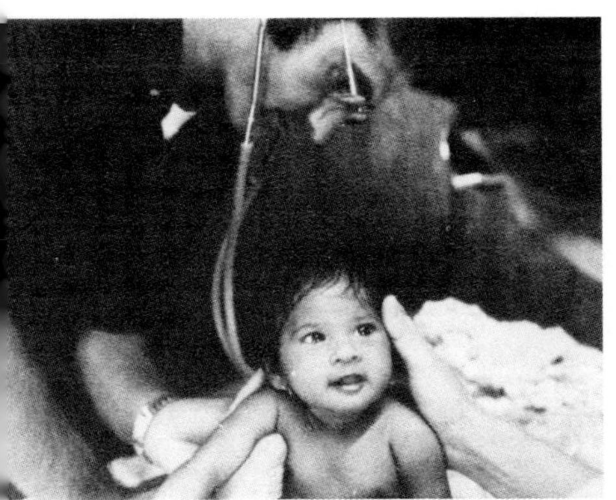

Dr. Larry Schacht examines a baby in the Jonestown clinic. When he wasn't caring for residents, Schacht was researching ways to kill them.

Under the watchful eye of a sitter, Kimo Prokes (standing) and John Victor Stoen splash in an inflatable wading pool in May 1978.

Jonestown's teenagers mug for the camera in 1978.

Maria Katsaris, one of Jones's mistresses and a member of his innermost circle, poses with a toucan in 1978.

Carolyn Layton, Jones's longtime mistress and right hand, poses with their son, Kimo, on the porch of the cottage she shared with Jones.

Congressman Leo Ryan in November 1977. A year later, he would investigate allegations of abuse and mistreatment in Jonestown, a decision that would cost him his life.

Jim Jones speaking in the Jonestown pavilion in October 1978, just a month before the tragedy.

A photographer accompanying Congressman Ryan to Guyana snapped this picture of Jonestown's entrance on his way into the compound on the morning of November 18, 1978. The sign hanging over the road reads: Greetings, Peoples Temple Agricultural Project. The building to the right is a security checkpoint.

Jim Jones (in the white shirt) introduces John Victor Stoen to an unidentified man while inner-circle members Harriet Tropp (left) and Carolyn Layton (right) look on.

Gang of Eight member and Concerned Relative Jim Cobb Jr. sits with his siblings in the Jonestown pavilion on November 17, 1978. From left: Ava Cobb Brown, Brenda Cobb, Jim Cobb Jr., and Joel Cobb. Only Jim Jr. would survive the tragedy.

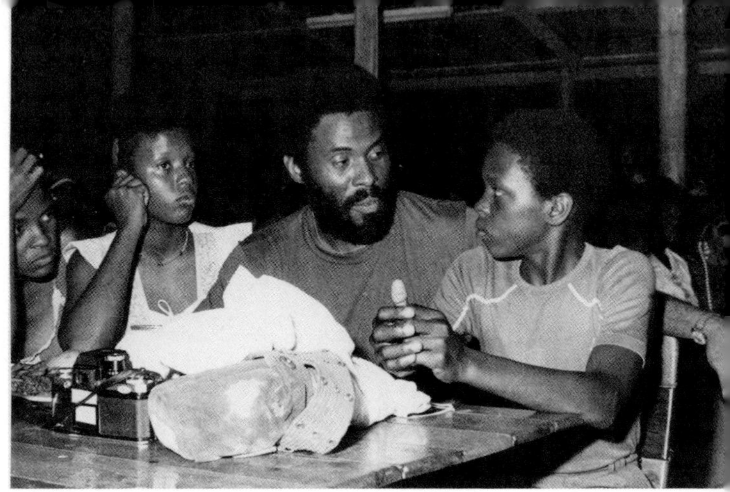

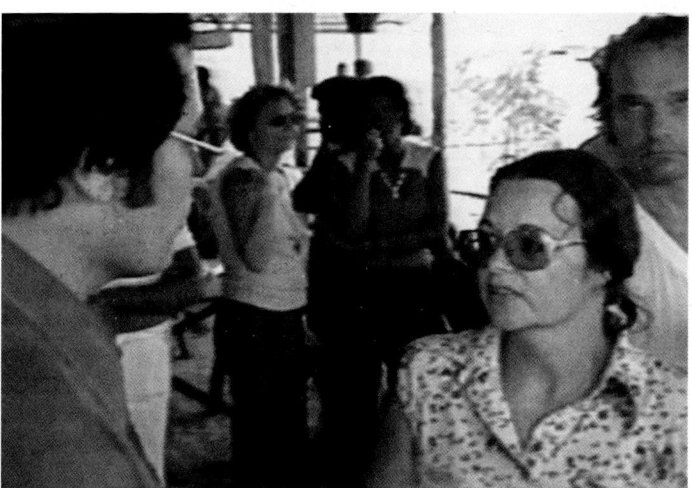

Edith Bogue, Tommy's mother, tells Jim Jones that her family is leaving. On the right stands Harold Cordell, owner of the smuggled-in transistor radio. In the background wearing sunglasses is Marceline Jones.

Christine Miller, the only voice of dissent heard on the Temple's final tape recording.

Al Simon, holding his daughter Summer, planned to leave with Congressman Ryan but was forced back by his wife, Bonnie, as well as Temple lawyers.

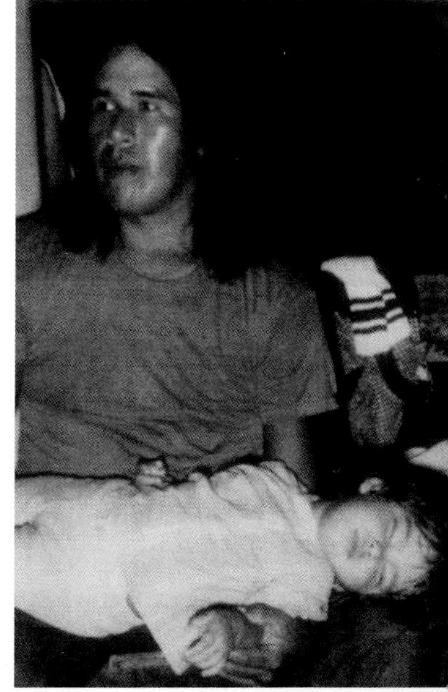

Stethoscopes and paper cups left strewn across the pavilion steps provide stark evidence of the tragedy.

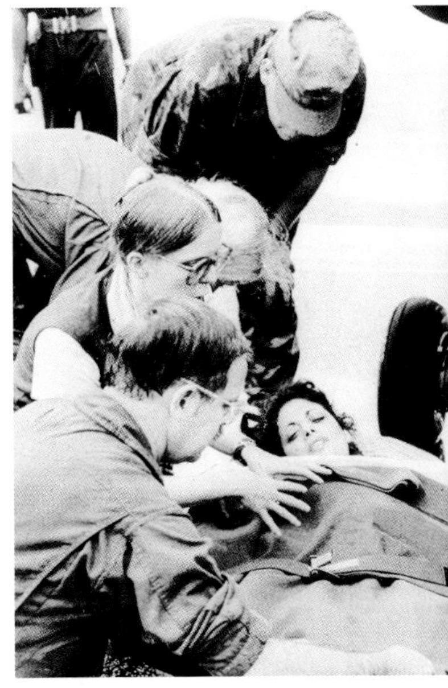

A badly wounded Jackie Speier is airlifted from Port Kaituma on November 19, 1978.

Larry Layton being taken into custody by the Guyanese police. He eventually stood trial in the United States and was found guilty of "aiding and abetting the conspiracy to murder Congressman Ryan." Sentenced to life in prison, he was paroled in 2002.

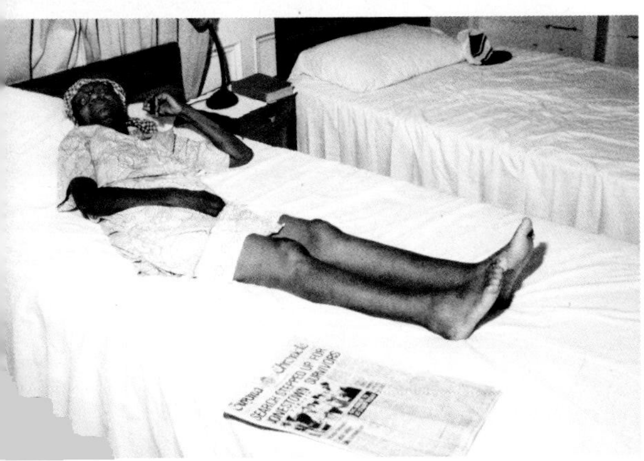

After being discovered in Jonestown, Hyacinth Thrash was transported to Georgetown, where she was besieged by reporters. One of them, with little respect for her privacy or grief, snapped this photo after placing a newspaper next to her on the bed.

United States military personnel stack aluminum caskets containing the remains of Jonestown residents in preparation for shipment to Dover Air Force Base in Maryland.

Congressman Ryan's body arrives at a San Francisco airport on November 20, 1978.

Reporter Tim Reiterman (foreground), a survivor of the attack at Port Kaituma, stands at the Jonestown Memorial in Evergreen Cemetery in Oakland, California, on the forty-fifth anniversary of the massacre. The plaques before him list the names of all who died in Guyana on November 18, 1978.

Eager to be rid of the bodies, medical examiners working for the United States government declared all the deaths in Jonestown suicides. They chose not to investigate further. While pathologists did perform a handful of perfunctory autopsies—on the bodies of Jim Jones, Annie Moore, and Carolyn Layton, among others—they did not look for any other answers. They did not take blood or tissue samples for analysis, nor did they examine the bodies for possible injection sites—despite the claim of Guyana's chief medical examiner that he saw many bodies with inoculation marks that he believed pointed to murder rather than suicide. Morgue workers *did* fingerprint each body before the embalming process in hopes of making an identification. But many of the victims, especially the children, did not have dental and medical records on file. They'd never been fingerprinted. No longer recognizable, most were never identified.

Other victims were identified but remained unclaimed. Most of these were African Americans who'd come from low-income neighborhoods. Their loved ones simply could not afford to have the bodies shipped across the country for private burial. Grief-stricken citizens were forced to leave their family members—in many cases, *numerous* family members—in a Delaware air force hangar. Wealthier families—mostly white—brought their loved ones home.

Brian Davis finally returned to his mother in Redding, California.

Carolyn Layton and Annie Moore were laid to rest in the Moore family plot in Davis.

Zipporah Edwards received a "decent Christian burial" in Los Angeles, thanks to her sister, Hyacinth.

As for Marceline Jones, she was buried in Richmond, Indiana, along with her children Lew and Agnes. (Their spouses and children went unidentified.) Jim Jones, however, did not rest beside them.

Instead, the body of the man the press called the most notorious cult leader of all time was cremated and his ashes scattered in the Atlantic Ocean.

The flag-draped casket containing Congressman Leo Ryan's body was eulogized by family, friends, and fellow members of Congress less than a week after he was slain, and his body was interred at Golden Gate National Cemetery in San Bruno, California. In 1983, President Ronald Reagan posthumously awarded him a Congressional Gold Medal for courage in the line of duty. In 2008 his former staffer Jackie Speier was elected to the House of Representatives. She served many of Ryan's former constituents.

While these burials took place, more than four hundred other caskets remained stacked in an air force hangar. Officials in nearby towns refused to bury them in their cemeteries, claiming that the remains of "cultists" would desecrate the grounds. They worried, too, about the grave becoming a pilgrimage site for the ghoulish and unsavory.

Fall turned to winter.

Winter turned to spring.

At last, the San Francisco Council of Churches scraped together the necessary funds to transport the remaining bodies to California. In May 1979—six months after the massacre—the caskets traveled across the country by moving van. They came to rest in Evergreen Cemetery in a single mass grave.

At first, just a small headstone marked the grave. But time passed. Grief and anger gave way to acknowledgment and perhaps a better understanding of the tragic and terrible human loss. Thirty-two years after the tragedy, in 2010, four memorial plaques were placed on the grave. The names of every person who perished at Jonestown—as well as those who died in Port Kaituma and Georgetown—were engraved on them. Even Jim Jones's name is found there because, as contributors to the Jonestown Memorial Fund explained, "all who died on November 18, 1978, are in need of mercy, love, and compassion."

Since the placement of those plaques, survivors, former members, friends, and family gather at this spot every November 18. They hug and sing, tell stories and eulogize. Sometimes Grace Stoen is there. So are Johnny and Jim Cobb, Stephan Jones, and others. For a long time Tommy Bogue refused to attend. "Why live in the past?" he'd ask. But in recent years even he has felt compelled to reconnect with the survivors of Peoples Temple.

Stephan claims these events are not only emotional but also healing. At one, a woman approached him. It was Congressman Ryan's daughter Patricia. When she introduced herself, Stephan felt taken aback. Then he apologized for his father's actions. Replied Patricia, "It's not your fault. You didn't do it, your father did."

Stephan says many of the members have remained close. They are still family.

He realizes he'll never understand the whole truth about Jonestown. But maybe, he suggests, that's not what matters most. Perhaps the more important questions are "What can we learn from what happened? What do we do now with that knowledge?" He pauses before adding, "So what? Now what?"

AUTHOR'S NOTE

After that terrible day in November 1978, hundreds of Peoples Temple survivors who never lived in Jonestown, and a few who did, were left to piece together their lives. So, too, were families who lost their children, parents, and siblings. Even more than forty years later, the events are difficult to talk about. And yet, nine people agreed to share their memories with me—both joyful and painful. Three of them spoke candidly about family members. With frankness and eloquence, they expressed their longings and regrets. They gave me details and context and stories never told before. And they never flinched from the truth. Though not all of these survivors are featured prominently in this book, each nudged me toward a deeper understanding of the topsy-turvy world of Peoples Temple—its often illogical groupthink; its beyond-fervent commitment to community; its fears, paranoia, and, yes, even fun.

"Don't forget to tell them we laughed," Mike Cartmell said before regaling me with stories about church skits and close friends and playing sax in the Peoples Temple band. He was there for the church's "good days," before Jonestown, and because he was the Joneses' son-in-law, his in-depth and often loving look at Jim and Marceline was eye-opening.

Nicole Valentine has been searching for memories of teenagers Mauri and Daren Janaro—two cousins she never even knew existed until recently. Her journey brought home the stigma and secretiveness that have surrounded survivors and family members. I can't imagine having to hide away such deep grief. "It's like losing them twice," Nicole said.

And then there is Stephan Jones. He has, he admits, finally forgiven his father. And yet he remains clear-eyed about Jim Jones. "He was a murderer in the very definition of the word," he said during our first conversation. Still, he made sure I understood that there was "something" in Jones's personality that could "just light people up." Stephan remembered a time in Jonestown when the preschoolers paraded past his cottage wearing paper hats and big smiles. "They were just beautiful, all [skin] colors, together and laughing." The sight brought him and his male bunkmates to tears. "We weren't embarrassed by that emotion," adds Stephan. "We recognized the beauty of it. . . . That was because of Jim Jones."

Everyone I spoke with agreed to do so for the same reason: They wanted to share their experiences with young people. Most had spent their teen years in Peoples Temple. Their hope is that stories from their youth will resonate with today's young audience—readers who might be particularly susceptible to peer pressure, charismatic leaders, and undue influence. Their stories are, says Stephan Jones, a "cautionary tale . . . It really *can* happen to anyone." But there is hope in the horror. Perhaps readers, after hearing this tragic story, will draw parallels between then and now. Perhaps they will recognize the destructive groups in their own midst. What will you make of their memories?

I am so grateful to Michael Touchette, Dr. Rebecca Moore, Fielding McGehee III, Mike Cartmell, Jordan Vilchez, Mike Carter, Debbie Layton, Nicole Valentine, and Stephan Jones. I have, indeed, been pulled into the "vortex." This book is so much richer because of you.

ACKNOWLEDGMENTS

No book is the work of just one person. It takes a team, and I am fortunate to have a brilliant one at Random House: Christa Angelios, Emily Hoffman, Alison Kolani, Angela Carlino, Cathy Bobak, Tessa Rudolph, Rebecca Vitkus, Amy Schroeder, Christine Ma, and last, but never least, the indomitable, wise, and kind Anne Schwartz, who never lets me off easy. Thank you for sticking with me all these years.

Thanks, too, to Debra Kaufman, collections rights and imaging coordinator at the California Historical Society; Regan Steinmel, reference librarian at the Indiana Historical Society; and Anna Culbertson, head of special collections at San Diego State University. Your tireless hunt for the obscure and overlooked has made this book much richer.

I am deeply grateful to Dr. Rebecca Moore, professor emerita of religious studies at San Diego State University, and her husband, Fielding M. McGehee III, for their extraordinary knowledge and understanding of Peoples Temple. Their decades of work, including their co-management of the substantive website Alternative

Considerations of Jonestown & Peoples Temple opened my eyes—and heart—to aspects of this story I hadn't considered.

Like most nonfiction, this book stands on the shoulders of writers who have gone before me. Thank you to Tim Reiterman, Jeff Guinn, Julia Scheeres, and Leigh Fondakowski for your impeccable research and gut-wrenching work.

Most of all, I am indebted to those who have courageously and honestly shared their Peoples Temple experiences through books, interviews, articles, and documentaries. Hyacinth Thrash, Leslie Wagner-Wilson, Deanna and Elmer Mertle, Laura Kohl Johnston, Thom Bogue, Tim Stoen, Jackie Spier, Yulanda Williams, and Eugene Smith, I bow to you all.

SOURCES

There is an avalanche of primary source material related to Peoples Temple. After the tragedy, FBI agents recovered four hundred audiotapes (nine hundred hours), as well as reams of documents and photographs, from both the Jonestown and Lamaha Gardens sites. These documents include members' medical records, committee meeting minutes, letters, diaries, radio communications, Temple membership cards, and much more. All documents collected and archived by the FBI begin with the prefix *RYMUR* (RYan MURder) and the digits *89-4286,* followed by additional numbers and letters for each document, and sometimes for each page of a document. Because these identification numbers were made by hand and by hundreds of different people, it is often difficult to decipher the entire number. Adding to this legibility problem are the swaths of redactions made by the FBI before releasing the documents under the Freedom of Information Act. This means that not every RYMUR file number listed below is complete, although I included as much of its identification number as possible. These documents can be viewed at vault.fbi.gov/search?SearchableText=Jonestown.

Audiotapes archived by the FBI begin with *Q* followed by a number. The Jonestown Institute generously provided the transcripts for many of these tapes. These can be read, and the tapes listened to, at jonestown.sdsu.edu.

Over the years, many survivors have shared their poignant, painful stories in interviews, articles, and books. Some have passed away. Others have said their piece. I am particularly indebted to Leslie Wagner-Wilson, Jeannie Mills (aka Deanna Mertle), Jim Cobb Jr., Thom Bogue, Jean Clancey, Hyacinth Thrash, Representative Jackie Speier, and journalist Tim Reiterman, whose remembrances helped shape this book.

Prologue: "The Horrors of Jonestown"

"strange religious cult": "1978 Special Report: 'Horrors of Jonestown,'" Hezakya Newz & Films, youtube.com/watch?V=pZ-63wvWycm.
"bodies of children": ibid.
"sipping from a bucket": ibid.
"These metal caskets": ibid.
"His people believed": ibid.
"to be God": ibid.
"Why in the world": ibid.
"baffled": ibid.
"I think you will find": ibid.
"Often these organizations": ibid.
"I was anticipating": ibid.
"No one joins": Michael Cartmell, interview with author.
"We were going": "1978 Special Report: 'Horrors of Jonestown.'"
"Most of us": ibid.

Cult: What Is It?

"a practice of religious": "Is it a cult, or a new religious movement?" Penn Today, penntoday.upenn.edu/news/it-cult-or-new-religious-movement.
"veneration": quora.com/Does-the-unwavering-support-by-Trumps-supporters-represent-a-cult-Dictionary-defines-cult-as-veneration-devotion-misplaced-or-excessive-admiration-to-particular-person-often-align-with-existing-religions-followers.
"brainwashed cultists": "1978 Special Report: 'Horrors of Jonestown.'"

PART ONE: BEGINNINGS

"To understand": Stephan Jones, interview with author.

Chapter One: One Weird Kid

"Move back": Guinn, 32.
"I can't move": ibid.
"a weird look": ibid.
"I've gone as far": RYMUR 89-4286-FF-7-a-1-FF-7-h-3.
"You go ahead": ibid.

"Manipulation was not": Stephan Jones, interview with author.
"the rejects of the community": ibid.
"immediate acceptance": ibid.
"I know that men": Hitler, *Mein Kampf.*
"He had a flair": Guinn, 41.
"a worm": RYMUR 89-4286-FF-7-a-1-FF-7-h-3.
"My worthless father": FBI Tape Q134.
"Get out of the way": Reiterman, 26.
"All men are": FBI Tape Q134.
"The experience": Scheeres, 6.

Chapter Two: Husband and Healer

"visibly touched": RYMUR 89-4286-BB-18-Z-62-BB-18-Z-68.
"I looked around": RYMUR 89-4286-O-I-B-L.
"[Marceline] was angelic": Guinn, 52.
"*I'm* not a healer": Jack Coe.
"You're tormented by": ibid.
"I believe": ibid.
"So, here it comes": ibid.
"Do you want": ibid.
"No": ibid.
"And you never": ibid.
"Lord, heal this": ibid.
"Touch your toes": ibid.
"Loosen up": ibid.
"How does your back": ibid.
"Wonderful": ibid.
"Raise your hands": ibid.
"If they can do it": RYMUR 89-4286-0-1-B-8.
"didn't work out": ibid.
"I perceive that": ibid.
"all this shit": ibid.
"I felt as if": RYMUR 89-4286-BB-18-2-64.
"I don't know how": RYMUR 89-4286-01-B-8.
"taking little notes": ibid.
"beat[ing] in [their]": Stephan Jones, interview with author.
"What's bothering you": Guinn, 69.
"Let's write": ibid.
"Unity proves": ibid.
"A wonderful lady": ibid.
"a single foreigner": Denne, "Inequality Remade."
"undesirable populations": ibid.
"better class": ibid.
"native white": ibid.
"See?": Guinn, 69.
"I love you": Reiterman, 47.

Chapter Three: Hyacinth and Zip

"TV church": Thrash, 46.
"It was like Jim": ibid., 47.
"door is open so wide": Scheeres, 10.
"I've found my church": Thrash, 47.
"It was wonderful": ibid., 48.
"Mikey, he's got it all": Michael Cartmell, interview with author.
"Here Comes Peter": RYMUR 89-4286-FF-1-95d.
"Here comes Peter": Nelson and Rollins, "Here Comes Peter Cottontail."
"Jim had": Thrash, 49.
"She was sold": ibid., 68.
"You have an ear": Reiterman, 54.
"Your ear will be": ibid.
"You're going to be": ibid.

Chapter Four: All a Facade

"so good": Thrash, 50.
"It seemed gross": RYMUR 89-4286-O-I-B-L.
"good versus evil": ibid.
"infiltrate the church": ibid.
"Now what": Reiterman, 61.
"I didn't think so": ibid.
"God for some": ibid; italics added.
"There was not": ibid.
"Some of you": ibid, 61–62.
"corrective fellowship": Devin, jonestown.sdsu.edu/?page-id=33220.
"no better than": RYMUR 89-4286-696.
"You will be": RYMUR 89-4286-1099.
"[He] was always": Thrash, 56.
"a rainbow family": RYMUR 89-4286-HH-6-A42.
"a living example": ibid.
"It's hard to understand": RYMUR 89-4286-0-1-B1-01-B-19.
"For some strange reason": ibid.
"Oh-boke needs": ibid.
"Oh . . . it was cruel": ibid.
"for outside show": Thrash, 73.
"so good and had": ibid., 57.

Chapter Five: Hanging On to Jim

"witness to integration": Thrash, 51.
"most white folks": ibid, 13.
"That really hurt": ibid., 51.
"I was afraid": ibid.
"Hyacinth, you have": ibid.
"You've had bad news": ibid.
"How do you explain": ibid., 52.
"Divine healing": ibid.
"[I] hung on to him": ibid., 53.
"I have received": Reiterman, 76.

Chapter Six: Strange Odyssey

"They became a part": Reiterman, 73.
"Look out": Jones, "Like Father, Like Son," jonestown.sdsu.edu/?page_id=17018.
"Bogeyman": Stephan Jones, interview with author.
"Stephan": Jones, "Like Father, Like Son."
"Is everything okay": ibid.
"I came running": ibid.

PART TWO: RELOCATING

"I was totally": Fondakowski, 266.

Chapter Seven: California Dreaming

"Eureka safe zone": Sims, "Standing in the Shadows of Jonestown," *North Coast Journal Weekly,* northcoastjournal.com/092503/cover0925.html.
"the migration": Kohl, jonestown.sdsu.edu/?page_id=81226.
"From the Ladies' Aid Society": California Historical Society, MS 4124, Box 2, Folder 38.
"sky god stories": RYMUR 89-4286-FF-7-a-1-FF-7-h-3.
"Who raises the dead": California Historical Society, MS 4124, Box 1, Folder 11.
"booming, stomping, rocking": Stephan Jones, interview with author.
"He had people hooked": ibid.

Chapter Eight: Joining Jim

"He was losing": Thrash, 54.
"Oh, it was": ibid., 62.
"doing things right": ibid., 66.
"We all helped": ibid., 65.
"I'm going": Reiterman, 101.
"big-city dances": ibid.
"If you got hurt": ibid., 102.
"You played football": ibid.

Chapter Nine: Reeling In Members

"It was the only subject": Rebecca Moore, interview with author.
"We had a saying": Amanda Montell, *Cultish: The Language of Fanaticism,* New York: Harper Wave, 2021, 61.
"appealed to anyone": "Nearly 40 Years Later, Jonestown Offers a Lesson in Demagoguery," *Fresh Air,* NPR, npr.org/transcripts/523348069.
"His vocabulary could": Montell, 58.

Chapter Ten: Carolyn

"This is good": Jones, "Like Father, Like Son."
"Look at how much": ibid.
"She will be": ibid.
"helpless and lost": ibid.
"His world": ibid.
"Your dad told me": ibid.
"Not only had I": ibid.
"I'm sorry": ibid.
"Thou shalt not": Exodus 20:14 (King James Version).
"needed this": Guinn, 168.
"Larry, I'm in love": Reiterman, 171.
"Up to now": Moore, *A Sympathetic History,* 89.
"I can't express": ibid.
"a charlatan": ibid.

Chapter Eleven: Brother Tim and God the Father

"refugees from": Barbour, jonestown.sdsu.edu/?who_died=tupper-rita-jeanette.
"I loved [Tim]": Jones, "My Dear Brother, Tim Tupper Jones," jonestown.sdsu.edu/?page_id=92969.
"We live and die": Reiterman, 145.
"There [is] no need": ibid., 146.
"I come as": ibid., 147.
"All right": ibid.
"I shall show you": ibid., 148.
"And I must say": ibid.
"If you still need": ibid.
"You prayed": ibid.
"No, it's not": ibid., 149.
"When your world": ibid.
"A lot of people": Thrash, 100.

Chapter Twelve: Secrets Behind the Temple's Doors

"the staff": Reiterman, 157.
"heavenly deceptions": ibid., 158.
"Only by surrendering": ibid., 158.
"know how special": ibid., 159.
"patronized in the [historical]": Taylor, 95.
"Jones was in essence": ibid.
"the loft": Reiterman, 162.
"At [my] first meeting": Guinn, 240.

"Five whacks": Mills, 290.
"Thank you, Father": ibid.
"crippled bitch": ibid.
"Remember": Cahill, 18.
"We did a lot": Stephan Jones, interview with author.
"Am I the only": ibid.
"It was peer": ibid.

PART THREE: RADICALIZING

"You got this guy": Fondakowski, 66–67.

Chapter Thirteen: Multiplying

"[When] a community": Taylor, 92.
"If you closed": ibid., 96.
"The 1970s were": ibid., 98.
"a black soul": ibid., 96.
"white power and privilege": ibid.
"The last two": Kilduff and Tracy, "Inside Peoples Temple."

Chapter Fourteen: Pill Popping and Paranoia

"very special": Guinn, 218.
"generous socialism": Mills, 179.
"Rifle shot": FBI Tape Q616.
"Tell them": Reiterman, 202.
"I could stick": ibid.

Chapter Fifteen: Truth by Trickles

"He's out to destroy": Reiterman, 219.
"Your father has": ibid.
"I won't kill": ibid., 220.
"Deep in my heart": Mills, 248.
"Calm down": Wright, 74.
"I'm all right": ibid.
"An overnight case": RYMUR 89-4286-Bulky-2233-BB-11.
"Made me want": ibid.
"A glob": ibid.

Chapter Sixteen: Going Communal

"Our life savings": Mills, 230.
"[I'm] feeding six hundred": Fondakowski, 108.
"Modesty is": Guinn, 191.
"It was like heaven": Thrash, 65.
"I just didn't know": ibid., 74.
"He knew he could": ibid., 76.
"But [he] never did": ibid., 77.
"She thought of it": ibid., 70.
"For I was hungry": Scheeres, 29.
"Posing as a purely": Abbott, jonestown.sdsu.edu/?page_id=64856#_ftnref51.

Chapter Seventeen: Annie

"hard sell": Rebecca Moore, interview with author.
"Oh God": ibid.
"The reason is": Moore, *The Jonestown Letters,* 76.
"Go, sell": Matthew 19:21 (New International Version).
"in the same way": Rebecca Moore, interview with author.
"You obviously think": Moore, *The Jonestown Letters,* 78.

Chapter Eighteen: "I Know a Place"

"realize how someone": Reiterman, 220.
"Mama, I don't": ibid.
"No": ibid.
"If you can't": ibid., 221.
"I've been out": ibid.
"crisis mode": Wood, jonestown.sdsu.edu/?page_id=29475.
"I've prophesized": FBI Tape Q1057-4.
"like electricity": Mills, 283.
"I tell you": FBI Tape Q1057-4.
"Never, never": ibid.
"Mmm-hmm": ibid.
"Amen, Father": ibid.
"one hell of a": ibid.
"Now what we have": ibid.
"I know a place": FBI Tape Q958.

Chapter Nineteen: Escape!

"Leave and you": RYMUR 86-4286-89-4286-Bulky-2018-C-1-A-7 (146).
"We know where": RYMUR 89-4286-X-3-c-1.
"keep your mouth": ibid.
"But don't tell": Reiterman, 221.
"I want to tell": ibid.
"Man": ibid., 222.
"For the past": "The Eight Revolutionaries (Original Document)," jonestown.sdsu.edu/?page_id=14077.
"If I had": FBI Tape Q1057-3.
"It was a test": Mills, 290.
"How many of you": ibid., 231.
"Revolutionary suicide does not": Newton, 5.
"We will go down": Mills, 231.
"I want to take": ibid.
"I don't want": ibid.
"[These] are people": ibid., 232.
"We could all": ibid.
"More than one hundred": ibid.

Chapter Twenty: Father's Grand Plan

"Peoples Temple Agricultural Project": "Progress Report, Summer 1977," jonestown.sdsu.edu/wp-content/uploads/2013/10/04-10-AgBkltSum77_sm.pdf.
"Temple boats loaded": Mills, 295.

Chapter Twenty-One: Pioneers

"And this is no joke": "Mike Touchette Interview (Text)," jonestown.sdsu.edu/?page_id=111238.
"pioneers": Stephan Jones, interview with author.
"Don't worry": Scheeres, 66.
"We cleared the jungle": Michael Touchette, interview with author.
"I got really good": ibid.
"This is where": ibid.
"We planned by ourselves": ibid.
"It got so": ibid.
"It was a lot": "Mike Touchette Interview (Text)," jonestown.sdsu.edu/?page_id=111238.
"[If] you had": ibid.

"We sit there": ibid.
"This new way": ibid.

Chapter Twenty-Two: Kimo

"I sent her away": Mills, 276.
"It was an astonishing": ibid.
"I'm the gladdest": Moore, *The Jonestown Letters,* 94.
"Aren't you excited": Moore, *A Sympathetic History,* 100.
"No": ibid.
"Instead, he was": Rebecca Moore, interview with author.
"is very cute": Moore, *The Jonestown Letters,* 94.

Chapter Twenty-Three: Tommy and Brian

"We both enjoyed": Bogue, jonestown.sdsu.edu/?page_id=34231.
"comrades in mischief": Sheeres, 72.
"Right here": Bogue, jonestown.sdsu.edu/?page_id=34231.
"Wouldn't you know": ibid.
"It made us miss": ibid.
"Well, I didn't": ibid.
"I couldn't believe": ibid.
"I almost cried": ibid.
"[I was] sent": ibid.

Chapter Twenty-Four: Death and Sacrifice

"I have something": Mills, 310.
"What are you doing": ibid.
"No, Father": ibid., 311.
"I don't want to die": ibid.
"Are there any other": ibid.
"I now know": ibid.
"I love socialism": RYMUR 89-4286-Bulky-2018-C-1-A-3-(1)-3 (104).
"A good socialist": ibid.
"We've got to go": ibid.
"so full of shit": Stephan Jones, interview with author.
"tap into something": ibid.
"It was torture": Jones, "Like Father, Like Son."

PART FOUR: EXODUS

"The thing [that's] important": Stephan Jones, interview with author.

Chapter Twenty-Five: Life in the Jungle

"It won't be": Stephan Jones, interview with author.
"I want you": ibid.
"I put every nail": ibid.
"I knocked down": ibid.
"I was building": ibid.
"Together we were": Mike Cartmell, interview with author.
"designated heir": ibid.
"No matter the goal": ibid.
"all right with her": "Serial 1303-17," jonestown.sdsu.edu/?page_id=91789.
"princess": Mike Cartmell, interview with author.
"I don't remember her": ibid.
"I stole away": ibid.
"high on the hog": FBI Tape Q693.
"ungrateful heifer": ibid.
"capitalist pig": ibid.
"wicked, wicked woman": ibid.

Chapter Twenty-Six: First Cracks

"And it broke": Fondakowski, 113.
"They started to tell": ibid.
"Do you believe them": ibid.
"What are you talking": ibid.

Chapter Twenty-Seven: Going to the Promised Land

"What do you think": Reiterman, 320.
"It's impossible": ibid.
"How many people": ibid.
"About one hundred fifty": ibid.
"Jonestown has turned": "Jonestown Promotional Film (Full Version)," Henry Bemis, youtube.com/watch?v=fDc-QFSnJoA.
"Rice and black-eyed": ibid.
"She left me one": Fagan, 5.

Chapter Twenty-Eight: "Inside Peoples Temple"

"Jim Jones is one": Kilduff and Tracy, "Inside Peoples Temple."
"beaten so severely": ibid.
"a kind of log": ibid.
"Why Jim Jones Should": ibid.
"An investigation of": ibid.
"federal courts": ibid.
"The story of Jim Jones": ibid.

Chapter Twenty-Nine: Father in Jonestown

"I was shocked": Fondakowski, 201.
"Everything changed": ibid.
"we absolutely enabled": ibid.
"whacked out": ibid.
"I think the essence": "Harriet Sarah Tropp Memo on Uglification of Jonestown," jonestown.sdsu.edu/?page_id=13220.
"shoot to kill": Maaga, 117.
"stop them": ibid.
"became a pattern": ibid.
"Jonestown is too beautiful": Morris, 345.
"I have people": Reiterman, 394.
"LOVE ONE ANOTHER": digitalcollections.sdsu.edu/do/472f8177-0510-4b70-a9d5-a15f04cb0843.
"Here's something": ibid.
"Ball of Fire": ibid.
"Keep chewing": ibid.
"Hell, no": ibid.
"Thank you, Father": ibid.

Chapter Thirty: God's Nurse and a Surprise for Tommy

"You don't tell God": Stephan Jones, interview with author.
"I just wanted you": Moore, *A Sympathetic History,* 306–307.
"However, within an hour": Bogue, "'I Want to Go with You but They Won't Let Me': Memories of My Friend Brian Davis."
Advanced Vocabulary: ibid.
"We took a dictionary": ibid.
"popped his cork": ibid.
"You, you, you": ibid.
"So we defined": ibid.
"We didn't feel": ibid.
"We hated it there": ibid.

PART FIVE: JONESTOWN

"You were faced": Fondakowski, 242.

Chapter Thirty-One: Hyacinth in the Promised Land

"Most of my day's": Thrash, 86.
"It was just something": ibid., 87.
"Jesus, what have I": ibid., 104.
"double feelings": ibid., 94.
"There were times": ibid.
"Work went from": Stephan Jones, interview with author.
"Hitler did his": RYMUR 89-4286-2018-C-11-d-14c.
"All rebels suffered": RYMUR 89-4286-C-3-A-1 (1).
"It's like you": Fondakowski, 164.
"I just sat at the back": Thrash, 94.
"I have entertained": RYMUR 89-4286-2233-FF-5-r-3.
"It would just be": Michael Touchette, interview with author.
"It was relief": ibid.
"With me, it went": Thrash, 94.

Chapter Thirty-Two: The Stoens and the Six-Day Siege

"child prince": Stoen, 87.
"Father was terribly": Layton, 101.
"the most compassionate": RYMUR 89-4286-BB-31-a-24.
"The way to get to Jim Jones": Hall, 32.
"a matter of life and death": Yates, jonestown.sdsu.edu/?page_id=111337.
"Alert": Wright, 76.
"white night": Wagner-Wilson, 83.
"hacked to death": Scheeres, 94.
"I've got a hell": FBI Tape Q948.
"Folks were getting": Thrash, 96.
"I'm hit": Reiterman, 363.
"Keep calm": ibid.
"We have fired": ibid.
"They'll let me": FBI Tape Q135.
"Thank you, Father": ibid.
"My God, if they won't": ibid.
"If I'm the only": ibid.
"Come and get us": FBI Tape Q948.
"rather die than return": Scheeres, 96.
"rather die than give up": ibid.
"rather die than endure": ibid.
"Who wants to commit": Wagner-Wilson, 87.

Chapter Thirty-Three: Gone Boys

"Then we'd be home free": Bogue, " 'I Want to Go with You but They Won't Let Me': Memories of My Friend Brian Davis."
"succulent Big Macs": ibid.
"Once it gets dark": ibid.
"It was going to be great": ibid.
"Do you hear that": ibid.
"A tractor's coming": ibid.
"You know about": FBI Tape Q933.
"Fourteen months": ibid.
"The anaconda": ibid.
"I'm aware of all": ibid.
"Thirty-six feet": ibid.
"Yes, Father": ibid.
"What kind of story": ibid.
"I was going to say": ibid.

"Do you believe this": ibid.
"No": ibid.
"Anybody got any questions": ibid.
"Shameful bastards": ibid.
"Goddamn white fascists": ibid.
"Vile filth": ibid.
"Enough": ibid.
"Neither of you": ibid.
"That's very honorable": ibid.
"Tie them to": ibid.
"Put them up against": ibid.
"I don't really": ibid.
"That's right": ibid.
"I don't": ibid.
"[Jones] thought": Bogue, "'I Want to Go with You but They Won't Let Me': Memories of My Friend Brian Davis."
"Get moving": ibid.
"We discovered something": ibid.
"We were at the point": ibid.
"No": ibid.
"Then just hit": ibid.
"No": ibid.
"Just do it": ibid.
"My thumb": ibid.
"learning crew": ibid.
"Side kick": ibid.

Chapter Thirty-Four: Death and Secrets

"very well": RYMUR 89-4286-O-1-B.
"How many of you": FBI Tape Q998.
"Do you ever": ibid.
"What does planning": ibid.
"I think a healthy": ibid.
"I want you to be": ibid.
"Some of you people": ibid.
"Be creative": RYMUR 89-4286-2233-EE-1-5-57.
"It would be terrorizing": RYMUR 89-4286-2233-EE-1-M-77.
"escorted to a place": RYMUR 89-4286-2233-EE-Ic28b.
"For many years": RYMUR 89-4286-2018-NIC-31d.

Chapter Thirty-Five: The Jonestown Team

"thrusting a middle finger": Stephan Jones, interview with author.
"What a folly": Smith, vault.si.com/vault/2007/12/31/escape-from-jonestown.
"Thank you for": Wright, 78.
"We gotta kill him": Reiterman, 454.
"The only way": ibid.
"Walk with me": Wright, 80.
"What's really up": ibid.
"I can't believe": ibid.
"Shadow [your brother]": ibid.
"I'm supposed to be": Reiterman, 455.
"I ain't got nothing": ibid.
"Don't give me": ibid.
"That's right": ibid.
"You know what": ibid.
Concerned Relatives: Reiterman, 408.

Chapter Thirty-Six: Exit Plans

"What did Jesus": Thrash, 100.
"Tim and Jimmy acted": Michael Touchette, interview with author.
"We ate good": ibid.
"Cyanide is one": RYMUR 89-4286-2233-EE-1-5-55x.
"We pretty much felt": Bogue, "'I Want to Go with You but They Won't Let

Me': Memories of My Friend Brian Davis."
"But . . . tell him nothing": ibid.

Chapter Thirty-Seven: The Congressman's Visit

"I do so as part": RYMUR 89-4286-2233-AA-1-b6.
"We prefer death": RYMUR 89-4286-2018-E-3-4-2(72).
"congressional hearings": Guinn, 416.
"I know we can't worry": RYMUR 89-4286-X-3-a-32a.
"No matter what": Reiterman, 470.
"I heard some congressman": RYMUR 89-4286-Q-161.
"We were enjoying": Stephan Jones, interview with author.
"You want to make good PR": Reiterman, 474.
"I told you": ibid.
"No": ibid.
"You don't have": ibid., 475.
"It was time to stop": Stephan Jones, interview with author.
"I'm the bad guy": Wright, 81.
"We're making a statement": ibid., 82.
"I want to remind you": Reiterman, 471.

Chapter Thirty-Eight: Friday, November 17

"It looks like": FBI Tape Q050.
"We'll try to get": Reiterman, 489.
"I am imploring you": Reiterman, 485.
"I hope to God": Scheeres, 209.
"The State Department": "40 Years Later, Rep. Speier Looks Back on Surviving Jonestown," *PBS News Hour*, youtube.com/watch?v=fAABLTU14TU.
"Letters brought in by Ryan": RYMUR 89-4286-2233-AA-1-e-1.
"I feel like a dying man": Reiterman, 493.
"I only said": ibid., 497–498.
"I felt embarrassment": ibid., 493.
"Our basketball team": ibid., 495.
"Now that's a coup": ibid.
And if, by chance: Creed and Masser, "The Greatest Love of All," lyrics.com/lyric/25031116/Whitney+Houston/Greatest+Love+of+All.
"I think you all know": FBI Tape Q048.
"See": Reiterman, 494.
"Oh, you dropped": Fondakowski, 224.
"He passed him": ibid.
"Vernon Gosney": ibid.
"You're the first": ibid., 225.
"You're in great danger": ibid.
"We have no transportation": ibid.
"You're in danger": ibid.
"We can't leave": ibid.

Chapter Thirty-Nine: Saturday Morning, November 18

"I'll whistle when": Reiterman, 506.
"People play games": "Jonestown Raw Full NBC Footage," youtube.com/watch?v=qP6rnNRF5Es.
"If it's so damn bad": ibid.
"We want to leave": ibid.
"Please don't go": ibid.
"You held us here": Scheeres, 214.
"I'm going to go get him": ibid., 215.
"Mom, so help me": ibid.
"It's not a trick": ibid.

"Mom is with us": ibid.
"We're gonna go back": "Jonestown Raw Full NBC Footage," youtube.com/watch?v=qP6rnNRF5Es.
"You don't have to": ibid.
"We're going to have": Guinn, 432.
"They're coming out": Reiterman, 513.
"In his emotion": ibid., 512.
"A pill": ibid., 513.
"I have strictly prohibited": "Jonestown Raw Full NBC Footage," youtube.com/watch?v=qP6rnNRF5Es.
"Come on": Bogue, "'I Want to Go with You but They Won't Let Me': Memories of My Friend Brian Davis."
"I want to go": ibid.
"I'll kill you": "Jonestown Raw Full NBC Footage," youtube.com/watch?v=qP6rnNRF5Es.
"I sense danger": Reiterman, 518.
"You're going to die": "Jonestown Raw Full NBC Footage," youtube.com/watch?v=qP6rnNRF5Es.
"Does this change things": Guinn, 434.
"It doesn't change": ibid.

Chapter Forty: Saturday Afternoon, November 18

"I've sent my avenging angels": Wright, 82.
"Jimmy's here": ibid.
"Dad": ibid.
"Where are your brothers": ibid.
"Let me see who": Reiterman, 524.
"I think we've got trouble": ibid., 525.
"Come on": ibid., 526.
"Duck down": Scheeres, 221.
"I was absolutely incredulous": Turner, 10.
"The pilot poured on": Reiterman, 533.
"They're coming back": ibid., 531.
"We're going to see": Wright, 83.
"Is this real": ibid.
"We might have to die": ibid.
"Okay, fine": ibid.
"Let's wait a minute": Jones, "Death's Night," jonestown.sdsu.edu/?page_id=40172.
"I believed Dad": Stephan Jones, interview with author.
"Tell them . . . not to do": Jones, "Death's Night."
"Please be them": Wright, ibid.
"Sharon killed": Jones, "Death's Night."
"Where are they": ibid.
"My memory of the rest": ibid.
"All that can be done": ibid.
"I was dizzy": ibid.

Chapter Forty-One: The End

"That so": Thrash, 109.
"Jim's going to be": ibid.
"He'll just have to come": ibid.
"I believe I'll wear": ibid., 109–110.
"We'll tell you": ibid., 110.
"There must be another": Fondakowski, 247.
"Tell me what": ibid.
"Dick, stop being": ibid.
"Is there a way": Guinn, 440.
"Is it quick?" ibid.
"Yeah, it's really": ibid.
"Okay, do what": ibid.

“How very much”: FBI Tape Q042.
“So, my opinion”: ibid.
“Well, I don’t see it”: ibid.
“Someday everybody”: ibid.
“I’m going to tell you”: ibid.
“I’m not ready”: ibid.
“I don’t think”: ibid.
“I look at the babies”: ibid.
“They also deserve more”: ibid.
“Right”: ibid.
“We all came”: ibid.
“And . . . have we”: ibid.
“No”: ibid.
“I tried to give you”: ibid.
“It’s suicide”: ibid.
“When we destroy”: ibid.
“We win when we go”: ibid.
“I have a right to say”: ibid.
“That’s what twenty”: ibid.
“I think I still”: ibid.
“You must prepare”: ibid.
“I’m not talking”: ibid.
“The best testimony”: ibid.
“Christine, you’re”: ibid.
“[Father] has saved”: ibid.
“You want to see”: ibid.
“What’s that”: ibid.
“You mean you want”: ibid.
“Do you actually”: ibid.
“He’s young”: ibid.
“I know”: ibid.
“That’s all”: ibid.
“I’m going to lay”: ibid.
“You mean”: ibid.
“Peace, peace, peace”: ibid.
“If you tell us”: ibid.
“It’s all over”: ibid.
“Please get us”: ibid.
“You’ve got to move”: ibid.
“I don’t want to die”: Scheeres, 231.
“No”: ibid.
“[The children] are not”: FBI Tape Q042.
“I’m looking at”: ibid.
“Please”: ibid.
“You can’t do this”: ibid.
“Mother, Mother, Mother”: ibid.
“Where’s the vat”: ibid.
“Lay down your life”: ibid.
“We didn’t commit”: ibid.
“My bed was behind”: Thrash, 110.
“Maybe the mercenaries”: ibid.
“I’ll see you”: Scheeres, 232.
“If one commits revolutionary”: Carter, jonestown.sdsu.edu/?page_id=31976.
“because everyone else was”: Stephan Jones, interview with author.
“Knowing my father”: ibid.
“I am 24 years”: RYMUR 89-4286-1894.
“It seems that everything”: ibid.
“What a beautiful place”: ibid.
“We died because”: ibid.

PART SIX: AFTER

“In my mind”: Fondakowski, 299.

Chapter Forty-Two: The Days After

“That’s funny”: Thrash, 110–111.
“Birdy”: ibid., 111.
“Birdy, what’s wrong”: ibid.
“Oh, my God”: ibid.
“Fear not”: ibid.
“All we can see”: RYMUR 89-4286-1.

"Lady, what are you": Thrash, 112.
"It was like": ibid., 113.
"She was laying": ibid.
"Where do you think": Guinn, 447.
"I don't want": ibid.
"Have a nice life": ibid.
"Hyacinth": Thrash, 113.
"No comment": ibid., 114.
"Those little babies": ibid., 121–122.
"Did he say": Wright, 83.

Chapter Forty-Three: Aftermath

"clean up the mess": Rebecca Moore, interview with author.
"Drinking the Kool-Aid": Chiu, "Jonestown: 13 Things You Should Know About Cult Massacre," *Rolling Stone,* May 29, 2020, rollingstone.com/feature/jonestown-13-things-you-should-know-about-cult-massacre-121974.
"I hated that people": ibid.
"It was the last time": Mike Cartmell, interview with author.
"Baby killers": ibid.
"It is inadequate to say": Hutchinson, jonestown.sdsu.edu/?page_id=61499.
"promise of agrarianism": "Discussing Peoples Temple," youtube.com/watch?v=J0z_ry7RHYw.
"But they never fully": ibid.
"decent Christian burial": ibid.
"all who died": "A Fact Sheet on the Jonestown Memorial Fund and the Memorial Stones," jonestown.sdsu.edu/?page_id=29501.
"Why live in the past?" Scheeres, 249.
"It's not your fault": Wright, 84.
"What can we learn": Stephan Jones, interview with author.

BIBLIOGRAPHY

BOOKS

Fondakowski, Leigh. *Stories from Jonestown.* University of Minnesota Press, 2013.

Guinn, Jeff. *The Road to Jonestown: Jim Jones and Peoples Temple.* Simon & Schuster, 2017.

Hall, John R. "The Apocalypse at Jonestown." In *Apocalypse Observed: Religious Movements and Violence in North America, Europe and Japan.* Routledge, 2000.

Hitler, Adolf. *Mein Kampf.* Translated by Ralph Manheim. Mariner Books, 2017.

Layton, Debbie. *Seductive Poison: A Jonestown Survivor's Story of Life and Death in the Peoples Temple.* Edwin Mellen Press, 1985.

Maaga, Mary McCormick. *Hearing the Voices of Jonestown.* Syracuse University Press, 1998.

Mills, Jeannie. *Six Years with God: Life Inside Rev. Jim Jones's Peoples Temple.* A&W Publishers, 1979.

Moore, Rebecca, comp. *The Jonestown Letters: Correspondence of the Moore Family, 1970–1985.* Edwin Mellen Press, 1986

Moore, Rebecca. *A Sympathetic History of Jonestown: The Moore Family Involvement in Peoples Temple.* Edwin Mellen Press, 1985.

Morris, Adam. *American Messiahs: False Prophets of a Damned Nation.* Liveright Publishing Company, 2019.

Newton, Huey P. *Revolutionary Suicide.* Penguin Books, 2009.

Reiterman, Tim, with John Jacobs. *Raven: The Untold Story of the Rev. Jim Jones and His People.* Jeremy P. Tarcher/Penguin, 2008.

Scheeres, Julia. *A Thousand Lives: The Untold Story of Hope, Deception, and Survival at Jonestown.* Free Press, 2011.

Stoen, Timothy Oliver. *Marked for Death: My War with Jim Jones the Devil of Jonestown.* Self-published, CreateSpace, 2015.

Taylor, James L. "Black Churches, Peoples Temple and Civil Rights in San Francisco." In *From Every Mountainside: Black Churches and the Broad Terrain of Civil Rights.* Edited by R. Drew Smith. SUNY Press, 2013.

Thrash, Catherine (Hyacinth), as told to Marian K. Towne. *The Onliest One Alive: Surviving Jonestown, Guyana.* Self-published, 1995.

Wagner-Wilson, Leslie. *Slavery of Faith.* Self-published, iUniverse, 2009.

ARTICLES AND ONLINE DOCUMENTS

Abbott, Catherine. "Communism, Marxism, and Socialism: Radical Politics and Jim Jones." Alternative Considerations of Jonestown & Peoples Temple. jonestown.sdsu.edu/?page_id=64856#_ftnref51.

Barbour, Kathryn. "Remembrance of Rita Jeanette Tupper." Alternative Considerations of Jonestown & Peoples Temple. jonestown.sdsu.edu/?who_died=tupper-rita-jeanette.

Bogue, Thom. "'I Want to Go with You but They Won't Let Me': Memories of My Friend Brian Davis." Alternative Considerations of Jonestown & Peoples Temple. jonestown.sdsu.edu/?page_id=34231.

Cahill, Tim. "In the Valley of the Shadow of Death: Guyana After the Jonestown Massacre." *Rolling Stone,* January 25, 1979.

Carter, Tim. "Murder or Suicide: What I Saw." Alternative Considerations of Jonestown & Peoples Temple. jonestown.sdsu.edu/?page_id=31976.

Chiu, David. "Jonestown: 13 Things You Should Know About Cult Massacre." *Rolling Stone,* May 29, 2020. rollingstone.com/feature/jonestown-13-things-you-should-know-about-cult-massacre-121974.

"Cult: Definition, Character & Behavior." study.com/learn/research/cult-characteristics-types-behavior.html.

Denne, Rebecca. "Inequality Remade: Residential Segregation, Indianapolis Public Schools, and Forced Busing." Indiana History Blog, February 16, 2017. blog.history.in.gov/inequality-remade-residential-segregation-indianapolis-public-schools-and-forced-busing.

"Does the unwavering support by Trump's supports represent a cult?" quora.com/Does-the-unwavering-support-by-Trumps-supporters-represent-a-cult-Dictionary-defines-cult-as-veneration-devotion-misplaced-or

-excessive-admiration-to-particular-person-often-align-with-existing-religions-followers.

"The Eight Revolutionaries (Original Document)." Alternative Considerations of Jonestown & Peoples Temple. jonestown.sdsu.edu/?page_id=14077.

"A Fact Sheet on the Jonestown Memorial Fund and the Memorial Stones." Alternative Considerations of Jonestown & Peoples Temple. jonestown.sdsu.edu/?page_id=29501.

Fagan, Kevin. "Haunted by Memories of Hell." *San Francisco Chronicle,* November 12, 1978, 5.

"Father Cares: The Last of Jonestown." NPR, October 18, 2016. npr.org/2016/10/18/497967228/father-cares-the-last-of-jonestown.

"Harriet Sarah Tropp Memo on Uglification of Jonestown." Alternative Considerations of Jonestown & Peoples Temple. jonestown.sdsu.edu/?page_id=13220.

Hutchinson, Sikivu. "No More White Saviors: Jonestown and Peoples Temple in the Black Feminist Imagination." Alternative Considerations of Jonestown & Peoples Temple. jonestown.sdsu.edu/?page_id=61499.

"Is it a cult, or a new religious movement?" *Penn Today,* penntoday.upenn.edu/new/it-cult-or-new-religious movement.

Jones, Stephan. "Death's Night." Alternative Considerations of Jonestown & Peoples Temple. jonestown.sdsu.edu/?page-id=40172.

Jones, Stephan. "Like Father, Like Son." Alternative Considerations of Jonestown & Peoples Temple. jonestown.sdsu.edu/?page_id=17018.

Jones, Stephan. "My Dear Brother, Tim Tupper Jones." Alternative Considerations of Jonestown & Peoples Temple. jonestown.sdsu.edu/?page_id=92969.

Kilduff, Marshall, and Phil Tracy. "Inside Peoples Temple." *New West,* August 1, 1977. jonestown.sdsu.edu/wp-content/uploads/2013/10/newWestart.pdf.

Kohl, Laura Johnston. "Migration and Emigration." Alternative Considerations of Jonestown Peoples Temple. jonestown.sdsu.edu/?page_id=81226.

"Michael Touchette Interview (Text)." Alternative Considerations of Jonestown & Peoples Temple. jonestown.sdsu.edu/?page_id=111238.

Moore, Rebecca. "Cult, New Religious Movement, or Minority Religion." erraticus.co/2018/08/29/cult-new-religious-movement-minority-religion/.

"Nearly 40 Years Later, Jonestown Offers a Lesson in Demagoguery." *Fresh Air,* NPR, April 11, 2017. npr.org/transcripts/523348069.

Peoples Temple Agricultural Project, "Summer Progress Report, 1977." Alternative

Considerations of Jonestown & Peoples Temple. jonestown.sdsu.edu/wp-content/uploads/2013/10/04-10-AgBkltSum77_sm.pdf.

Risling, Ken. "Angel of Death, My Beloved." Alternative Considerations of Jonestown & Peoples Temple. jonestown.sdsu.edu/?page_id=81199.

Ross, Devin. "Culture, Charisma and Peoples Temple." Alternative Considerations of Jonestown & Peoples Temple. jonestown.sdsu.edu/?page-id=33220.

"Serial 1303-17." Alternative Considerations of Jonestown & Peoples Temple. jonestown.sdsu.edu/?page_id=91789.

Sims, Hank. "Standing in the Shadows of Jonestown." *North Coast Journal Weekly.* northcoastjournal.com/092503/cover0925.html.

Smith, Gary. "Escape from Jonestown: How Basketball Gave Life to a Son and Grandson of the Infamous Cult Leader Jim Jones." *Sports Illustrated Vault,* vault.si.com/vault/2007/12/31/escape-from-jonestown.

Turner, Wallace. "A Survivor Who Hid in a Treetop All Night Tells of the Shootings." *New York Times,* November 22, 1978.

Walker, Barbara. "The Front Line in Ballad and Thought." Alternative Considerations of Jonestown & Peoples Temple. jonestown.sdsu.edu/?page_id=18452.

Woods, Nora. "Jonestown as a Reflection of American Society." Alternative Considerations of Jonestown & Peoples Temple. jonestown.sdsu.edu/?page_id=29475.

Wright, Lawrence. "Orphans of Jonestown," *New Yorker,* November 22, 1993.

Yates, Bonnie. "John Victor Stoen: The Unfortunate Son." Alternative Considerations of Jonestown & Peoples Temple. jonestown.sdsu.edu/?page_id=111337.

VIDEOS

"40 Years Later, Rep. Speier Looks Back on Surviving Jonestown." *PBS NewsHour.* youtube.com/watch?v=fAABLTU14TU.

"1978 Special Report: 'Horrors of Jonestown.'" Hezakya Newz & Films. youtube.com/watch?V=pZ-63wvWycm.

"Discussing Peoples Temple: Social, Cultural, and Political Influences on the Movement." California Historical Society. youtube.com/watch?v=J0z_ry7RHYw.

"Jack Coe: Message to the Modern Day Church." Revival Channel. youtube.com/watch?v=s8jMgs6q_FM.

"Jonestown Promotional Film (Full Version)." Henry Bemis. youtube.com/watch?v=fDc-QFSnJoA.

"Jonestown Raw Full NBC Footage 1978." Val Preston. youtube.com/watch?v=qP6rnNRF5Es.

OTHER SOURCES

Creed, Linda, and Michael Masser. "The Greatest Love of All." lyrics.com/lyric/25031116/Whitney+Houston/Greatest+Love+of+All.

Exodus 20:14. King James Bible Online. kingjamesbibleonline.org/Exodus-20-14.

Matthew 19:21. Bible Hub. biblehub.com/matthew/19-21.htm.

Nelson, Steve, and Jack Rollins. "Here Comes Peter Cottontail." lyrics.com/lyric/7458879/Gene+Autry/Peter+Cottontail.

IMAGE CREDITS

INSERT 1

Page 1, top: Photo courtesy Stephan Jones, the Jonestown Institute.

Page 1, bottom: Photo courtesy California Historical Society, MS-3791_1853_34.

Page 2, top: Indiana Historical Society, M0205.

Page 2, bottom: Photo courtesy Stephan Jones, the Jonestown Institute.

Page 3, top: Photo courtesy Grace Jones, the Jonestown Institute.

Page 3, bottom: ms0516-hf-16-12, Jones Family Memorabilia Collection, 1962–2002. Photo courtesy Special Collections & University Archives, San Diego State University Library; Stephan Jones, the Jonestown Institute.

Page 4, top: ms0516-hf-23-11, Jones Family Memorabilia Collection, 1962–2002. Photo courtesy Special Collections & University Archives, San Diego State University Library; Stephan Jones, the Jonestown Institute.

Page 4, bottom: ms0516-hf-39-14, Jones Family Memorabilia Collection, 1962–2002. Photo courtesy Special Collections & University Archives, San Diego State University Library; Stephan Jones, the Jonestown Institute.

Page 5, top: Photo courtesy California Historical Society, MS-3791_1536_26.

Page 5, bottom: Photo courtesy Doxsee Phares, the Jonestown Institute.

Page 6, top: Photo courtesy California Historical Society, PC 010.05.0481.

Page 6, bottom: Photo courtesy California Historical Society, PC 010.07.0728.

Page 7, top left: Photo courtesy California Historical Society, MSP-3800_ALB10 _Davis_Brian_1.

Page 7, top right: Public domain. Photo recovered by the FBI and released under the Freedom of Information Act, through the Jonestown Institute.

Page 7, bottom: Photo courtesy Claire Janaro, the Jonestown Institute.

Page 8, top: Public domain. Photo recovered by the FBI and released under the Freedom of Information Act, through the Jonestown Institute.

Page 8, bottom: Public domain. Photo recovered by the FBI and released under the Freedom of Information Act, through the Jonestown Institute.

INSERT 2

Page 1, top: Photo courtesy Doxsee Phares, the Jonestown Institute.

Page 1, middle left: Photo courtesy California Historical Society, MSP-3800_ALB14_Jones_Agnes.

Page 1, middle right: Public domain. Photo recovered by the FBI and released under the Freedom of Information Act, through the Jonestown Institute.

Page 1, bottom: Photo courtesy California Historical Society, MSP-3800_ALB02_Edwards_Zipporah.

Page 2, top: Public domain. Photo recovered by the FBI and released under the Freedom of Information Act, through the Jonestown Institute.

Page 2, bottom: MS0183-48-1-022, Peoples Temple Collection (1972–1990). Photo taken by FBI agents and released under the Freedom of Information Act, courtesy Special Collections & University Archives, San Diego State University Library, and the Jonestown Institute.

Page 3, top left: Public domain. Photo recovered by the FBI and released under the Freedom of Information Act, through the Jonestown Institute.

Page 3, top right: MS0183-78-1-063, Peoples Temple Collection (1972–1990). Photo courtesy Special Collections & University Archives, San Diego State University Library; John V. Moore, the Jonestown Institute.

Page 3, middle left: Public domain. Photo courtesy the Jonestown Institute.

Page 3, bottom right: MS0183-78-1-058, Peoples Temple Collection (1972–1990). Photo courtesy Special Collections & University Archives, San Diego State University Library; John V. Moore, the Jonestown Institute.

Page 4, top: Public domain. Photo courtesy the Jonestown Institute.

Page 4, middle: MS0183-78-1-053, Peoples Temple Collection (1972–1990). Photo courtesy Special Collections & University Archives, San Diego State University Library; John V. Moore, the Jonestown Institute.

Page 4, bottom: MS0183-48-10-006, Peoples Temple Collection (1972–1990). Photo courtesy Special Collections & University Archives, San Diego State University Library; John V. Moore, the Jonestown Institute.

Page 5, top left: Collection of the U.S. House of Representatives.

Page 5, top right: Public domain. Photo recovered by the FBI and released under the Freedom of Information Act, through the Jonestown Institute.

Page 5, middle: Public domain. Photo recovered by the FBI and released under the Freedom of Information Act, through the Jonestown Institute.

Page 5, bottom: Photo courtesy California Historical Society, PC 010.07.0730.

Page 6, top: Public domain. Photo recovered by the FBI and released under the Freedom of Information Act, through the Jonestown Institute.

Page 6, middle: Public domain. Photo recovered by the FBI and released under the Freedom of Information Act, through the Jonestown Institute.

Page 6, bottom left: Photo courtesy California Historical Society, MSP-3800 _ALB05_Miller_Christine.

Page 6, bottom right: Public domain. Photo recovered by the FBI and released under the Freedom of Information Act, through the Jonestown Institute.

Page 7, top left: Public domain. Photo taken by FBI agents and released under the Freedom of Information Act, through the Jonestown Institute.

Page 7, middle right: Bettmann/Getty Images.

Page 7, middle left: Ken Hawkins/Alamy Stock Photo.

Page 7, bottom: Ken Hawkins/Alamy Stock Photo.

Page 8, top: U.S. National Archives and Records Administration, NAID 6413440.

Page 8, middle: U.S. National Archives and Records Administration, NAID 6400288.

Page 8, bottom: Photo courtesy Mark Gallaga, the Jonestown Institute.

INDEX

ABOUT THE AUTHOR

CANDACE FLEMING is the versatile author of many award-winning books for young adults and children. Among numerous other accolades, she has won the Boston Globe–Horn Book Award for Nonfiction, the Los Angeles Times Book Prize, and the Sibert Medal. She lives outside of Chicago with her husband, Caldecott Medal–winning illustrator Eric Rohmann.